CREATING THE
CORPORATE FUTURE

CREATING THE CORPORATE FUTURE

**PLAN OR BE
PLANNED FOR**

RUSSELL L. ACKOFF

**The Wharton School
University of Pennsylvania**

JOHN WILEY & SONS
New York · Chichester · Brisbane · Toronto

71544

Library of Congress Cataloging in Publication Data

Ackoff, Russell Lincoln, 1919–
   Creating the corporate future.

  Includes bibliographical references and index.

   1. Corporate planning. I. Title.
HD30.28.A25   658.4'012   80-28005
ISBN 0-471-09009-3

Printed in the United States of America

10 9 8 7 6 5 4 3 2 1

To
ALEC

to whom
this is
a rededication

Look before,
or you'll find yourself behind

BENJAMIN FRANKLIN

PREFACE

A good deal of the corporate planning I have observed is like a ritual rain dance; it has no effect on the weather that follows, but those who engage in it think it does. Moreover, it seems to me that much of the advice and instruction related to corporate planning is directed at improving the dancing, not the weather. I have no objection to the inclusion of aesthetic considerations in planning; to the contrary, I insist on it, but not at the expense of the proper function of planning—*creation of the corporate future*. To the extent that we can control the future we do not have to forecast it (just as we do not forecast the weather in our own homes because we control it). To the extent that we can respond rapidly and effectively to changes that we neither control nor expect (as in driving an automobile), we need not forecast them. The better we can adapt to what we do not control, the less we need to control. Therefore the goal of this book is not to enable managers to prepare better forecasts of the future and to better prepare for what is forecast. It is to enable them to increase their control of the future and their ability to respond effectively to what they do not control.

This is not a textbook. It does not review what others have written on the subject. It is a presentation of my own concept of corporate planning, one that has been less influenced by the writings of others than by my experience in planning and my reflections on it. For this reason I am sure that many of the ideas expressed here have been expressed by others. I apologize to all those whom a more ardent scholar would have cited. If this work has any originality, it is more likely to lie in the way the ideas are put together than in the ideas themselves.

None of this is to say that I have not been influenced by others. I have, but this has taken place primarily by working and discussing my work with them. I am particularly indebted to David Badger and John Purnell, Vice Presidents of Corporate Planning and Development of Mars, Inc. and Anheuser-Busch Companies, respectively. They have provided me with both invaluable opportunities to learn and examples of what good planning is. I am also greatly indebted to my colleagues who share my trials and tribulations: George Calhoun, Peter Davis, Jamshid Gharajedaghi, Aron Katsenelinboigen, Hasan Ozbekhan, and Wladimir Sachs.

Over the years more students have contributed to my education than

I can possibly acknowledge, but I do want to thank Elsa Vergara in particular for her always cheerful and cheering help.

Of those who work independently of me but in parallel, I have special debts to Stafford Beer, Fred Emery, Donald Schon, and K. D. Tocher. They have affected my thinking a great deal.

It would be impossible to express too often my gratitude to Thomas A. Cowan and C. West Churchman, who started me off and are likely to finish me off as well.

Finally, I want to express my gratitude to Pat Brandt, who so organizes me that I occasionally have time after work to do some writing.

Russell L. Ackoff

Philadelphia, Pennsylvania
February 1981

CONTENTS

CREATING THE
CORPORATE FUTURE

PART ONE

———

BACKGROUND

CHAPTER ONE

———————

OUR CHANGING CONCEPT OF THE WORLD

There is a certain relief in change, even though it is from bad to worse; as I have found in travelling in a stage-coach, that it is often a comfort to shift one's position and be bruised in a new place.

WASHINGTON IRVING

Change itself is constantly changing. This is reflected in the widespread recognition of its accelerating rate. For example, the speed with which we can travel has increased more in our lifetimes than it has over all the time before our births. The same is true for the speed with which we can calculate, communicate, produce, and consume.

Change has always been accelerating. This is nothing new, and we cannot claim uniqueness because of it. There are, however, some aspects of the changes we are experiencing that are unique. These are responsible for much of our preoccupation with change.

First, although technological and social change have been accelerating almost continuously, until recently this has been slow enough to enable people to adapt, either by making small occasional adjustments or by accumulating the need to do so and passing it on to the next generation. The young have always found it easier than the old to make the neces-

3

sary adjustments. Newcomers to power have usually been willing to make changes that their predecessors were unwilling to make.

In the past, because change did not press people greatly, it did not receive much of their attention. Today it presses hard and therefore is attended to. Its current rate is so great that delays in responding to it can be very costly, even disastrous. Companies and governments are going out of business every day because they have failed to adapt to it or they have adapted too slowly. Adaptation to current rapid changes requires frequent and large adjustments of what we do and how we do it. As the eminent student of management Peter Drucker [25] put it, managers must now manage discontinuities. The changes in management required to handle change have become a major concern to all those associated with it.

Human beings seek stability and are members of stability-seeking groups, organizations, institutions, and societies. Their objective may be said to be "homostasis," but the world in which this objective is pursued is increasingly dynamic and unstable. Because of the increasing interconnectedness and interdependence of individuals, groups, organizations, institutions, and societies brought about by changes in communication and transportation, our environments have become larger, more complex, and less predictable—in short, more turbulent. The only kind of equilibrium that can be obtained by a light object in a turbulent environment is dynamic—like that obtained by an airplane flying in a storm, not like that of the Rock of Gibraltar.

We can drive a car down a deserted turnpike in good weather with few changes of direction and acceleration; hence we do so without giving it much conscious thought. The worse the weather and the road, and the heavier the traffic (hence the more unpredictable the driving of others), the more we have to concentrate on our driving and the more frequently we have to change our direction and speed.

As Alvin Toffler [80] pointed out, either we do not respond at all or we do not respond quickly enough or effectively enough to the changes occurring around us. He called our paralysis in the face of change-demanding change Future Shock. One of the objectives of this book is to overcome such paralysis.

The second unique characteristic of the changes we face is more subtle than the first and, perhaps, even more threatening. It was first brought to our attention by Donald A. Schön [68]. To paraphrase his argument, as the rate of change increases, the complexity of the problems that face us also increases. The more complex these problems are, the more time it takes to solve them. The more the rate of change increases, the more the problems that face us change and the shorter is the life of the solutions we find to them. Therefore, by the time we find solutions to many of the problems that face us, usually the most important ones, the problems have so changed that our solutions to them are no longer relevant or effective; they are stillborn. In other words, many of our solutions are to problems that no longer exist in the form in which they were solved. As a result we are falling further and further behind our times.

Little wonder, then, that to many experts on change it appears critical that we learn how to forecast it more accurately and as early as possible, to prepare for it more effectively, and to respond to it more rapidly when we have not anticipated it. They see the solution to the problems created by accelerating change in improved forecasting, learning, and adaptation.

There is no doubt that such improvements would reduce some of the social pressure brought about by accelerating change, but it is neither the only path we can follow nor the best one. It is better to develop greater immunity to changes that we cannot control, and greater control over the others. Many changes that occur need not occur; and many that do not occur could have. Most of the changes that people worry about are consequences of what they have done or failed to do, however unintentionally.

Although change in general may be inevitable, particular changes are not. To those changes that do occur we must, of course, learn how to adapt more rapidly and effectively. Therefore, in this book considerable attention is given to learning and adaptation. However, because control of change is preferable to responsiveness to it, control receives even more attention.

Acceleration of change takes place in our minds as well as in our environment. There is no doubt that we have become increasingly sensitive to changes in our environment, and that we now perceive changes that once would have been ignored. We are, perhaps, more finely tuned to pick up change than any previous generation.

The most important change taking place, I believe, is in the way we try to understand the world, and in our conception of its nature. However, the large and growing literature on change and its management focuses on its objective rather than subjective aspects. It assumes that most of the managerial problems created by change derive from its rate. This may be true, but it is apparent that we cannot deal with change effectively unless we understand its nature. This means understanding it in general, not just in particular instances. One of my students, who was better at asking questions than at answering them, grasped this point and put it into a very succinct question: *What in the world is happening in the world?*

It is hard to conceive of a question that is easier to ask and harder to answer. Nevertheless, each of us frames an answer to it, consciously or unconsciously. Our answer constitutes our *Weltanschauung*, our view of the world. This view has either an implicit or explicit impact on just about everything we think and do.

Because the way I proceed in this book is itself greatly affected by my view of the world, I present it here. I do so with the hope that it will enable others to understand better where I am coming from, and that it will support my contention that we cannot cope effectively with change unless we develop a better view of the world. Any view of the world is necessarily hypothetical, and mine is no exception. My view, like any other, will have to stand tests of its effectiveness in developing ways of coping with both the rate and content of change.

About the time of World War II the age we were in began to end, and a new age began to take its place. We are still in the period of transition from one age to another, standing with one foot in each. As the two ages draw further apart we feel increasing strain, and will continue to do so until we place both feet firmly in the age we are entering. We can, of course, step the other way and try to live our lives in a dying age. By so doing, however, we accelerate the demise of the institutions and the culture that are affected by such maladaptive behavior.

By an *age* I mean a period of history in which people are held together by, among other things, use of a common method of inquiry and a view of the nature of the world that derives from its use. Therefore, to say we are experiencing a change of age is to assert that both our methods of trying to understand the world and our actual understanding of it are undergoing fundamental and profound transformations.

THE MACHINE AGE

I believe we are leaving an age that can be called the *Machine Age*. In the Machine Age the universe was believed to be *a machine that was created by God to do His work*. Man, as part of that machine, was expected to serve God's purposes, to do His will. This belief was combined with another even more ancient in origin, man had been created in the image of God. This meant that man believed himself to be more like God than anything else on Earth. This belief is reflected in the way God was depicted in the art of the age: in the image of man. In a sense, men were taken to be "demigods."

From these two beliefs—that the universe was a machine created by God to His work, and that He had created man in His image—it obviously followed that *man ought to be creating machines to do his work*. The Industrial Revolution was a product of this inference. Not only did the idea of mechanization derive from the world view of the Machine Age, but all the important characteristics of the Industrial Revolution and the culture associated with it were derived from the methodology and basic doctrines on which this view rested. Let us see how.

In the Middle Ages the expected lifespan was short, between twenty and thirty–five years at different times. Infant and child mortality was very high. The population was frequently and devastatingly plagued. During their lives most people never traveled more than a few miles from their places of birth. There was little personal freedom. Poverty and deprivation were widespread. For these and many other reasons the intellectual life of the time focused on the inner spiritual life and afterlife. Let us listen to one witness, the historian Edward Maslin Hulme [43] who illustrates the typicality of these views.

> The intellectual strength of the Middle Ages did not lie in scientific knowledge and achievement, but in a vivid quickening of the spiritual imagination. . . The medieval man had little ability to look things squarely in the face; he had no clear-eyed perception of the visible world. It was not his practice to deal in an objective way with the facts of the actual world about him. All things were veiled with a mist of subjectivity. . . The speculative life was held to be vastly more important than the practical life. The world was but a house of probation.(p.124)

> The ideal life of the Middle Ages was one closed about with the circumscribing walls of a cloister. . . Its vision . . . ignored as much as possible the world of nature and the world of men, but it opened upon the infinite. (p.60)

The art of the age reflected this orientation by focusing on man's spiritual and afterlife, not on the content and context of everyday life.

> In the Middle Ages painting was merely the hand maid of the Church. Its function was not to reveal to men the beauty of the present world, but to help him win salvation in the next. (p.116)

Little wonder, then, that curiosity was not taken to be a virtue.

> In the age of faith curiosity was a cardinal sin. The idea that it is a duty or that it is a part of wisdom to find out the reality of things was quite foreign to the times. (p.64)

The Renaissance that took place in the fourteenth and fifteenth centuries was a reawakening or, literally, a *rebirth*. In a sense man reentered the world of nature in which he lived by noticing it, becoming curious about it, and inquiring into it. In the Middle Ages

Revelation was the sole source of truth. But when Peter the Hermit preached the first Crusade he unconsciously helped to set in motion forces that resulted in the Renaissance. Travel incited the curiosity of men. . . Men became filled with curiosity not only to know the civilization of other countries, but to learn something of men who had lived in distant ages and who had been activated by different ideals of life. This curiosity came to be a powerful and important force. . . It produced a revival of learning and research, it resulted in invention and discovery. . . It initiated the experimental method. It implanted in the hearts of men the desire to study and to know the world for themselves, unencumbered by the bonds of authority. (p.64)

Renaissance men confronted nature with awe, wonder, and childlike curiosity. They tried to unravel its mysteries much as children do today, *analytically*. I do not mean that these intellectual ancestors were unsophisticated. I mean that their science was naive in a literal sense, "having natural or unaffected simplicity."

Analysis

Children given something they not understand—a radio, a clock, or a toy—are almost certain to try to take it apart to see how it works. From an understanding of how the parts work they try to extract an understanding of the whole. This three-stage process—(1) taking apart the thing to be understood, (2) trying to understand the behavior of the parts taken separately, and (3) trying to assemble this understanding into an understanding of the whole—became the basic method of inquiry of the age initiated by the Renaissance. It is called *analysis*. No wonder that today we use *analysis* and *inquiry* synonymously. For example, we speak of "analyzing a problem" and "trying to solve a problem" interchangeably. Most of us would be hard pressed if asked to identify an alternative to the analytical method.

Commitment to the analytical method induces observation and experimentation, which, in fact, brought about what we think of today as modern science. Over time, the use of this method led to a series of questions about the nature of reality, the answers to which formed to world view of the Machine Age.

Reductionism

According to the viewpoint of the Machine Age, in order to understand something it has to be taken apart conceptually or physically. Then how does one come to understand its parts? The answer to this question is obvious: by taking the parts apart. But this answer obviously leads to another question: Is there any end to such a process? The answer to this question is not obvious. It depends on whether one believes that the world as a whole is understandable in principle, if not in practice. In the age initiated by the Renaissance it was generally believed that complete understanding of the world was possible. In fact, by the mid-nineteenth century many leading scientists believed that such understanding was within their grasp. If one believes this, then the answer to the second question must be yes. Given the commitment to the analytical method, unless there are ultimate parts, *elements*, complete understanding of the universe would not be possible. If there are such indivisible parts and we come to understand them and their behavior, then complete understanding of the world is possible, at least in principle. Therefore, the belief in elements is a fundamental underpinning of the Machine-Age view of the world. The doctrine that asserts this belief is called *reductionism*: all reality and our experience of it can be reduced to ultimate indivisible elements.

Formulated so abstractly, this doctrine may not appear to be familiar; but it is very familiar to most of us in its specific manifestations. In physics, for example, with the work of the nineteenth century English chemist John Dalton people generally came to accept a speculation of Democritus and other ancient Greek philosopher as well as the seventeenth century French philosopher Descartes: all physical objects are reducible to indivisible particles of matter, or *atoms*. These elements were believed to have only two intrinsic properties: mass and energy. Physicists tried to build their understanding of nature on a foundation of an understanding of these elements.

Chemistry, like physics, had its elements. They appeared in the familiar Periodic Table. Biologists believed that all life was reducible to a single element, the *cell*. Psychology was not so parsimonious; it postulated a number of elements at different times. It began with psychic atoms, *monads*, but gave them up in favor of *simple ideas* or *impressions*, later called *directly observables* and *atomic observations*. Fundamental *drives*, *needs*, and *instincts* were added. Later, however, Freud returned to psychic atoms to explain personality. He used three elements—the *id, ego,* and *superego*—and energy, the *libido*, to "explain" human behavior. Linguists tried to reduce language to indivisible elements of sound called *phonemes*; and so on and on.

In every domain of inquiry men sought to gain understanding by looking for elements. In a sense, Machine-Age science was a crusade whose Holy Grail was the element.

Determinism

Once the elements of a thing had been identified and were themselves understood it was necessary to assemble such understanding into an understanding of the whole. This required an explanation of the *relationships* between the parts, or how they interacted. It is not surprising that in an age in which it was widely believed that all things were reducible to elements it was also believed that one simple relationship, *cause-effect*, was sufficient to explain all interactions.

Cause-effect is such a familiar concept that many of us have forgotten what it means. It may be helpful, therefore, to review its meaning. One thing is said to be the cause of another, its effect, if the cause is both *necessary* and *sufficient* for its effect. One thing is necessary for another if the other cannot occur unless the first does. One thing is sufficient for another if the occurrence of the first assures the occurrence of the second. The program directed at explaining all natural phenomena by using only the cause-effect relationship led to a series of questions whose answers provided the remaining foundations for the Machine-Age view of the world.

First, the following question arose: Is everything in the universe the effect of some cause? The answer to this question was dictated by the prevailing belief in the possibility of understanding the universe completely. For this to be possible, everything had to be taken as the effect of some cause, otherwise they could not be related or understood. This doctrine was called *determinism*. It precluded anything occurring by either chance or choice.

Now, if everything in the universe is caused, then each cause is itself the effect of a previous cause. If we start tracing back through the chain of causes do we come to a beginning of the process? The answer to this question was also dictated by the belief in the complete understandability of the universe. It was yes. Therefore, a *first cause* was postulated and taken to be God. This line of reasoning was called the "cosmological proof of the existence of God." It is significant that this proof derived from the commitment to the cause-effect relationship and the belief in the complete understandability of the universe.

Because God was conceptualized as the first cause, He was taken to be the *creator*. As we will see, not all concepts of God attribute this function to Him, or even attribute individuality or "Himness" to Him.

The doctrine of determinism gave rise to yet another critical question to which philosophers of the Machine Age devoted much of their time. How can we explain free will, choice, and purpose in a deterministic universe? There was no generally accepted answer to this question, but this did not create a problem because there was widespread agreement on this much: the concept of free will or choice was not needed to explain any natural phenomenon, including the behavior of man.

Some held that free will was an illusion granted to us by a merciful God who realized how dull life would be without it. Man was thought to be like a fly who, riding on the trunk of an elephant, believes he is steering it. This belief makes the ride more interesting and the elephant does not mind.

Another important consequence of the commitment to causal thinking derives from the acceptance of a cause as sufficient for its effect. Because of this a cause was taken to explain its effect *completely*. Nothing else was required to explain it, *not even the environment*. Therefore, Machine-Age thinking was, to a large extent, *environment-free*; it tried to develop understanding of natural phenomena without using the concept of environment. For example, what does the word "freely" in the familiar "Law of Freely Falling Bodies" mean? It means a body falling in the absence of any environmental influences. The apparent universality of such laws (and there were many) does not derive from their applicability to every environment for, strictly speaking, they apply to none; it derives from the fact that they apply *approximately* to most environments that we experience.

Perhaps even more revealing of the environment-free orientation of Machine-Age science is the nature of the place in which its inquiry was usually conducted, the *laboratory*. A laboratory is a place so constructed as to facilitate exclusion of the environment. It is a place in which the effect of one variable on another can be studied without the intervention of the environment.

Mechanism

The concept of the universe that derives from the exclusive use of analysis and the doctrines of reductionism and determinism is *mechanistic*. The world was viewed *as* a machine, not merely like one. The universe was frequently compared to a hermetically sealed clock. This is a very revealing comparison, implying that it had no environment. Like a clock, its behavior was thought to be determined by its internal structure and the causal laws of nature.

The Industrial Revolution

This revolution had to do with the replacement of man by man-made machines as a source of work. Its two central concepts were *work* and *machine*. Whatever else was thought of work, it was believed to be *real*, particularly after the Reformation. Because all real things were believed to be reducible to atoms and atoms had only two intrinsic properties, mass (matter) and energy, work was conceptualized as the application of energy to matter so as to change its properties. For example, the movement of coal and its transformation into heat (energy) were considered to be work. Thought, however, was not taken to be work because it did not involve the application of energy to matter.

A machine was considered any object that could be used to apply energy to matter. Not surprisingly, it was believed that all machines were reducible to elementary machines: the lever, pulley, wheel and axle, and inclined plane (of which the wedge and screw are modifications).

The mechanization of work was greatly facilitated by reducing it to a set of simple tasks. Therefore, work was *analyzed* to reduce it to its *elements*. These elements were tasks so simple that they could only be done by one person—for example, tightening a screw or driving a nail. Then many of the work elements were mechanized. Not all were because either the technology required was not available or, although available, it was more costly than the use of human labor. Therefore, people and machines, each doing elementary tasks, were aggregated to do the whole job. The result was the industrialized production and assembly line that forms the spine of the modern factory.

The benefits of the Industrial Revolution are too obvious to dwell on here. They were many and significant. The same can be said of its costs. However, there is one cost which we have only recently become aware of, derived from what might be called the irony of the Industrial Revolution. In our effort to replace ourselves with machines as a source of energy, we reduced our work to elementary tasks designed to be simple enough to be done by machines, eventually if not immediately. In this way *we were reduced to behaving like machines*, doing very simple repetitive tasks. Our work became dehumanized. This is the source of one of the most critical problems facing us today, our alienation from work.

The nature of the workplace developed during the Industrial Revolution was dictated by the application of the analytical method to work. If there were another way of thinking about work, it would be possible to conceive of another kind of workplace, one very different from the kind that we know today. This possibility is one that recently has been given much thought. I will return to it after we have seen what the alternative way of thinking is.

On Looking Backward and Forward

The Machine Age is largely history, but part of it still lives. The very brief account of its history that I have given is not a conventional one, hence it is subject to controversy. In contrast, the Systems Age lies largely in the future; nevertheless, my account of it is equally controversial. Such controversy, however, revolves around what we want it to be because, as I will argue, to a large extent the future can be what we want it to be. The Systems Age emerges from a new vision, a new mission, and a new method. Therefore, in describing it my rhetoric changes from narrative to persuasive as I try to convince the reader to share the vision, mission, and method with which I believe we can create this new age.

I present the Systems Age as emerging dialectically from the Machine Age. The Machine Age is a thesis, and its meaning and implications only become clear when its antithesis is fully developed. This development is taking place now, in the period of transition from one age to another, just as it took place for the Machine Age during the Renaissance. The Systems Age, as I see it, is a synthesis of the Machine Age and its antithesis, which is still being formulated. Their synthesis, however, has already begun to emerge and is being disclosed more clearly as time goes on.

The Systems Age is a movement of many wills in which each has only a small part to play, even those who are trying to shape it deliberately. It is taking shape before our eyes. It is still too early, however, to foresee all the difficulties that it will generate. Nevertheless, I believe the new age can be trusted to deal with them. Meanwhile there is much work to be done, much scope for greater vision, and much room for enthusiasm and optimism.

My account of the Machine Age was a hurried resume of the past because I am eager to face the future. The brevity of my account depreciates the magnificent efforts of the past four centuries to cope effectively with reality. The origins of the Systems Age lie in this past, hence the problems it confronts are inherited, but those of us who intend to have a hand in shaping the new age are trying to face them in a new way. Now let us see what that way is.

THE SYSTEMS AGE

No age has a starting point; it emerges imperceptibly in bits and pieces that eventually combine, first to produce an awareness that something fundamental is happening, then to provide a new world view.

Doubts about a prevailing world view usually begin with the appearances of *dilemmas*. A dilemma is a problem or question that cannot be solved or answered within the prevailing world view and therefore calls it into question (see Kuhn [47]). We have already considered one such question: how can we account for free will in a mechanistic universe? In physics, Heisenberg's *Uncertaintly Principle* presented another such dilemma. He showed that within the prevailing paradigm in physics two critical properties of point particles could not be determined simultaneously; as the accuracy of the determination of one increases, the accuracy of the other decreases. This called into question the belief that the world is completely understandable, even in principle.

Then there was the dilemma that arose as all the king's men tried and failed to put Humpty Dumpty together again. Some things, once disassembled, could not be reassembled. The essential properties of other things could not be inferred from either the properties of their parts or their interactions, as for example, the personality or intelligence of a human being. More recently, in their studies of servomechanisms, machines that control other machines, Arturo Rosenblueth and Norbert Wiener [66] argued that such machines could only be understood if they were assumed to display choice and goal-seeking behavior. Choice and mechanism, however, are incompatible concepts. This dilemma had a special significance which is discussed later in this chapter.

In the latter part of the last century and the early part of this one, dilemmas arose with increasing frequency in every field of inquiry. Investigators confronted with dilemmas in one field gradually became aware of those arising in other fields and the similarities among them. They also became aware of the fact that the prevailing mechanistic view of the world and the beliefs on which it was based were increasingly being brought into question. This awareness was intensified by events that took place just before, during, and immediately after World War II.

This war took science and scientists out of their laboratories and into the "real world" in an effort to solve important problems arising in large, complex organizations—military, governmental, and corporate. Scientists discovered that the problems they faced could not be disassembled into ones that fit neatly into any one discipline and that the interactions of the solutions of disassembled parts were of greater importance than the solutions considered separately. This in turn led to the formation of interdisciplinary efforts. In the late 1930s, Operational Research, an interdisciplinary activity, emerged out of the British military establishment to deal with the management and control of its complex operations.

By the 1950s interdisciplinary scientific activities proliferated. These included the management sciences, decision sciences, computer sciences, information sciences, cybernetics, policy sciences, peace science, and many others. The overlap of interest among them and the similarities in their practices led to a search for a theme common to all of them.

By the mid-1950s it was generally recognized that the source of similarities of the interdisciplines was their shared preoccupation with the behavior of *systems*. This concept gradually came to be recognized as one that could be used to organize an increasingly varied set of intellectual pursuits. Of greater importance, however, was the fact that it revealed the fundamental dilemma of the Machine Age and suggested how its world view might be modified to escape the horns of that dilemma. It is for this reason that I refer to the emerging era as the *Systems Age.*

The Nature of a System

Before we can begin to understand the change in world view that the focus on systems is bringing about, we must first understand the concept of systems itself.

A system is a set of two or more elements that satisfies the following three conditions.

1. *The behavior of each element has an effect on the behavior of the whole.* Consider, for example, that system which is, perhaps, the most familiar to us: the human body. Each of its parts—the heart, lungs, stomach, and so on—has an effect on the performance of the whole. However, one part of the body, the appendix, is not known to have any such effect. It is not surprising, therefore, that it is called the appendix which means "attached to," not "a part of." If a function is found for the appendix, its name would probably be changed.

2. *The behavior of the elements and their effects on the whole are interdependent.* This condition implies that the way each element behaves and the way it affects the whole depends on how at least one other element behaves. No element has an independent effect on the system as a whole. In the human body, for example, the way the heart behaves and the way it affects the body as a whole depends on the behavior of the brain, lungs, and other parts of the body. The same is true for the brain and lungs.

3. *However subgroups of the elements are formed, each has an effect on the behavior of the whole and none has an independent effect on it.* To put it another way, the elements of a system are so connected that independent subgroups of them cannot be formed.

A system, therefore, is a whole that cannot be divided into independent parts. From this, two of its most important properties derive: every part of a system has properties that it loses when separated from the system, and every system has some properties—its essential ones—that none of its parts do. An organ or part of the body, for example, if removed from the body does not continue to operate as it did before removal. The eye detached from the body cannot see. On the other hand, people can run, play piano, read, write, and do many other things that none of their parts can do by themselves. No part of a human being is human; only the whole is.

The essential properties of a system taken as a whole derive from the *interactions* of its parts, not their actions taken separately. Therefore, *when a system is taken apart it loses its essential properties.* Because of this—and this is the critical point—*a system is a whole that cannot be understood by analysis.*

Realization of this fact is the primary source of the intellectual revolution that is bringing about a change of age. It has become clear that a method other than analysis is required for understanding the behavior and properties of systems.

Systems Thinking

Synthesis, or putting things together, is the key to systems thinking just as analysis, or taking them apart, was the key to Machine-Age thinking. Synthesis, of course, is as old as analysis—Aristotle dealt with both—but it is taking on a new meaning and significance in a new context just as analysis did with the emergence of the Machine Age. Synthesis and analysis are complementary processes. Like the head and tail of a coin, they can be considered separately, but they cannot be separated. Therefore, the differences between Systems-Age and Machine-Age thinking derives not from the fact that one synthesizes and the other analyses, but from the fact that systems thinking combines the two in a new way.

Systems thinking reverses the three-stage order of Machine-Age thinking: (1) decomposition of that which is to be explained, (2) explanation of the behavior or properties of the parts taken separately, and (3) aggregating these explanations into an explanation of the whole. This third step, of course, is synthesis. In the systems approach there are also three steps:

1. Identify a containing whole (system) of which the thing to to be explained is a part.
2. Explain the behavior or properties of the containing whole.
3. Then explain the behavior or properties of the thing to be explained in terms of its *role(s)* or *function(s)* within its containing whole.

Note that in this sequence, synthesis precedes analysis.

In analytical thinking the thing to be explained is treated as a whole to be taken apart. In synthetic thinking the thing to be explained is treated as a part of a containing whole. The former *reduces* the focus of the investigator; the latter *expands* it.

An example might help clarify the difference. A Machine-Age thinker, confronted with the need to explain a university, would begin by disassembling it until he reached its elements; for example, from university to college, from college to department, and from department to faculty, students, and subject matter. Then he would define faculty, student, and subject matter. Finally, he would aggregate these into a definition of a department, thence to college, and conclude with a definition of a university.

A systems thinker confronted with the same task would begin by identifying a system containing the university; for example, the educational system. Then such a thinker would define the objectives and functions of the educational system and do so with respect to the still larger social system that contains it. Finally, he or she would explain or define the university in terms of its roles and functions in the educational system.

These two approaches should not (but often do) yield contradictory or conflicting results: they are complementary. Development of this complementarity is a major task of systems thinking. Analysis focuses on *structure*; it reveals *how things work*. Synthesis focuses on *function*; it reveals *why things operate as they do*. Therefore, analysis yields *knowledge*; synthesis yields *understanding*. The former enables us to *describe*; the latter, to *explain*.

Analysis looks *into* things; synthesis looks *out of* things. Machine-Age thinking was concerned only with the interactions of the parts of the thing to be explained; systems thinking is similarly concerned, but it is additionally occupied with the interactions of that thing with other things in its environment and with its environment itself. It is also concerned with the *functional* interaction of the parts of a system. This orientation derives from the preoccupation of systems thinking with the *design* and *redesign* of systems. In systems design, parts identified by analysis of the function(s) to be performed by the whole are not put together like unchangeable pieces of a jigsaw puzzle; they are designed to fit each other so as to work together *harmoniously* as well as efficiently and effectively.

Harmony has to do not only with the effect of the interactions of the parts on the whole, but also with the effects of the functioning of the whole and the interactions of the parts on the parts themselves. It is also concerned with the effects of the functioning of the parts and the whole on the containing system and other systems in its environment. This concern with harmony has important implications in the management of systems—implications that are explored below.

There are considerable differences between what might be called analytical and synthetic management. To a large extent this book is devoted
to illuminating these differences. One such difference is worth noting
here. It is based on the following systems principle:

*If each part of a system, considered separately, is made to operate as efficiently
as possible, the system as a whole will* not *operate as effectively as possible.*

Although the general validity of this principle is not apparent, its validity in specific instances is. For example, consider the large number of
types of automobile that are available. Suppose we bring one of each of
these into a large garage and then employ a number of outstanding automotive engineers to determine which one has the best carburetor. When
they have done so, we record the result and ask them to do the same for
engines. We continue this process until we have covered all the parts
required for an automobile. Then we ask the engineers to remove and
assemble these parts. Would we obtain the best possible automobile? Of
course not. We would not even obtain an automobile because *the parts
would not fit together;* even if they did, *they would not work well together. The performance of a system depends more on how its parts
interact than on how they act independently of each other.*

Similarly, an all-star baseball or football team is seldom if ever the best
team available, although one might argue that it would be if its members
were allowed to play together for a year or so. True, but if they became
the best team it is very unlikely that all of its members would be on the
new all-star team.

The current methodology of management is predominantly based on
Machine-Age thinking. When managers are confronted with large complex problems or tasks, they almost always break them down into solvable or manageable parts; they "cut them down to size." Then they
arrange to have each part solved or performed as well as possible. The
outputs of these separate efforts are then assembled into a "solution" of
the whole. Yet we can be sure that the sum of the best solutions obtained from the parts taken separately is *not* the best solution to the
whole. Fortunately, it is seldom the worst.

Awareness of this conflict between parts and the whole is reflected in
the widespread recognition of the need for *coordinating* the behavior of
the parts of a system. At the same time, however, measures of performance are set for the parts that bring them into conflict. Formulation of
these measures is commonly based on the assumption that the best performance of the whole can be reduced to the sum of the best performances of its parts taken separately. The systems principle, however,

asserts that this is not possible. Therefore, another and more effective way of organizing and managing the parts is required. One is considered below.

The application of systems thinking, whether to management or the world, like the application of Machine-Age thinking, raises a number of fundamental questions. The answers to these questions provide the doctrines from which a systems view of the world derives. Let us see how.

Expansionism

In systems thinking, increases in understanding are believed to be obtainable by expanding the systems to be understood, not by reducing them to their elements. Understanding proceeds from the whole to its parts, not from the parts to the whole as knowledge does.

If the behavior of a system is to be explained by referring to its containing system (the suprasystem), how is the behavior of the suprasystem to be explained? The answer is obvious: by reference to a more inclusive system, one that contains the suprasystem. Then the fundamental question—Is there any end to this process of expansion? Recall that when the corresponding question arose in the Machine Age—Is there any end to the process of reduction?—the answer was dictated by the belief that, at least in principle, complete understanding of the universe was possible. In the early part of this century, however, this belief was shattered by such dilemmas as that formulated by Heisenberg. As a result, we have come to believe that complete understanding of anything, let alone everything, is an *ideal* that can be approached continously but *can never be attained.* Therefore, there is no need to assume the existence of an ultimate whole which if understood would yield the ultimate answer.

This means that we are free to believe or not in an all-containing whole. Since our understanding will never embrace such a whole, even if it exists, it makes no practical difference if we assume it to exist. Nevertheless, many individuals find comfort in assuming existence of such a unifying whole. Not surprisingly, they call it God. This God however, is very different from the Machine-Age God who was conceptualized as an individual who had created the universe. God-as-the-whole cannot be individualized or personified, and cannot be thought of as the creator. To do so would make no more sense than to speak of man as creator of his organs. In this holistic view of things man is taken as a part of God just as his heart is taken as a part of man.

Many will recognize that this holistic concept of God is precisely the one embraced by many Eastern religions which conceptualize God as a system, not as an element. It is not surprising, therefore, that in the past two decades many of the young people in the West—products of the emerging Systems Age—turned to religions of the East.

The East has used the concept of a system to organize its thinking about the universe for centuries, but it has not thought about systems scientifically. There is some hope, therefore, that in the creation of systems sciences the cultures of the East and West can be synthesized. The twain may yet meet in the Systems Age.

The doctrine of expansionism has a major effect on the way we go about trying to solve problems. In the Machine Age, when something did not work satisfactorily, we looked for improvement by manipulating the behavior of its parts; we looked for solutions from within and worked our way out from the interior only when we failed there. In the Systems Age we look for solutions from without and work our way in when we fail there. The reasons for and effects of this reversal of direction will become apparent when we consider the differences between Machine-Age and Systems-Age planning.

Producer–Product

The Machine Age's commitment to cause and effect was the source of many dilemmas, including the one involving free will. At the turn of the century the American philosopher E. A. Singer, Jr., showed that science had, in effect, been cheating.* It was using two different relationships but calling both cause and effect. He pointed out, for example, that acorns do not cause oaks because they are *not* sufficient, even though they are necessary, for oaks. An acorn thrown into the ocean, or planted in the desert or an Artic ice cap does not yield an oak. To call the relationship between an acorn and an oak "probabilistic" or "nondeterministic causality," as many scientists did, was cheating because it is not possible to have a probability other than 1.0 associated with a cause; a cause completely determines its effect. Therefore, Singer chose to call this relationship "producer–product" and to differentiate it from cause–effect.†

Singer went on to ask what the universe would look like if producer–product is applied to it rather than cause–effect. One might think of Singer's question in this way: an orange, when sliced vertically, yields a cross-sectional view that is very different from the view revealed when it

---

*Singer showed this in a series of papers published between 1896 and 1904. His work is best presented in a posthumors publication [74].

†Much after Singer, Sommerhoff [77] independently came up with very similar result. What Singer called "producer–product," Sommerhoff called "directive correlation."

is sliced horizontally. Yet both are views of the same thing. The more views we have of a thing, the better we can understand it. Singer argued similarly about the universe.

As Singer [74] and Ackoff and Emery [7] have shown, the view of the universe revealed by viewing it in terms of producer-product is quite different from that yielded by viewing it in terms of cause-effect. Because a producer is only necessary and not sufficient for its product, it cannot provide a complete explanation of it. There are always other necessary conditions, coproducers of its product. For example, moisture is a coproducer of an oak along with an acorn. These other necessary conditions taken collectively constitute the acorn's *environment*. Therefore, the use of the producer-product relationship requires the environment to explain everything whereas use of cause-effect requires the environment to explain nothing. Science based on the producer-product relationship is environment-*full*, not environment-*free*.

A law based on the producer-product relationship must specify the environment(s) under which it applies. No such law can apply in every environment, because if it did no environmental conditions would be necessary. Thus there are no universal laws in this view of the universe. For example, we have learned more recently that the law that everything that goes up must come down is not universally true. (Unfortunately, some things that we have put up with the intention that they not come down, nevertheless have done so.) Environmentally relative laws can use probabilistic concepts in a consistent and meaningful way. In an environment in which all the necessary coproducing conditions are not specified—hence may or may not be present—it is not only meaningful but it is useful to speak of the probability of production. For example, we can determine the probability of an acorn producing an oak in a specified environment in which some of the relevant properties are not known. Therefore, the probability determined is the probability that the unspecified but necessary environmental conditions are present.

Teleology

Singer [74] showed by reasoning that is too complicated to reproduce here that in the producer-product-based view of the world, such concepts as choice, purpose, and free will could be made operationally and objectively meaningful. (See also Ackoff and Emery [7].). A system's *ends—goals, objectives, and ideals—*could be established as objectively as the number of elements it contained. This made it possible to look at systems *teleologically,* in an output-oriented way, rather than deterministically, in an input-oriented way.

Objective teleology does not replace determinism, which is an objective *a*teleology; it complements it. These are different views of the same thing, but the teleological approach is more fruitful when applied to systems.

Centuries ago Aristotle invoked teleological concepts to explain why things, inanimate as well as animate, behaved as they did; but he employed a *subjective* teleology. Among those who carry on in his spirit are some psychologists who try to explain human behavior by invoking such (unobservable, they claim) intervening variables as beliefs, feelings, attitudes, and drives which at best are only observable by those who have them. In an objective teleology, beliefs, feelings, attitudes, and the like are attributable to human beings because of *what they do*; hence are observable. These properties are derived from observed regularities of behavior under varied conditions. Such concepts do not lie behind behavior, but *in* it; hence are observable. In an objective teleology functional characteristics of systems are not treated as metaphysical forces, but as observable properties of the systems' behavior.

The ideas and concepts developed by Singer were largely ignored for the first half of this century. Sommerhoff's were ignored as well, but for a shorter time. It was not until the concept of teleological mechanisms* and the dilemma contained in it came into the focus of science's attention that the work of Singer and Sommerhoff came to be recognized as significant. Their work solved this dilemma. A teleological system and a deterministic machine are two different aspects of the same thing. These antithetical points of view are synthesized in the concept of reality emerging in the Systems Age.

Systems-oriented investigators focus on teleological (goal seeking and purposeful) systems. In the Machine Age, even human beings were thought of as machines. In the Systems Age, even machines are thought of as parts of purposeful systems. We now believe that a machine cannot be understood except by reference to the purpose for which it is used by the purposeful system of which it is a part. For example, we cannot understand why an automobile is like it is without understanding the purposes for which it is used. Moreover, some machines, teleogical mechanisms, are seen to have goals, if not purposes, of their own.

Ordinary machines serve the purposes of others but have no purposes of their own. *Organisms* and *organizations* are systems that usually have purposes of their own. However, the parts of an organism (i.e, heart, lungs, brain) do not have purposes of their own, but the parts of an organization do. Therefore, when we focus on organizations we are con-

*Such mechanisms were brought to the attention of science by Frank et al [33].

cerned with three levels of purpose: the purposes of the system, of its parts, and of the system of which it is part, the suprasystem.

There is a functional division of labor among the parts of all types of systems. A set of elements or parts, all of which do the same thing, does not constitute a system; it is an aggregation. For example, a collection of people waiting for a bus does not constitute a system, nor does a collection of clocks all ticking away on the same shelf. Each part of a system has a function in the system, and some of these must differ. To organize a system, as we will see, is to divide its labor functionally among its parts and to arrange for their coordination.

The Postindustrial Revolution

To complete this account of the change of age that we are in, we should consider the effect of systems thinking on the Industrial Revolution.

The conversion of the Industrial Revolution into what has come to be called the *Postindustrial Revolution* has its origins in the last century. Scientists who explored the use of electricity as a source of energy found that it could not be observed easily. Therefore, they developed such *instruments* as the ammeter, ommeter, and voltmeter to observe it for them. The development of instruments exploded in this century, particularly after the advent of electronics and sonar and radar. Look at the dashboard of a large commercial airplane, or even one in an automobile. These instruments *generate symbols* that represent the properties of objects or events. Such symbols are called *data*. Instruments, therefore, are observing devices, but they are not machines in the Machine-Age sense because they do not apply energy to matter in order to transform it. The technology of instrumentation is fundamentally different from that of mechanization.

Another technology with this same characteristic emerged when the telegraph was invented in the last century. It was followed by the telephone, wireless, radio, television, and so on. This technology, like that of instrumentation, has nothing to do with mechanization; it has to do with the *transmission of symbols*, or *communication*.

The technologies of observation and communication formed the two sides of a technological arch that could not carry any weight until a keystone was dropped into place. This did not occur until the 1940s when the *computer* was developed. It too did no work in the Machine-Age sense; *it manipulated symbols logically*, which, as John Dewey [24] pointed out, is the nature of *thought*. It is for this reason that the computer is often referred to as a thinking machine.

Because the computer appeared at a time when we had begun to put things back together again, and because the technologies of observation, communication, and computation all involve the manipulation of symbols, people began to consider systems that combine these three functions. They found that such systems could be used to *control* other systems, to *automate*. Automation is fundamentally different from mechanization. Mechanization has to do with the replacement of *muscle*; automation with the replacement of *mind*. Automation is to the Postindustrial Revolution what mechanization was to the Industrial Revolution.

Automatons are certainly not machines in the Machine-Age sense, and they need not be purposeless. It was for this reason that they came to be called teleological mechanisms. However, automation is no more an essential ingredient of the systems approach than is high technology in general. Both come with the Systems Age and are among its producers as well as its products. The technology of the Postindustrial Revolution is neither a panacea nor a plague; it is what we make of it. It generates a host of problems and possibilities that systems thinking must address. The problems it generates are highly infectious, particularly to less-technologically developed cultures. The systems approach provides a more effective way than previously has been available for dealing with both the problems and the possibilities generated by the Postindustrial Revolution, but it is by no means limited to this special set of either or both.

CONCLUSION

Well, there it is: a tentative answer to the question—what in the world is happening in the world? My response to it is an attempt to make some sense out of what is going on and to equip us to cope with it more effectively. In particular, I hope to show that this response has important and useful implications to managers. Curiously, I have found managers more willing to embrace the systems approach and its implication than academics. Managers are more inclined than academics to try something new and judge it on the basis of its performance. Their egos are not as involved as the academics' in the acceptance or rejection of a view formulated by another. Academic evaluations tend to be based on the subjective opinions of peers, not on any objective measure of performance. Fortunately, in this connection the corporate manager has a more effective and exacting taskmaster: the "bottom line," the performance of the managed system.

CHAPTER TWO

OUR CHANGING CONCEPT
OF THE CORPORATION

Corporation, n. *An ingenious device for obtaining individual profit without individual responsibility.*

AMBROSE BIERCE

Corporations and the way we conceptualize them have evolved a great deal in the last hundred years. The modern corporation is a product of the Industrial Revolution, which, in turn, was a product of the Machine Age. Recall that in this age Western man conceptualized the universe as a machine created by God to do His work. Furthermore, man took himself to be a part of this machine and to have been created in the image of God. The Industrial Revolution was a consequence of man's efforts to imitate God by creating machines to do his work.

THE CORPORATION AS A MACHINE

The industrial organizations produced by the Industrial Revolution were taken to be related to their creators, their owners, much as the universe was to God. They were thought of as machines whose function was to serve their creators by providing them with an adequate return on their

25

investment of time and money. Therefore, the principal, if not the only, function of such organizations was to make a profit.

In corporations so conceived, employees were treated as replaceable machines or machine parts even though they were known to be human beings. Their personal objectives, however, were considered irrelevant by employers. Employment involved an implicit acceptance by employees of the employer's right to treat them as though they were machines. Furthermore, the very simple repetitive tasks they were given to do were designed as though they were to be performed by machines.

Even managers were treated as machine parts. According to E. E. Jennings [45]:

> Private life [of managers] ceased to exist apart from company life. The higher a man went, the more responsibility and, hence, less freedom to live privately. . . Family life became just another *cog in the corporate machine*. (p.29)

This conception of corporation as machine was tenable only as long as the following conditions held:

1. The owner had and could exercise virtually unlimited power over his employees—he could hire, fire, and otherwise reward or punish them much as he saw fit.
2. The threat to employees of economic destitution resulting from unemployment was large and real.
3. The skills required of workers were generally low, hence easily obtainable.
4. The levels of education and aspiration of ordinary workers were relatively low.

These conditions prevailed in the United States until the early part of this century. To be sure, workers objected to them almost from the beginning. Over time the number of objectors and the intensity of their objections grew. This growth kept pace with that of corporations.

After the turn of the century the conditions necessary to support the mechanistic concept of the corporation began to change. First, opportunities for company growth generally exceeded what could be internally financed. Therefore, many privately owned companies "went public," or incorporated. Their ownership was dispersed among a large group of anonymous stockholders who seldom came into direct contact with workers. In effect, God disappeared. He became an abstract spirit rather than a concrete presence. Management emerged as a clergy that interpreted their god's desires and administered its will on the workers.

Second, the emergence of a management distinct from ownership was accompanied by the growth of unionization, social welfare, and the economy, each of which reduced the threat of economic destitution that faced the labor force.

Third, increasing mechanization required greater skills of workers. The more skills they acquired, the more difficult and costly it became to replace them.

Finally, the increase of compulsory education and the passage of laws restricting use of child labor raised the levels of education and aspiration of those entering the work force. They became less willing to accept a machinelike work life.

The mechanistic concept of the corporation could not stand up to this barrage of change.

THE CORPORATION AS AN ORGANISM

After World War I a new concept of the corporation gradually emerged: the corporation as an *organism*. So conceptualized, the corporation was taken to have a life and purposes of its own. Its principal purposes, like those of any organism, were believed to be *survival and growth*. Corporate profit came to be viewed in much the same way as oxygen is to an organism—necessary, but not the reason for its existence.

Because of the continued dispersion of corporate ownership and its increasingly transitory nature due to speculation on the stock exchange, the claims made by management of access to God by revelation became less believable. Managers had to accept full responsibility for their decisions.

Management was characterized as the brain or head of the firm and employees as its organs. Because organs are less easily replaced than machines or machine parts, their health and safety became corporate concerns. Working conditions became the focus of union–management negotiations. However, the concept and the nature of work itself were not called into question except when they affected health and safety.

Workers, their work places, and the society that contained them continued to change. Such change was greatly accelerated by World War II, when exceptional demands were made on both managers and workers. It became apparent that how workers felt about their work had a large effect on how much work they did and how well they did it. When work became less satisfying, output decreased. As Philip Shakeoff [69] wrote in the *The New York Times* when commenting on a study issued by the U.S. Department of Health, Education and Welfare, "A changing American work force is becoming pervasively dissatisfied with dull, unchallenging and repetitive jobs, and this discontent is sapping the economic and social strength of the nation."

As automation was introduced and spread, the technical content of many jobs increased significantly; hence learning became an essential part of these jobs. The investment in the education and training of workers became a major one, making their replacement even more costly. Furthermore, the greater the skills required of a worker, the more difficult it became for his boss to tell him how to do his work. Few managers, for example, could instruct computer programmers or airline pilots. Managers could specify the kind of output or performance they wanted but not how it was to be obtained. In this way the increase in the technological content of work brought about increased freedom of, and dependence on, nonmanagerial employees.

As the skills of workers increased, the less inclined they were to give blind loyalty to their employing organizations. They began to think of themselves as professionals. Therefore, their personal aspirations and work-related requirements became increasing concerns to employers seeking their skills. This, as E. E. Jennings [45] observed, applied equally to managers:

> Then came World War II . . . and innovation was needed at all levels; no one person could possibly know enough to maintain corporate viability.
>
> Corporations began placing their chips on young men not yet mesmerized by the loyalty ethic. . .
>
> Young executives grew self-confident that they could manage their own careers.. . . When they saw upward mobility arrested, they opted for opportunities elsewhere. . .
>
> The most mobile had the best chance to achieve and acquire experience; mobility bred competency that in turn bred mobility. Rapid executive turnover became a fact of life. (p.29)

The immense flood of talented young executives that poured into business would alone have disposed of the idea of the corporation as a machine, even without worker dissatisfaction. The major role of this new group of managers, as Jennings observed, was *innovation*, the exact antithesis of machinelike behavior. The idea of a corporation as an organism was harder to discredit. To be regarded as the brain of a corporation had a seductive appeal. But the brain merely proposes; the body, other human beings, and the environment taken together dispose. In the turbulent environment of post-World War II, managers quickly perceived that their major problem was managing people. Those who had returned from the service were no longer willing to be treated in the mechanistic way that the military had treated them. They insisted on consideration of their individual aspirations and hopes. Therefore, their treatment as purposeful individuals of intrinsic as well as extrinsic value could hardly be avoided.

The new entrants into the work force were raised in families and educated in schools that were increasingly permissive. The products of permissiveness did not submit easily to authority. Furthermore, the continued development of the welfare state made economic destitution even less real. For these reasons and others the work ethic was significantly undermined.

Finally, in the post–World War II period the accumulated effects of the behavior of industrial organizations on their social and physical environments were increasingly seen as bad. The social responsibility of the corporation became a major public issue. Consumerism and environmentalism were launched, and the energy crisis added considerable fuel to these fires. Such movements pushed government toward more intervention in the conduct of business.

THE CORPORATION AS AN ORGANIZATION

For all the foregoing reasons and others, the concept of a corporation as an organism has become less tenable. A new concept has begun to emerge: the corporation as an *organization*. The corporation, of course, has always been thought of as an organization, but the implications of this have only recently come into collective consciousness.

An organization is (1) a purposeful system that is (2) part of one or more purposeful systems, and (3) parts of which, people, have purposes of their own. The first of these properties disposes of the concept of a corporation as a machine. The second denies that it is environment free. The third renders inapplicable the analogy of a corporation as an organism. These negative inferences from the properties of an organization simply clear the way to what these properties imply in an affirmative sense. This is a longer story.

We have become increasingly aware of the interactions of these three levels of purpose: societal, organizational, and individual; and that how well a corporation performs depends on how it is affected by both the people who are part of it and the systems of which it is part. Additionally, we are beginning to see more clearly that how an organization's parts affect it depends on how it affects them; and, similarly, the way in which the containing system affects it depends on how it affects that system. To put it another way, management is seen as having three major interdependent types of responsibility: first, to the purposes of the system they manage (*control;*)second, to the purposes of the people who are part of the managed system (*humanization*); and third, to the purposes of the containing system and other systems that it contains (*environmentalization*).

Humanization problems have become pervasive and critical in contemporary society. Problems between races, the women's liberation movement, the generation gap, the third-world problem, and alienation from work are examples. In each, purposeful individuals who are part of the same system organize to protest the way they are treated by their containing system.

Environmentalization problems such as ecological consideration and consumerism are also pervasive and critical. Such problems are created when purposeful individuals or organizations in the environment of a system organize to protest the way they are affected by that system. The environmentalization problem arises outside an organization; the humanization problem within it.

The task of management is seen increasing as that of directing the corporation to satisfy the three types of demand that are placed on it. To a large extent the difficulty of this task derives from the fact that the three sets of demands, and even the demands within each set, are often incompatible. Effective management in the face of this sort of conflict requires a clear concept of an organization's functions relative to its parts and the system of which it is part, as well as its own purposes. We now turn to the development of such a concept.

The Stakeholder View of the Firm

The way we conceptualize a corporation affects the way we look at and describe its activities. To conceptualize a corporation as an organization is to see it as its *stakeholders* do. Stakeholders are all those inside or outside an organization who are directly affected by what it does. Therefore, they include all those whom managers should take into account, including managers themselves. From their perspectives a corporation engages in six types of exchanges (see Figure 2.1):

1. An exchange of money for work with *employees.*
2. An exchange of money for goods and services with *suppliers.*
3. An exchange of goods and services for money with *customers.*

4. An exchange of money paid later for money received now with *investors* and *lenders*.
5. An exchange of money paid now for money received later with *debtors*.
6. An exchange of money for goods, services, and regulation with *government* (e.g., water, waste collection and disposal, and fire and police protection).

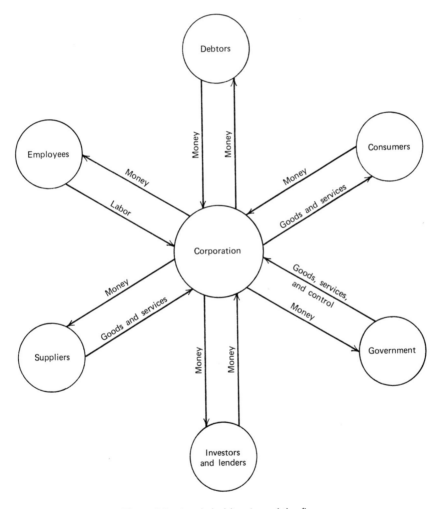

Figure 2.1 A stakeholder view of the firm.

An examination of the flow between a corporation and its stakeholders reveals that, in a very general sense, a corporation does two things: it consumes, and it makes consumption possible. It makes consumption possible by making goods and services available, and by providing others with money with which they can purchase goods and services. The wealth produced by a corporation is the difference between the consumption it makes possible and its own consumption. Clearly, one societal function of industrial and commercial corporations is the production of wealth. Not so clear is the fact that it has another equally important societal function: the distribution of income through which consumption is made possible.

Employment is the principal means by which income is distributed in industrialized societies, whatever their politics. If corporations fail to provide enough employment to perform this function satisfactorily (as has been the case, for example, in many less developed countries) their governments have no alternative but to take over all or part of it. Increased social welfare and government employment (through nationalization of corporations, for instance) are two of the more common ways by which such a takeover is achieved.

There are not many examples of governments that run wealth-producing organizations efficiently. Furthermore, because welfare institutions are not wealth-producing, the cost to society of having its government distribute income is generally larger than that of having it done by private corporations. Nevertheless, some feel that doing so is worth the additional cost because it can yield a more equitable distribution of wealth than a private distribution system. As yet, no exclusively private system for distributing wealth in a society has been able to eliminate poverty, but some public and some combined public–private systems have.

Some governments are reluctant to control or take over the task of creating and maintaining employment but feel obliged to do so because private corporations fail to do the job adequately. Increased governmental regulation of corporate behavior is a consequence. For example, the governments of many European countries have made it very difficult for employers to fire anyone. Unions have joined governments in forcing corporations to treat wages as virtually a fixed cost. This can, but need not, be disastrous to corporations. Whether it is depends on how management reacts to it.

Most private corporations attempt to maximize the return on the investment in their fixed assets, facilities and equipment. Profit enables them to provide a return to their investors. This way of looking at a corporation, although commonplace, is arbitrary. It derives from earlier conditions that have changed or are changing: shortage of capital and a commodity-like labor market. Relevant social values are also changing; for example, as societies develop, their tolerance for poverty decreases.

Legislation, regulation, and labor contracts are making it increasingly difficult to treat the cost of labor as a variable and, therefore, as an expense. Social pressure is forcing managers to attempt to maximize the return on a relatively fixed cost of labor. In a sense, the cost of labor is changing from an expense to an investment. This does not mean, however, that the need to increase the productivity of labor or of facilities and equipment is less pressing, but it does require a higher level of management skill to determine how to use a relatively fixed work force productively. This implies that when workers are replaced by machines, new productive work must be found for them. Since growth is also an objective of most corporations, this need not place much of an additional burden on management. However, it requires coordination of growth and increases of productivity. (One can argue moralistically that an organization that cannot increase its productivity does not deserve to grow.) It is not at all unlikely that efforts to maximize the return on labor would yield larger corporate profits than efforts to maximize return on fixed assets. In any event, pressure for this changeover in management perspective is more likely to grow than to diminish in the foreseeable future.

Corporations have a social responsibility not merely for distributing wealth, but for doing so equitably. *Equity* in this context does not necessarily mean *equally*, not even in communist societies. Its most widely accepted meaning implies the elimination of poverty. Poverty refers to a level of income that reduces opportunities for self-realization and life expectancy.

When management and labor disagree on what is a fair distribution of the wealth created by a corporation, at least one of these parties feels that it is being exploited by the other. It is this feeling that leads one or both parties to seek a larger portion of the pie. The consequence is inflation. Inflation, of course, has many other sources, but this is a major one. For this reason the rate of inflation is an indicator of social dissatisfaction with the distribution of wealth. This is as true between nations as it is within them, which is apparent from the behavior of the OPEC countries in the recent past.

To return to the question of the appropriate objective of a corporation conceptualized as an organization. It is *not* to serve any one of its stakeholder groups to the exclusion of any of the others. *It is to serve all of them by increasing their ability to pursue their objectives more efficiently and effectively.*

This corporate objective seems to imply that a corporation should have no purpose of its own. It should be no more than an instrument of others. This, however, is a great deal. Just as serving patients is a purpose of a doctor, serving stakeholders should be a purpose of a corporation. It is a purpose rather than a function because the corporation can display choice with respect to this objective; it can reject it. The corporation has choice of both ends and means. This kind of discussion would be meaningless if the corporation did not have such a choice. It is only because it does that it is meaningful to speak of what its purpose *should* be.

In the Machine Age a corporation was conceptualized as a mechanical tool of its owners. The organizational concept developed here differs from this in two ways. First, it views the corporation as an instrument of *all* its stakeholders. From society's point of view, serving the interests of investors may not be as important as serving the interests of one or more other types of stakeholder. This is clearly the case where public utilities are concerned. It seems apparent that, in general, corporations are more important to their employees than they are to their investors in the sense that in the event of the demise of a corporation, the average loss suffered by its employees would be relatively greater than that suffered by its investors.

Second, a corporation is purposeful, capable of selecting its own objectives and the means for pursuing them. Therefore, the objective formulated here cannot be imposed on it. It is a matter of corporate choice.

The objective—to increase the ability of its stakeholders to pursue their objectives—is equivalent to enabling them to improve their standard of living and quality of life. An increase in a corporation's ability to develop its stakeholders is corporate development. Such development has meaning only for purposeful systems. It is a term whose meaning is not obvious and therefore requires discussion.

THE CONCEPT OF DEVELOPMENT

The discussion of development that follows is necessarily philosophical. This is another way of saying that it is based on important and fundamental beliefs, attitudes, and commitments.

Most managers currently think of corporations as organisms, not as organizations. Therefore, they see growth as an objective that is second only to survival. To be sure, they speak of "corporate development," but they normally think of it as equivalent to corporate growth. *Growth and development are not the same thing.* Growth can take place with or without development, and development can take place with or without growth. For example, a cemetery can grow without developing; so can a rubbish heap. A nation, corporation, or an individual can develop without growing.

Growth, strictly speaking, is *an increase in size or number.* Organisms can increase in size and populations can increase in number. Corporate growth, therefore, refers to either an increase in size or an increase in some measurement of performance such as gross sales, share of market, number of employees, or net earnings. Growth is also used metaphorically as, for example, when we apeak of a person growing up, meaning becoming more mature. In such usage we refer to an increase in certain functional qualities, not structural quantities.

Growth usually occurs in organisms without choice. Nevertheless, purposeful systems can deter or accelerate their growth by the choices they make; for example, human beings can do so by choice of diet and corporations by choice of investments. If a physically normal human being has a compulsion to grow we consider this condition to be pathological. Medical science increasingly treats obesity combined with a compulsion to eat as a pathology. However, if a corporation or a society has such a compulsion, not only do we consider it natural, but also laudable. Why? Because we assume that physical or economic growth and social or corporate development are causally connected, if not the same thing. Neither is the case. Nevertheless, if limits to growth threatened a society's or corporation's survival, one could understand its preoccupation with growth, but not even the authors of *The Limits to Growth* [52] say that this is the case. Limits to growth do not limit development.

First consider what development of a person means. Contrary to what many believe, development is not a condition or state defined by what a person has. It is *a process in which an individual increases his ability and desire to satisfy his own desires and those of others.* It is an increase in capacity and potential, not an increase in attainment. It is more a matter of motivation, knowledge, understanding, and wisdom than it is of wealth. It has less to do with how much one has than with how much one can do with whatever one has. This is why Robinson Crusoe and the Swiss Family Robinson are paradigms of development.

Development is more closely related to the quality of life than it is to the standard of living. If we give wealth to an underdeveloped people they do not thereby become developed. If we give them knowledge and understanding, they are thereby developed. It has become increasingly apparent that increases in the standard of living are not necessarily accompanied by increases in the quality of life. In fact, many now argue that in at least some of the economically most advanced countries, increases in the first have brought decreases in the second.

Where the initial standard of living and quality of life are low, increases in wealth are often associated with improved quality of life and for this reason many governments focus on standard of living. However, this is not necessarily true. To many American Indians, for example, the surrounding white society is seen to have a higher standard of living but a lower quality of life than they do.

This is *not* to say that wealth is irrelevant to development or quality of life; it is very relevant. How much people can *actually* improve their quality of life and that of others depends not only on their knowledge and motivation, but also on what instruments and resources are available to them. For example, a man can build a better house with good tools and materials than he can without them. On the other hand, a developed man can build a better house with whatever tools and materials he has than a less developed man with the same resources. In other words, a developed man with limited resources can often improve his quality of life and that of others more than a less developed man with unlimited resources.

Because development consists of a desire and an ability, it cannot be given to or imposed on one person by another. Nor can a government develop the governed, or a corporation its employees. The most they can do is *encourage* and *facilitate* such development. Development is not like the practice of medicine, but like teaching. One cannot prescribe development; but, although one cannot learn or become motivated for another, one can encourage and facilitate another's learning and motivation.

The quality of life that people can actually realize is the joint product of their development and the resources available to them. Although this implies that limited resources may limit the improvement of the quality of life, it does *not* imply that they limit development. Development is a *potentiality* for improvement, not the actual improvement of the quality of life or the standard of living.

Limits to Growth and Development

A limit is a quantity that a variable cannot exceed. For example, nothing can move faster than light; the speed of light is a limit. There is a maximum speed at which an automobile can travel on a flat highway. Limits, like growth, are structural in nature; that is, they refer to physical properties of things. But we loosely apply the term to functional properties as well; this is a figurative, not a literal, application. For example, what we refer to as a speed limit on a highway clearly does not limit the speed at which we travel. The limit to the speed at which an automobile can travel need not limit its driver. She can take an airplane if she wants to

travel faster. Therefore, the limiting effects of physical limits on purposeful individuals and systems can be removed either by changed desires or
technological developments that remove or raise the limit. A limited resource limits us only if we want to do something that requires more of
that resource than is available and there is no suitable substitute in sufficient supply. A limited resource ceases to be limiting if our need for it
decreases or if we learn how to use it more efficiently and effectively;
that is, *if we develop.* The more developed a person of system is, the less
he or she or it is limited by resources.

Constraints on the growth of a society or a corporation usually lie in its
environment, but the principal constraints on its development lie within
it. To put it another way, the principal limits to growth are external,
imposed from without; the principal limits to development are internal,
self-imposed.

Development and Competence

An unlimited ability to satisfy one's desires and those of others can be
called *omnicompetence.* This term has connotations significantly different from those of *omnipotence.* Omnipotence connotes unlimited
power, authority, or force. Competence does not imply either authority
or force. the only power it implies is the power *to* (the ability or capacity
to perform effectively), not *over* (might or authority). Omnipotence implies control of others; omnicompetence implies self-control.

The philosopher E. A. Singer, Jr., [72 and 73] pointed out that the
unlimited ability to satisfy desires is a *necessary ideal* of all people—past,
present, and future—because no matter what men want, they must want
the ability to obtain it. Thus the desire for competence necessarily accompanies all desire, even the desire for absence of desire, or Nirvana.
Because omnicompetence is an ideal implying the ability to attain any
other ideal, it can be thought of as a *meta-ideal.* To develop, then, is to
make progress toward this meta-ideal.

Societies, institutions, corporations, and other types of social entity are
created and supported by individuals to enable them to pursue their
goals, objectives, and ideals more efficiently and effectively. They are
instruments of their members. At least one of their purposes, therefore,
should be to perform this function efficiently and effectively. Social
groups, including corporations, are developed to the extent that they
desire and are capable of increasing the development of all those who
are effected by them.

Of those affected by a social system, those who are part of it are
usually the most affected; they spend more of their time with it than

others. The corporation is a work environment for its employees but not for any of its other stakeholders. For this reason the corporation has a special responsibility to encourage and facilitate the development of all its employees, not just its managers or potential managers.

What can a social system, particularly a society, do to encourage and facilitate the development of its members? The answer to this question lies in an analysis of the conditions necessary for an individual's continuous progress toward omnicompetence.

The ancient Greek philosophers identified four pursuits individually necessary and collectively sufficient for the development of man: *truth, plenty, good*, and *beauty*.

1. The pursuit of *truth* is the *scientific* and *technological* function of society. It consists of encouraging and facilitating the production of the information, knowledge, and understanding required by individuals to select the most efficient means available and to develop increasingly efficient means.

A corporation can contribute to this societal function formally through its own research and development activities, and through its support of such activities by others. It can add to the store of information, knowledge, and understanding available to its society and its own members. To do so may not be its principal function, but it is an important one. To the extent that a corporation fails to make its information, knowledge, and understanding available for noncompetitive use by others, it retards societal development. Making them available, however, does not require providing them cost free.

2. The pursuit of *plenty* is the *economic* function of society. It consists of encouraging and facilitating the provision to individuals of the physical and mental resources they require in the pursuit of their ends. Doing so involves the production and distribution of such resources— making them generally available, making their availability known, providing access to them, and protecting them against appropriation or destruction.

As I have already observed, the principal societal role of the corporation in society is economic: to produce and distribute wealth. Other social institutions are also so engaged. Government plays an indispensable role in providing resources and services (e.g., water and waste disposal), and in protecting property against appropriation (through the police and military) and destruction (through flood control, for example).

Education, it should be noted, is a way of distributing mental resources—information, knowledge, and understanding. Therefore, to the extent that a corporation encourages and facilitates the education of its members, it contributes to their development.

3. The pursuit of the *good* is the *ethical–moral* function of society. It is directed at removing conflict between objectives within individuals (peace of mind) and between individuals (peace on Earth).

Unless conflict within an individual is removed, he or she will have some objectives toward which progress cannot be made. The same is true for at least some of the individuals involved in conflict with others.

The *ethical–moral* function is carried out in the main by educational, religious, psychiatric, and legal institutions, as well as the family. The corporation does not have a significant societal role here except with respect to its own members. It has the same ethical–moral responsibilities to its members in their work place as society has to its members in their social environment. Corporations that take this responsibility seriously do such things as offer employee assistance programs providing services directed at removing internal conflict, and ombudsmen who attempt to remove conflict between individuals and the organization or its parts. Formalized grievance procedures are directed to the same end. As discussed later in the chapter, conflict within a corporation can be a major deterrent to its development.

4. The pursuit of *beauty* is the *aesthetic* function of society. This function requires more extended treatment because it is the least understood and, I believe, currently the most critical of the four. The mystery associated with aesthetics is reflected in the fact that throughout history very few systemic philosophers have been able to incorporate it in their philosophies. Of the few who have, the results have been more like appendices to their philosophies than integral parts of them. On the other hand, very few of those who have been preoccupied with aesthetics have made a significant contribution to our understanding of science, economics, ethics, or morality. Historically, aesthetics has been the black sheep of the philosophical family.

This disconnectedness of aethetics is reflected in the fact that managers have some idea of what the science, economics, and the ethics or morality of management mean, but they often have no idea what the aesthetics of management means. It has long been assumed that aesthetics and management have little to do with each other.

Most would agree that at least so-called developed societies have made scientific and economic progress. Fewer, but still some, would argue that ethical and moral progress has also been made. Hardly anyone, however, would argue that we have made any significant aesthetic progress: that we can either produce better art or appreciate natural or man-made beauty more than our predecessors.

My concern with aesthetics derives from my belief that lack of progress in this domain is responsible for one of our most critical social problems: *a decreasing quality of life.* To support this belief I must first clarify the nature of the aesthetic function in society. Because so little is known or understood about aesthetics, almost any assertion made about it is bound to generate intense controversy. However, I see no way of getting a grip on the quality of life unless we engage in and work our way through such controversy. My concern is with both the quality of life in general and the quality of work life in particular.

Aesthetics: A Philosophical Perspective

It may well be that we humans are unique in our ability to formulate and pursue ideals, desired states that we can never attain but to which we can always come closer. If we are to pursue any ideal continuously, we must never be willing to settle for anything less; that is, we must never be either permanently discouraged or completely satisfied. Therefore, whenever we attain one objective we must seek another—one that is more desirable and whose attainment moves us closer to the ideal. Thus, we must always be able to find new possibilities for progress and new sources of satisfaction. We must always be able to generate visions of something more desirable than what we have and we must be motivated to pursue these visions.

Singer [73] argued that the aesthetic function is to *inspire*: to create visions of the better and give us the courage to pursue it, whatever short-run sacrifices are required. Inspiration and aspiration go hand in hand. Art, therefore, consists of the works of people capable of stimulating new aspirations and inspiring commitment to their pursuit. We call this capability *beauty*.

In *The Republic*, Plato conceived of art as a potentially dangerous stimulant that could threaten society's stability. He saw it producing dissatisfaction with things as they are, hence disrupting the status quo. Therefore, he believed that art would be dangerous in an ideal society, one in which all problems would have been solved or be solvable. For him dissatisfaction in such a state could bring nothing but retrogression.

For most of us today such a society as Plato's Republic would not be ideal. We would prefer a state in which there are still an unlimited number of problems to be solved and objectives to be pursued. Why? Because there is at least as much satisfaction to be derived from the pursuit of solutions and ends as there is in attaining them. An ideal state for us, therefore, is not one in which we have everything, but one in which there is always more to be had, and we have the ability and desire to obtain it. This, of course, encompasses nonmaterial as well as material things.

In contrast to Plato, Aristotle conceptualized art as a cathartic, a palliative for dissatisfaction, hence as a producer of stability and contentment. He saw art as something from which one extracts satisfaction here and now. Where Plato saw art as *creative*, Aristotle saw it as *recreative*.

These apparently contradictory views of Plato and Aristotle are actually complementary because they are concerned with two different aspects of the same thing. Art is both creative and recreative; these are the inseparable head and tail of the aesthetic coin. Recreation is the extraction of pleasure from the here and now. It is a reward for past effort. It provides the "pause that refreshes," thereby recreating the creator. We could not maintain continuous pursuit of something we can never attain without payoffs along the way. Art is also creative: it inspires us to further progressive efforts. It both pulls us toward the future and pushes us from the past.

Aesthetics: A Psychological Perspective

The objective of decision making appears to be the selection of a *means* that will bring about a desired outcome, an *end*. Assuming this to be the case, a number of scientists have developed a theory of "rational" decision making from which they infer that when a rational decision maker is confronted with alternative means all of which produce the same outcome, he or she should have no preference among them. Unfortunately for the theorists, when most apparently rational people are in such situations they are *not* indifferent to the alternative means.

For example, brown shoes may be just as efficient for walking as black ones, but most of us prefer one to the other because one pleases us more than the other. A preference for a fountain pen, ball point, felt tip, or pencil exists despite an awareness of the fact that each works as well as the others for recording a message or writing a letter.

Therefore, either most people are irrational or the theory of rational decision making is irrational. I believe the latter to be the case because people have rational preferences among means regardless of their consequences. Means have value in themselves.

Ends and means are relative concepts, relative to how large a segment of behavior we consider. We buy a book in order to read. We read in order to learn. We learn in order to earn, and so on. Therefore, means have two kinds of value: (1) an *instrumental* or *extrinsic* value that lies in their chance of bringing about a desired outcome, an end; and (2) an *intrinsic* value that has to do with the satisfaction they bring about independent of what outcome they produce, their value as ends in themselves.

Our preferences for means that are independent of what ends they lead to is part of what is meant by a person's or organization's style. Style is a matter of taste; it has to do with the satisfactions we derive from what we do rather than why we do it. Our individuality lies as much in our style as in the ends we pursue and the efficiency with which we pursue them.

The importance of style in corporate life is obvious. For example, three executives who wanted to diversify the company they owned in order to be challenged more and to become more involved in their business which pretty well ran itself. In their words, they wanted "to get more *fun* out of it." Fun is a matter of aesthetics and recreation, not science, economics, ethics, or morality.

Another example: a major corporation's profits have been suffering recently because of its commitment to producing only the highest quality products in the field. Its cost of materials is now inflating more rapidly than are its competitors', but it refuses to adulterate its products or abbreviate the processes by which they are made.

Degrading its products would significantly reduce the satisfaction that the managers derive from their work and their pride in the company. This too is a matter of aesthetics.

Finally, there are two separate districts of the Federal Reserve banking system that have exactly the same functions. Nevertheless, they differ significantly in the way they are organized and carry out their functions. The atmospheres in these two banks are very different. The differences cannot be explained in scientific, economic, or ethical–moral terms; they are aesthetic, or stylistic, in character.

Ends, in contrast to means, are usually taken to have only intrinsic value, value that lies in the satisfaction their attainment brings. As we have seen, however, ends are also means. Every attainable end has consequences; it leads to further outcomes which, in turn, have their consequences. Therefore, any attainable end must have extrinsic value that derives from its efficiency in producing desirable consequences. To measure such efficiency, a target consequence is required, but such a target is not provided by an end that has further consequences. Therefore, the target must be an ideal, an ultimate consequence. The extrinsic value of an end lies in the amount of progress its attainment brings toward one or more ideals.

In science, for example, where the ideal of zero error is pursued, a reduction of error produced by a research effort constitutes progress, hence has extrinsic value. Similarly, a corporation may have as one of its ideals "production at no cost." An effort that reduces production costs, therefore, yields both satisfaction with the improvement, its intrinsic value, and with the progress made toward the ideal, its extrinsic value.

Quality of Life

In the Machine Age, life, and every aspect of it, was taken apart by analysis. Work, play, and learning were separated and kept separate by institutions dedicated exclusively to one of them; for example, factories, country clubs, and schools. In the Western world attitudes toward business and work have been dominated by the Protestant, if not the Puritan, ethic. This ethic separates work from play and learning, and views it as an *ascetic*, not an aesthetic, activity. Most people, even today, think of work as something necessary and necessarily unpleasant. The lack of satisfaction derived from work was once rationalized as a kind of earthly purgatory in which sin is expiated and virtue is gradually accumulated. This rationalization has lost its persuasiveness during this century. The generations born after World War II are increasingly alienated from work that is not satisfying and has no intrinsic value.

Quality of life, including work life, derives from the satisfactions one receives from life's intrinsic value; and from a sense of progress toward ideals brought about by what is accomplished, its extrinsic value. Now it is easy to identify the sources of our current concern with the deteriorating quality of life.

Less and less satisfaction is being derived by more and more people from the ordinary things they do, such as taking a walk or a drive, attending school, shopping, or working. This decrease in satisfaction is a consequence of a deterioration in the aesthetic properties of our environment and what we do within it.

The feeling that our quality of life is deteriorating also derives from the growing belief that much of the increasingly rapid cultural and technological change is, to use the vernacular, getting us nowhere. This means we have no sense of progress toward an ideal or such properties of an ideal state as peace of mind, peace on earth, equality of opportunity, and the elimination of poverty. A sense of progress toward an ideal gives meaning to life, converts mere existence into significant living by making choice meaningful. Today there is a growing belief that we are not in control of our futures. This, in turn, tends to make us view our choices as meaningless. Fatalism and resignation degrade the quality of life. Alienation from work derives in part from a reduced quality of work life, from work that is not satisfying in itself and does not provide a sense of progress toward ideals.

Toward improved quality of life

I have argued that it is the responsibility of every social system, including corporations, to try to improve the quality of life of all those they directly affect. To do so it appears necessary to be able to measure quality of life. Ackoff and Emery [7] have constructed measurements of both satisfaction with one's current state and progress toward an ideal. They are, however, too difficult to use in practical situations.

Because measurements of the quality of life are at best very difficult to obtain, easier to obtain social indicators are often used in their place; for example, the crime rate, number of occupants per dwelling unit, and morbidity rates. The use of such indicators raises a fundamental methodological problem. Their effectiveness depends on how well they correlate with the measurements for which they are a substitute. But since we do not have adequate measurements with which to determine their correlation, they cannot be evaluated properly. Therefore, their use is justified by their subjectively perceived correspondence to their proponents' subjectively made qualitative judgments of the quality of life. This, however, also gives rise to a major methodological problem: whose judgment, made when and where, should be used? What confidence can be placed in such judgments? Furthermore, if we justify the use of indicators by their correlation with such judgments, why not use the judgments themselves? This, of course, is just what many do.

Must we wait until an ability to measure the quality of life is developed before social-system designers, planners, and managers can make effective efforts to improve it? Instead, must we go ahead without the precision and accuracy required?. Or is there an alternative approach to the quality-of-life problem in which measurement is not required but can yield efficient and effective attacks on it? I believe there is such an alternative.

The problems associated with efforts to improve the quality of life of others, including their work life, arises because the others lack either the opportunity or the ability to do it for themselves. Managers and planners who have the opportunity, even if not the ability, to improve the quality of life *of others* require measurement of it. However, if those ordinarily planned for had the opportunity and the ability to make such improvements themselves, the measurement problem disappears. What is required is that individuals be able to evaluate their own quality of life, that they have an opportunity to improve it, that they be encouraged to do so, and that their efforts to do so be facilitated. Therefore, the planning problem is not how to improve the quality of life of others, but how to enable them to do so for themselves and to learn continually how to do so more effectively. This reformulated problem can be solved by encouraging and facilitating the participation of the others in the design of and planning for the organizations and institutions of which they are part.

Those who participate in the redesign of and planning for their organization or institution cannot help but put their stylistic preferences into their designs and plans. Nor can they refrain from incorporating pursuit of their ideals into these designs and plans. Therefore, the kind of organizational and institutional planning that is most responsive to the styles and ideals of stakeholders is participative planning, particularly the kind discussed in Chapter 3.

ORGANIZATIONAL TYPES

I have argued that social systems—societies, institutions, and organizations, including corporations—should facilitate the development of their stakeholders, particularly their members. If this argument is accepted, it is the responsibility of those who manage or govern such systems to see to it that this function is carried out efficiently and effectively.

The relationship between governors and governed and managers and managed is a matter of *politics*. Politics is a matter of *power*; who has control over whom. Humans, being political animals must engage in political activity even if doing so consists of withdrawal from active political concerns. Because such withdrawals have an effect on the well-being of the stakeholders of the social system, they can hardly be considered to be nonpolitical, or above and beyond politics. For example, abstention from voting in a democracy is a powerful political tool. However, it is not such behavior or even direct political involvement that is my concern here; rather it is with the political philosophy of institutions and organizations, particularly corporations. The relationship between political philosophy and politics is the same as the plot of a drama and its dialogue. The two components are distinct but interact strongly.

The position that a government or management takes with respect to power, possibly in contrast to the position it proclaims, can be characterized along two scales having to do with ends and means. One has to do with who selects the ends to be served by a social system, and the other with who selects the means it uses.

At one extreme of the ends-selection scale is the selection by *one* person of the ends to be pursued by the social system as a whole. This extreme can be called *ends autocracy*. At the other extreme *all* those who hold a stake in a system have a hand in selecting the ends to be pursued by that system. This extreme can be called *ends democracy*. A number of intermediate positions can be found between these two extremes. For example, the choice of ends can be made by a small group—an executive committee or a board—whose members are not selected by those they control. Closer to the other extreme is the case in which an elected body such as a congress or parliament makes the choices for the whole.

A similar scale can be constructed with respect to means selection. Its extremes are *means autocracy* and *means democracy.*

Social systems, including corporations, can be characterized by their positions in the space defined by these two scales (see Figure 2.2). Their positions in this space define their political philosophy. Consider the four corners of this space.

In *ends-autocratic-means-autocratic* social systems one person has the power to make all decisions that affect members of the system. Such is the case in a society governed by an absolute monorch or dictator. Absolute power may, of course, be concentrated in a small group rather than an individual as, for example, in a junta.

Many societies, prisons, military organizations, churches, and *corporations* are organized in this way. Autocratic organizations and institutions are plentiful even in societies whose governmental structure is not autocratic. On the other hand, there are industrial organizations in autocratic societies that are managed in a democratic way.

An autocratic political structure does not preclude decentralization of decision making, but when it is decentralized, lower-level decisions can always be overridden by those of higher authority and, ultimately, by the

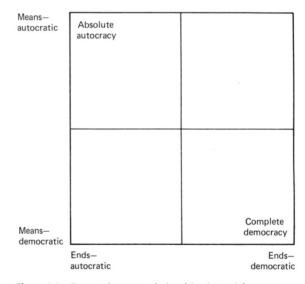

Figure 2.2 Types of power relationships in social systems.

highest authority. Decentralized units in an autocratic organization are never autonomous.

The power relationship between government and governed and management and managed may be quite different from the structure of government or management itself; that is, the power relationships within government or management may differ from those *between* government and governed or management and managed. For example, the government of a democratic state can be organized autocratically. The highest governmental authority may have complete control over others in government yet be completely controlled by the governed. On the other hand, an autocratic governing body such as an executive council can itself be organized democratically. Most corporations in the United States are ends- and means-autocratic but their managements are increasingly organized as ends-autocratic and means-democratic.

In *ends-autocratic–means-democratic* social systems ends are imposed on the governed or managed, but they select means by themselves. Autonomous work groups, which are becoming common in industrial establishments, are organized in this way. Their tasks or objectives are assigned to them, but they are free to select whatever means they want in pursuit of these ends. Units of a guerrilla army and political parties often have the same type of organization. The order to desegregate schools issued by the Supreme Court of the United States is an imposition of an end on communities that are free to design and select the means by which this end is to be obtained.

The current move in many corporations to management by objectives is a move toward this type of power distribution *within* managment, whereas the use of autonomous work groups affects the relationship between managers and managed.

In *ends-democratic–means-autocratic* social systems an ultimate authority has complete control over the means employed, but the ends are selected by those served by the organization. Welfare institutions—hospitals, nursing homes, old-age homes, and many schools—are organized in this way. For example, in principle at least, a hospital is supposed to serve the interests of its patients who, nevertheless, have little or no control over the means selected to do so. Means selection is controlled by an authority. The rationale behind such a power distribution lies in the assumption that individuals do not know how, or are not capable of, taking care of themselves as well as some experts do. A type of doctor-patient relationship holds between governors and the governed or managers and the managed.

In *ends-democratic–means-democratic* social systems the governed or managed select both ends and means. Government and management are seen as service organizations responsible to the governed and managed. In such a political structure the only legitimate objective of government or management is service to members of the system. In a sense, therefore, such a government or management is an instrument of the governed or managed.

Many organizations whose members are free to associate with it or not are organized in this way; for example, farm cooperatives, most professional societies, and social clubs. Small communities governed by town meetings are similarly organized. Industrial organizations in Europe have been moving in this direction under legislative pressure.

Now recall my earlier assertion that a government or management cannot develop the governed or managed, but it can and should encourage and facilitate such development. Since development requires increasing competence, and omnicompetence is an ideal of all, to the extent that a social system encourages and facilitates development it is ends-democratic. Furthermore, since development requires both learning and motivation, it takes place best among those who participate in decisions that affect them, including development-related decisions. Therefore, a social system trying to develop its members as effectively as possible should also be means-democratic.

A cautionary note: the preceding discussion implies nothing about the relative merits of capitalism and communism. These two "isms," strictly speaking, have nothing to do with the issue of autocracy versus democracy. Unfortunately, they are frequently treated as though they do. The "isms" have to do with the ownership of the means of production and the way wealth and poverty are distributed. In principle, communism may be either autocratic, as it clearly was in the Soviet Union under Stalin, democratic, as it is and has been in a number of communes set up in capitalistic countries. On the other hand, capitalism may be either autocratic, as it clearly was under Franco in Spain, or democratic. Furthermore, there is no causal relationship between the "isms" and the rate of development in social systems. There are instances of both communist and capitalist societies that have developed rapidly, and instances in which neither type has made much progress.

SUMMARY

Because the line of argument in this chapter has been complex, a comprehensive summary of it follows. The concept of a corporation has evolved from one that was mechanistic to one that was organismic, and from organismic to organizational. Viewed as a machine it was taken to have no purpose of its own, but to be an instrument for use by its owners in pursuit of their profit objective. Viewed as an organism the corporation was taken to have survival and growth as its principal purposes. Conceptualized in either of these ways the corporation was seen to have no responsibility to the purposes of its parts, its employees. However, viewed as an organization the corporation was seen to have such a responsibility to all of its stakeholders and to society, the larger system of which it is part.

The economic role of a corporation in society consists of making consumption possible by creating wealth and distributing it. It has a responsibility for doing this in a way that does not degrade the quality of life, either within the corporation or in its environment. Its principal purpose should be to develop itself and to encourage and facilitate the development of all its stakeholders, particularly its members.

Development is the process of increasing one's desire and ability to satisfy one's own desires and those of others. Because development so conceived is at least as much a matter of motivation and learning as of wealth, it can take place with or without resources. Therefore, shortages of resources that limit growth do not necessarily limit development. Nevertheless, the quality of life that can be obtained at any stage of development depends on the resources that are or can be made available. However, the effect of development on resources is more important than their effect on development: the more developed a purposeful system or individual is, the less dependent it is on external resources and the more effectively it can use and create resources to improve quality of life.

Development implies an increase in competence. Competence sufficient to attain any end or to make unlimited progress toward any ideal, *omnicompetence*, is necessarily a meta-ideal of humanity because we can desire nothing without simultaneously desiring the ability to obtain it.

A proper role of social system is to encourage and facilitate the development of its members. Doing so requires that it carries out four functions: the scientific, the economic, the ethical–moral, and the aesthetic. These correspond to the pursuit of truth, plenty, good, and beauty, respectively.

Of the four functions the aesthetic is least understood. Quality of life is primarily a matter of aesthetics; it involves satisfactions derived from what we do, no matter how trivial. These are satisfactions in the intrinsic values of the means we employ. Quality of life also involves a sense of progress toward ideals, ends that can never be obtained but toward which unlimited progress is possible. Measurement of these two types of satisfaction may be possible in principle, but not in practice; nor can we develop appropriate substitutes without the measurements themselves. Therefore, such measurements are necessary for those whose objective is to design, plan for, and develop a society or organization in which the quality of life *of others* is improved. An alternative strategy is available, however, that does not require such measurement (even though it could benefit from it): to design, plan, and develop social systems in which each member of the system can participate and thus bring more of his own future under his control. Involvement in such a future-creating process is itself a way of developing and a source of satisfaction. Therefore, it yields an improved quality of life.

The key to development and improved quality of life is *not* planning *for* or measurement of others; but enabling them to plan and measure for themselves. There is deep wisdom in the motto of an indigenous self-development group in Mantua, one of Philadelphia's black ghettos: *Plan or be planned for*. To make participative planning possible is to make an art of living.

The relationship between government/management and governed/managed is political: it involves the distribution of power. Social systems can be characterized along two scales: one running from ends-autocratic to ends-democratic, and the other from means-autocratic to means-democratic. Because a government or management cannot develop the governed or managed, but can only encourage and facilitate their development, and because individual development takes place most effectively in situations in which individuals can participate in making decisions that affect them, it is an ends-democratic and means-democratic type of social system that can best facilitate and encourage development.

The controversy between communism and capitalism is not connected to the autocracy–democracy issue. The former are types of economy, not relationships between government and the governed. Either capitalism or communism may be organized democratically or autocratically.

The appropriate response to limited growth is unlimited development. The key to unlimited development is choice that is limited only to the means and ends that do not obstruct the freedom of choice of others.

CHAPTER THREE

OUR CHANGING CONCEPT OF PLANNING

Plan, v.t. *To bother about the best method of accomplishing an accidental result.*

AMBROSE BIERCE

In the last chapter a concept of planning began to emerge that differs significantly from the ones that prevail. It is a concept of planning as an activity *within* which development takes place, not merely as an activity whose output may contribute to development.

An even more fundamental difference exists between those who believe in planning and those who do not, whatever concept of it. To plan or not seems always to have been a matter of temperament, even among animals. Recall the familiar fable of the grasshopper and the ant. (In a little-known modern version of the fable, James Joyce refers to the "gracehoper.") Some people refuse to plan, at least consciously; they prefer just to let things happen. Nevertheless, these antiplanners cannot avoid being affected by the planning of others, and they are often victimized rather than benefitted by it. From this derives the significance of the previously quoted motto: *Plan or be planned for.* It is a matter of elementary justice that people be permitted to plan for themselves.

Most conventional planning is carried out by professional planners *for* others. To such planners, participative planning means taking into account the desires, hopes, and expectations of others as they, the experts, see them; these are taken to be subject to economic, legal, moral, and practical constraints, again as the experts see them. The one thing that most professional planners feel they cannot do is allow those who are affected by their planning to "meddle" (i.e., participate) in it. To do so, they believe, is to vulgarize the process and to diminish the appreciation by others of the special competence they have. In contrast, here participation means direct involvement in the planning process of all those who can be affected by it directly.

The concept of planning developed here differs in another significant way from conventional concepts. Most planners consider a plan to be an aggregation of the solutions to each of a set of problems (threats and opportunities) that are dealt with independently. Therefore, a corporate plan is seen as a collection of the plans separately prepared for each of the parts of the whole. In contrast, the type of planning proposed here proceeds from a treatment of the whole to the interaction of the parts, and then finally to the parts themselves. The justification for doing so arises out of a concept of planning that involves dealing with *interdependent* problems. It this were not the case—that is, if planning involved only independent problems—it would be nothing but multiple problem solving. Let me explain.

A set of two or more interdependent problems constitutes a *system*. The French call such a system a *problematique*; for lack of a corresponding word in English, I call it a *mess*. (It seems appropriate to think of planning as mess management.)

A mess, like any system, has properties that none of its parts have. These properties are lost when the system is taken apart. In addition, each part of a system has properties that are lost when it is considered separately. The solution to a mess depends on how the solutions to the parts *interact*. Therefore, a plan should be more than an aggregation of independently obtained solutions to the parts of a mess. It should deal with messes as wholes, systemically.

In brief, planning is here conceptualized as a participative way of dealing with a set of interrelated problems when it is believed that unless something is done, a desirable future is not likely to occur; and that if appropriate action is taken, the likelihood of such a future can be increased.

A TYPOLOGY OF PLANNING

The concept of planning developed here is best understood by contrasting it with the alternative concepts that currently prevail. The essential

Table 3.1   The Four Basic Orientations to Planning

Orientation	Past	Present	Future
Reactive	+	−	−
Inactive	−	+	−
Preactive	−	−	+
Interactive	+/−	+/−	+/−

+ = a favorable attitude; − = an unfavorable attitude.

differences between these concepts derive from their temporal orientations. The dominant orientation of some planners is to the past, *reactive*;
others to the present, *inactive*; and still others to the future, *preactive*
(see Table 3.1). A fourth orientation, *interactive*, the one developed here,
regards the past, present, and future as different but inseparable aspects
of the mess to be planned for; it focuses on all of them equally. It is
based on the belief that unless all three temporal aspects of a mess are
taken into account, development will be obstructed.

The four basic planning orientations are like the primary colors; they
seldom appear in their pure form. Most of the planning we see, like
colors, are mixtures; nevertheless, they are usually dominated by one of
the four pure types. In most corporations we can find examples of all the
basic orientations. Furthermore, the orientations change from time to
time, from person to person, and from situation to situation.

These orientations are not intended to be taken as general psychological or sociological types, but simply as convenient ways of characterizing
certain surprisingly pervasive ways of managing and planning. Therefore,
when I personify these orientations by referring to "inactivists," "reactivists," and so on, these are only a figure of speech.

Finally, it should be understood that there are strengths in inactivism,
reactivism, and preactivism even though my treatment of them will em-
phasize their weaknesses. However, I will try to indicate what these
strengths are.

Reactivism

Reactivists are satisfied neither with things as they are nor with the way
they are going. However, they like the way things once were. Therefore,
they seek to return to a previous state by *unmaking* the relevant intervening changes. They tend to be nostalgic about the past and to romanticize
it. Caught in the tide of change, they try to swim against it in an effort to
return to the shore from which it has pulled them. They tend to enter the

future facing the past, hence they have a better view of where they have been than of where they are going.

Because reactivists believe that technology is the principal cause of change, it is their principal enemy. Throughout history they have resisted it and sought to return to a "simple life." For example, early in the Industrial Revolution the Luddite movement in England dedicated itself to destroying the machines and factories that its members believed were destroying the quality of life. Jean Jaques Rousseau led a similarly motivated back-to-nature movement during the French Enlightenment. John Ruskin and William Morris tried to initiate a similar retreat from industrial technology in Victorian England. More recently, in the 1960s, many young dissidents went back to primitive farming so they could cast off the yoke of modern technology. They found philosophical support in the writings of Jacques Ellul [28], a French mystic, who attributed most of our current ills to technology, which he believed to be a manifestation of the devil. He argued that technology is no longer under our control and that, like Frankenstein's monster, it now controls its former masters.

The methodology of the reactivist's approach to problems is that of the Machine Age: every current problem once did not exist. Something happened to bring it about. What happened and what was its cause? Find the cause, then repress, suppress, or remove it and the problem will disappear. For example, when alcoholism became a significant problem in the United States after World War I, reactivists sought and found its apparent cause, alcohol. Therefore, they tried to prohibit its use. This "cure" did not work; alcohol was kept available illegally, thereby nourishing organized crime, which became at least as serious a problem as alcoholism. Despite this failure, when narcotic addiction later became a major problem in the United States, under pressure from reactivists narcotics were prohibited, with an equal lack of success.

Because reactivists are hostile to technology, they usually support the arts and humanities in what C. P. Snow [76] called "the war of the two cultures." They would rather deal with people and values than with artifacts and efficiency. Their evaluations and judgments are rooted in morality, not in science. They are more comfortable thinking qualitatively than quantitatively, looking for answers in experience and history, rather than in Scientific experiments. They associate knowledge, understanding, and wisdom with age because they believe experience is the best teacher and that the best place to acquire it is in the "school of hard knocks."

Because reactive managements base themselves on experience and history, they tend to rely on old organizational forms, usually an authoritarian paternalistic hierarchy. They think of their organizations as machines and manage them in an ends- and means-autocratic way.

Although reactive organizations are ruled from the top down, they are planned from the bottom up. Reactive planning is usually initiated by a chief executive who, for instance, tells his or her immediate subordinates to provide a corporate plan in twelve months. He or she instructs them to submit plans for their parts of the organization in eleven months, allowing the executive time to integrate their submissions. The second-level managers similarly instruct their immediate subordinates giving them ten months for their submissions. This process continues until it reaches the lowest level of the organization. The lowest-level manager is usually given virtually no time (and sometimes even less) to prepare a plan. (Note that this process corresponds to the first step of analysis: it reduces the corporation to its elements.)

The lowest-level manager begins planning by listing current deficiencies in his or her unit. Then he or she designs projects directed at finding and removing their causes. Estimates of the costs and benefits of each project are prepared and, based on these, priorities are set. A subset of the projects is then selected, assuming the availability of more resources than the manager actually expects to receive. This selection is then sent up to the immediate superior. The superior adjusts and edits the submissions he or she receives, often adds a "fudge factor," and passes the output up one level. This process continues until an aggregation of projects reaches the top where a final selection is made, thus completing the analytical process.

Reactive planning deals with problems separately, not systemically, thereby missing the essential properties of the whole and many of the important properties of the individual parts. Furthermore, it is based on the mistaken belief that if we get rid of what we do not want, we will have what we do want. This is obviously false. When television viewers are confronted with programs they do not want they can easily get rid of them by changing the channel. It is quite likely, hoever, that when they do they will get another program that they like even less.

Planning in reactive organizations is normally taken as a prerogative of management. Professional planners and people "on the line" are seldom included, although staff personnel are sometimes used to work up the details. Consultation with, let alone participation of, stakeholders is rare.

Reactive planning tends to be ritualistic, like an Indian rain dance performed at the end of the dry season. It has no effect on the weather that follows, but sometimes it makes those who engage in it feel good. In general there is more concern with the dancing than the weather; hence when experts are consulted it is usually for improvement of the dancing.

It is not surprising that reactive corporations tend to be those whose products or services are being replaced because of technological developments in the hands of others. The railroads are an example. I have heard many railroad executives react to their plight by saying that there is nothing wrong with their industry that elimination of trucks and the Interstate Commerce Commission would not cure.

The reactive orientation has three principal attractions. First is the sense of, and respect for, history from which some things can be learned. Not everything that occurs is new; much of it has occurred before. Second, it embodies a feeling for continuity and avoids abrupt, disruptive, and poorly-understood changes. Finally, it preserves traditions that tend to make those affected feel secure. It keeps people on familiar ground and thus provides them with a sense of stability; however, often in reality the ground beneath them is crumbling.

Inactivism

Inactivists are satisfied with things as they are. They are unwilling to return to a previous state and they do not like the way things are going. Therefore, they try to *prevent* change. Their objectives are survival and stability. Caught in the tide of change, they try to anchor themselves in a fixed position.

Inactive managements may not believe that the current condition is the best one possible, but they believe that it is either good enough or as good as can be reasonably expected. They are satisfied with things as they are and seek no more than to keep them that way: to *satisfice*, to do well enough. They believe that most change is either temporary or illusory and that their affairs, even in an unstable state, will come back to equilibrium if left alone. Their policy, therefore, is "hands off." They believe that if nothing is done, little or nothing will happen, and that is what they want.

They believe that it is the intervention of others in the course of events, however well intentioned, that messes things up. Inactivists delay reacting to the messes created by others until a crisis arises; that is, until their survival or stability is threatened. Therefore, they practice crisis management and brinksmanship. Even in crises, however, they do the least that is required to return to equilibrium. They do not try to find the causes of crises and remove them; they try only to alleviate the threat they present. Inactivists try to remove the discomfort caused by an ailment rather than cure it because they believe that organizations will cure themselves if left alone.

Inactive policies have been systematically formulated and defended by the political scientists Hirschman and Lindblom [39] who call the supporting doctrine "disjointed incrementalism." They advise treating each problem separately, disjointedly, and by doing as little as possible. Some refer to such a strategy as "muddling through."

Contrary to what their name suggests, inactivists are very active. Even when there are no crises, which is seldom the case, it takes a lot of work to keep things from happening. Many people want to do things to bring about change. They must be kept busy in activities that accomplish nothing. It is not surprising, therefore, that bureaucracy and red tape are among the indispensable instruments of inactivists. In addition, they go in heavily for gathering facts, an endless process: all the facts are never in, and until they are there is no reason to make a decision. Unlike reactivists who are historically oriented, inactivists are oriented toward current events, news. Keeping up to date is a task that can keep a large number of people busy without requiring them to accomplish anything.

Because awareness of what is going on is more important to an inactive management than past experience, managers are generally selected for their grasp of current events rather than history. For such a grasp they require access to those "in the know." Connections tend to be of more importance than competence.

Perhaps the most effective instrument of inactivism is the *committee*, in whatever form it takes—study groups, councils, task forces, or commissions. These make it possible to occupy large numbers of people in activities that seldom have any issue. When a committee does come up with recommendations for action these can always be referred to another committee for evaluation and review. This process can usually be extended long enough for the problem that initiated it to change sufficiently to make the committee's work outdated. If recommendations are produced in time for action and cannot be ignored, they can be accepted but put out for implementation with insufficient resources or management so that their failure is virtually assured. Such actions are taken for appearance rather than effect.

Inactive organizations value manners more than efficiency. They are preoccupied with conventions, customs, rules, and correct behavior. Conformity is valued more than creativity. Disloyalty is regarded as a cardinal sin. For these reasons inactive organizations tend to be means-autocratic and ends-democratic. They see themselves serving the interests of their stakeholders, particularly their investors and customers, and knowing better than they how to do so efficiently and effectively. They pursue stability by trying to be indispensable to those they serve and those who serve them.

The type of organization that can best survive inactive management is one whose survival is independent of its performance; that is, one that is subsidized. Little wonder that they resist efforts to measure their performance. Many examples of inactivism can be found among government agencies, but also among service departments in corporations. Perhaps the best example is the typical university, which has been characterized as being as difficult to change as a cemetery, and for the same reasons.

Inactive organizations do well when current environmental forces are actually favorable to them. There are obviously situations in which doing nothing is better than doing anything. Some problems do solve themselves or fade away if left alone. Furthermore, even in an environment that is virtually completely uncontrollable and turbulent, although inactivists may not do well by doing nothing, often do no worse than those who try to do something. Finally, because they act cautiously, they seldom make mistakes of catastrophic proportion. When they die, they do so slowly.

Preactivism

Preactivism is the dominant style of management in the United States today. Its adherents are unwilling to return to a previous state or to settle for things as they are. They believe the future will be better than either the present or the past. Therefore, they seek to *accelerate* change and exploit the opportunities that it brings. They try to ride the tide, seeking its leading edge so they can get to where it is going before anyone else. Then they try to stake a claim and collect a toll from those who arrive later.

Like reactivists, preactivists believe technology is the principal cause of change, but, because they think change is good, they look favorably on technology. They believe that there are few problems technology cannot solve. Therefore, to reactivists, preactivists appear to be technocrats who are trying to push us over a precipice into the technological inferno that lies below. To preactivists, reactivists seem to be incurable romantics and ineffectual humanists who resist the inevitable and are out of touch with reality.

Unlike inactivists, preactivists are not willing to settle for doing well enough; they want to do as well as possible, to *optimize*. In their search for the best they rely on all the paraphernalia that science and technology can provide. They are captivated by such quantitative science-based techniques as linear programming, planning and program budgeting, risk analysis, and cost-effectiveness studies. They tend to treat each new technique and technology as a panacea.

Because they believe that technological developments will make the future very different than the past, preactivists place little reliance on experience. They rely on experiment. To preactivists experience is too slow, too imprecise, and too ambiguous a teacher. They view organizations as organisms and structure them as ends-autocratic and means-democratic. They believe in management by objectives. Therefore, their organizations tend to be means-permissive, decentralized, and informal. They value inventiveness rather than conformity, and like to be the first to try new things. Their principal objective is growth—to become bigger, obtain the largest share of market, cover more countries, and produce more products than anyone else: to be "number one."

Planning in a preactive organization consists of *predicting* the future and *preparing* for it. Preparation involves taking steps to minimize or avoid future threats and, of greater importance, to exploit future opportunities. Preactivists are more concerned about missing an opportunity than about committing an error. Unlike inactivists, they believe that errors of commission are less costly and easier to correct than errors of omission.

Of the two parts of planning, prediction and preparation, prediction is the more important. Preactivists believe that it is more difficult to predict accurately than it is to prepare effectively for an accurately predicted future. Perfect preparations for an inaccurately predicted future are of no value. Therefore, they put a great deal of effort into improving forecasting. They have supported the develpment of "futurology" and a number of new ways of trying to foresee the future. The oracles they heed are usually dressed in scientific garb and equipped with a computer.

Preactive planning, unlike that of the reactivists, proceeds from the top down. It usually begins with a forecast of environmental conditions by a professional planning staff. Then those at the top prepare a statement of corporate objectives and formulate a broad strategy for the organization as a whole. This output in passed down to the next level where appropriate lower-level objectives are set and programs are developed for their pursuit. (Programs are systems of projects.) These are passed down further and at each successive level the process is repeated.

On the Accuracy of Forecasts

Because preactive planning is critically dependent on the accuracy of forecasts, it is important to understand the conditions under which perfectly accurate forecasts could be obtained. There are three such sets of conditions.

First, if a system and its environment did not and could not change, and we knew its state at any one moment of time then, of course, we would know its state at any other moment of time, including the future.

Clearly, these conditions do not exist, but even if they did, preparation would not be possible because it requires change.

Second, perfectly accurate forecasts would be possible if a system and its environment were, or were part of, a deterministic system that obeyed the laws of cause and effect, and the state of this system at any moment of time and the relevant laws were perfectly known. These are the conditions that were believed to pertain to the universe in the Machine Age. If the future of a system that could be so predicted were determined, it would not be subject to change; hence preparation would be meaningless. Preparation presupposes choice but determinism presupposes a lack of it.

Third, we would be able to predict the future perfectly if it were completely under our control, if we were omnipotent. If this were the case, forecasting would be meaningless because we would be able to bring about any future we desired.

In the first two of these situations perfect prediction would be possible but preparation would not. In the third situation we would be able to prepare perfectly, but prediction would be meaningless. Therefore, there is an indeterminacy involved in preactive planning: the more accurately we can predict, the less effectively we can prepare. On the other hand, the more effective our preparations, the less we need to forecast.

Preactive planners do not believe this argument presents a dilemma. They respond to it by pointing out that what they predict is not the future of the system planned for but that of its environment, over which they have no control. They predict the environment and prepare the system. This response assumes that the environment is determined but that the system that is part of it has choice. This is not possible: no part of a deterministic system can exercise choice.

In response to this last argument preactivists point out that we can predict the weather, although not perfectly, and prepare for it; and that we benefit from doing so. They are right about the weather because *our preparations for it have no effect on it.* This is not the case, however, in corporate planning where what corporations do has an effect on their environment. It is precisely because what is forecasted in corporate planning is affected by what corporations do that forecasting is so imperfect.

The last position of defense of the preactivist is based on the assumption that the future, after all, is not determined and therefore cannot be predicted with perfect accuracy. They claim, however, that they can identify *possible futures* and, in some cases, assign probabilities to them. Then they can plan for each and implement the correct one once they know what the future is. This is called *contingency planning.* It is useful when *all* the possible futures can be identified and there are sufficient resources to prepare for each. The major changes in a system's environment, however, are often ones that cannot be anticipated.

In recent history examples of such changes were the closing of the Suez Canal, the discovery of oil in the North Sea and Mexico, and the inflation of grain prices following the large sale of grain to the U.S.S.R. by the United States. The range of possible futures is too large for us to be able to identify each one. Unlikely critical events are certain to occur precisely because choice is involved. Choice is creative and thus inherently unpredictable. To the extent that what we call choice is predictable, it is not choice.

Perhaps the greatest difficulty in preactive planning derives from the fact that the further ahead we try to forecast, the greater the error is likely to be. This is apparent, for example, with respect even to the weather. Therefore, effective preparation is restricted at best to the relatively near future. Planning based on forecasting cannot deal effectively with more than the relatively short run.

Despite the methodological problems inherent in the preactive orientation, its predominance among American managers and planners attests to its attractiveness. It is widely perceived as useful, as it undoubtedly is. It is often better than nothing. It has great appeal because of its close association with modern science and technology, from which it obtains much of its prestige. Preactivists' acceptance and advocacy of change give them a progressive stance at the frontiers to the future. Their preoccupation with the future gives the impression that they have it well in hand.

Unlike reactivists and inactivists who are firmly rooted in the Machine Age and are generally unaware of the change of age that is taking place, preactivists know that something is up, but they do not have a clear vision of it. They embrace and exploit the technology of the Systems Age but apply it to situations that are conceptualized in Machine-Age terms. Furthermore, they retain Machine-Age methodology. They are the ones previously referred to who stand with one foot in each age and, therefore, feel an increasing strain as the two ages draw apart.

The fourth orientation, *interactivism*, arises out of a self-conscious effort to develop a methodology of management and planning that is firmly rooted in the Systems Age.

Interactivism

Interactivists, sometimes called proactivists, are not willing to return to a previous state, to settle for things as they are, or to accept the future that appears to confront them. The combination of these attitudes seems to imply a cynicism that requires resignation from the world, but this is not the case. It is not the case because interactivists deny an assumption made, usually implicitly, by inactivists, reactivists, and preactivists: that the future is largely out of our control and, therefore, the most that can be controlled is *our* future within *the* future. Interactivists believe that *the* future depends at least as much on what we and others like us do between now and then as it does on what has happened until now. Therefore, they maintain, the future is largely subject to creation. From this derives the interactive concept of planning as *the design of a desirable future and the invention of ways to bring it about.*

As stated earlier the inactivist tries to hold a fixed position in a moving tide; the reactivist tries to swim against it; and the preactivist tries to ride with it along its leading edge. The interactivist tries to control it. This may seem impossible, but recall that man has changed the direction of rivers, moved them from one place to another, and put arable land where oceans once rose and fell with the tides.

Interactivists, unlike reactivists, do not see technology and change as evil; and unlike the preactivists they do not see them as necessarily good. The effects of technology, they believe, depend on how we use it, and how well we use it depends on humanistic as well as scientific considerations. Science, as the interactivist sees it, involves the search for similarities among things that are apparently different. On the other hand, the arts and humanities look for differences among things that are apparently similar. One seeks the general, the other the unique. Like the head and tail of a coin, they are distinct but not separable. We may, however, look at one without seeing the other.

To deal effectively with any problematic situation two things are required. First, we must determine what the situation has in common with other situations that we have previously experienced. This tells us what part of our available knowledge is relevant. Science enables us to do this. Second, we must also know how the situation we face is unique and therefore requires knowledge not yet available to us. The arts and humanities enable us to do this. To put it another way, the arts and humanities reveal the questions yet to be answered and the values yet to be obtained; science provides answers to these questions and efficient ways of pursuing these values. (A technocratic culture runs the risk of getting the right solutions to the wrong problems. A humanistic culture runs the risk of getting the wrong solutions to the right problems.) Like preactivists, interactivists rely on experiments rather than experience to find solutions to problems wherever they can. Like the reactivists, however, they rely on experience rather than experiment to reveal the problems that require solution.

Recall that inactivists are willing to settle for doing well enough, to *satisfice*; preactivists want to do as well as possible, to *optimize*. Interactivists want to do better in the future than the best we are capable of doing now, to *idealize*. Therefore, interactivists focus on improving performance over time rather than on how well they can do at a particular time under particular conditions. Their objective is to maximize their ability to learn and adapt, to develop.

Learning and adaptation are taken as key requirements because of the accelerating rate of social change. No societal or corporate problem stays solved for long, and the duration of the solution reduces as the rate of change increases. Furthermore, the solution to any problem creates new and often more difficult problems. The progress of science, for example, has derived as much from the progression from simple to complex problems as it has from the progression from complex to simple solutions.

Recall that inactivists focus on not doing things that should not be done (avoiding errors of commission), and preactivists on doing things that should be done (avoiding errors of omission). Inactivists try to avoid both but they are more concerned with two other types of error that are generally ignored: asking the wrong questions or solving the wrong problems and not asking or not solving the right ones. They believe we fail more often because of an inability to face the right problems than because of an inability to solve the problems we face.

The interactivist believes our failure to address the right problems arises from a lack of awareness of what we are striving for *ultimately*. Humans are more than ends-seeking animals; we are *ideal-seeking*. Curiously, however, this characteristic of humans is ignored in all approaches to planning other than the interactive.

There are three types of ends that people pursue:

1. *Goals*: those ends that we can expect to attain within the period covered by planning.
2. *Objectives*: those ends that we do not expect to attain within the period planned for but which we hope to attain later, and toward which we believe progress is possible within the period planned for.
3. *Ideals*: those ends that are believed to be unattainable but towards which we believe progress is possible during and after the period planned for.

Planning ought to involve explicitly all three types of ends, but it seldom does. Which types are taken into account determine whether planning is *operational, tactical, strategic,* or *normative* (see Table 3.2).

Table 3.2 Types of Planning and Planning Postures

Types of planning	Means	Goals	Objectives	Ideals	Associated with
Operational	Choose	Given	Given	Given	Inactivism
Tactical	Choose	Choose	Given	Given	Reactivism
Strategic	Choose	Choose	Choose	Given	Preactivism
Normative	Choose	Choose	Choose	Choose	Interactivism

Operational planning consists of selecting means for pursuing goals that are either given, set, or imposed by a higher authority, or are accepted by convention; for example, planning to produce an amount of product specified by a higher authority. Such planning is usually short-range.

Inactivists engage in operational planning despite their negative attitude toward planning in general. Their goal, to keep things as they are, is given, but they must select the means by which this is to be accomplished.

Tactical planning consists of selecting means and goals for pursuing objectives that are either given, set, or imposed by a higher authority, or are accepted by convention. For example, a company's objective, to obtain market leadership in the next ten years, may be imposed on its marketing department. That department may then decide to reduce the gap between the company and the current market leader by a specified amount (its goal) in the period covered by its five-year plan. It then selects the means by which it will try to do so. Such planning tends to be medium-range.

Reactivists engage in tactical planning. They must select the previous states to which to return (their goals) and, of course, the means to do so.

Strategic planning consists of selecting means, goals, and objectives, but ideals are either given, imposed by a higher authority, accepted by convention, or, as is usually the case, not formulated. Such planning tends to be long-range.

Preactivists engage in strategic planning, holding in view a period longer than the one for which planning is done. In this sense they are more far-sighted than either reactivists or inactivists.

Normative planning requires the explicit selection of means, goals, objectives, and ideals. Such planning is indefinitely extended. It has no fixed horizon.

Interactivists engage in normative planning. As will be seen, not only do ideals play an important role in such planning, but they play the *key* role.

The four types of planning—operational, tactical, strategic, and normative—are obviously increasingly general. Operational planning is not only of the shortest range but it also tends to focus on small subsystems of the organization planned for and to deal with them independently. Tactical planning has an intermediate-range perspective and deals with the interactions between subsystems and their interactions with the organization as a whole. Strategic planning is longer-range and encompasses not only internal relationships but also those between the organization as a whole and its "transactional" environment, that with which it interacts directly and on which it has some influence. Normative planning is indefinitely extended and deals with all internal and external relationships including those between the organization and its contextual environment, which it has no influence over but which influences it.

My presentation of the four orientations to planning has, of course, been biased. I am a proponent of the interactive approach and advocate it because I believe it provides the best chance we have for coping effectively with accelerating change, increasing organizational complexity, and environmental turbulence. Moreover, it is the only one of the four orientations that explicitly addresses itself to increasing individual, organizational, and societal development and improving quality of life.

So much for an overview of the basic approaches to planning. The remainder of this book is devoted to developing the interactive concept of corporate planning. Before turning to that task, however, it may be helpful to set the stage by considering two aspects of such planning: its operating principles and its content.

OPERATING PRINCIPLES OF INTERACTIVE PLANNING

The way interactive planning is carried out depends on three operating principles: the *participative* principle, the principle of *continuity*, and the *holistic* principle.

The Participative Principle

Most planners and consumers of plans believe that the principal benefit of planning comes from use of its product, a plan. The interactivist denies this. He asserts that *in planning, process is the most important product.* Therefore, the principal benefit of it derives from engaging in it.

It is through participation in interactive planning that members of an organization can develop. In addition, participation enables them to acquire an understanding of the organization and makes it possible for them to serve organizational ends more effectively. This, in turn, facilitates organizational development. Just how all this can come about is a subject to which considerable attention is given below.

The participative principle has two important effects on the way interactive planning is carried out. First, it implies that no one can plan effectively for someone else. It is better to plan for oneself, no matter how badly, than to be planned for by others, no matter how well. The reason for this derives from the meaning of development: an increase in one's desire and ability to satisfy one's own desires and those of others. This ability and desire are not increased by being planned for by others, but by planning for oneself.

In interactive planning, plans are not prepared by internal or external planning units and then submitted to executives for approval. Rather, executives engage directly in the planning process. Doing so is one of their major responsibilities. Furthermore, all those who are normally planned for are also given an opportunity to engage in the process. How such comprehensive participation can be organized is the subject of the next section.

In one sense, involvement in planning is like playing a game that one wants to win, but the winning of which is not the principal benefit to be obtained from the play. The principal benefit lies in what one obtains from the play itself. If this were not the case, it would not be a game. Play is converted to work when winning a game becomes more important than playing it. Similarly, the planner for whom the plan is more important than the planning sacrifices much of the satisfaction and benefit to be derived from engaging in it. Planning should be fun as well as productive. If it is, it enhances the quality of the work life of the participants and enables them to develop.

The second important effect on the way interactive planning is carried out is to be found in a question about the proper role of professional planners and planning units inside or outside the organization planned for. If their role is not to prepare plans for others, what is it? Is is to encourage and facilitate the planning of others for themselves. Professionals should provide whatever motivation, information, knowledge, understanding, wisdom, and imagination are required by others to plan effectively for themselves.

A Design for Participative Planning

The design presented here is idealized in the sense that it may be very difficult if not impossible to realize, but it can usually be approximated quite closely. Some of the difficulties involved in using it will be considered after it has been described.

I use a simple three-level conventionally structured organization to describe the design (see Figure 3.1). However, the design can be applied to organizations of any size and structure. The three levels in the example could be corporate, divisional, and departmental. Each box in Figure 3.1 represents a unit: the collection of people working at that level in a particular function. The small circle at the top of each box represents the head of that unit. All members of a unit are given an opportunity to participate in planning for that unit.

The essential elements of the design are the (planning) boards which are represented in Figure 3.1 by the larger circles. The head of each unit, who leads the planning for his unit, reports to a board. Each board except

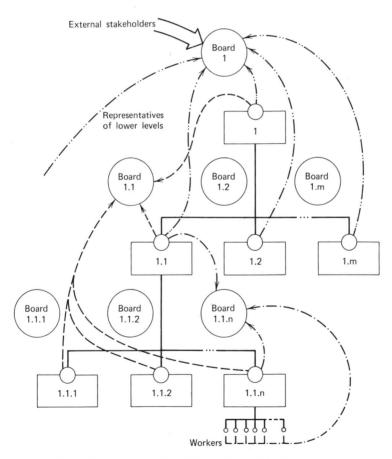

Figure 3.1 An organizational design for participative planning.

those at the top and bottom, which are treated separately below, consist of the following members:

1. The head of the unit reporting to it—for example, the head of unit 1.1 is a member of board 1.1.
2. The immediate superior of the head of the unit—for example, the head of unit 1 is a member of board 1.1 (and also boards 1.2, . . ., 1.m).
2. The immediate subordinates of the head of the unit—for example, the heads of units 1.1.1, 1.1.2, . . . , and 1.1.n are members of board 1.1.

Thus three levels are present on each board. All unit heads other than those at the top and bottom, are members of boards at three levels: the one immediately above, their own, and the ones immediately below. Therefore, in an organization that has five levels in it, managers in the middle interact with all five levels: two higher in the boards of their immediate superiors, and two lower in the boards of their immediate subordinates. The extensiveness of such vertical interaction makes effective integration of unit planning possible. The need for such integration is discussed below.

At the lowest level all members of the unit are members of their unit's board. This brings the workers at the bottom into contact with two levels of management, their immediate superior and his immediate superior. If the size of the lowest-level units are large, this makes for too large a board, one that cannot operate effectively. For this reason the basic work unit should be small, perhaps no more than ten people. Reducing the size of these units need not increase the number of lowest-level managers required. If the work teams are set up as autonomous work groups, they can select and rotate leadership among themselves. Then no additional managers are required, and each autonomous work group can have its own board in which all of its members participate along with the manager to whom it reports. The board of the lowest-level manager then contains the leaders of the autonomous work groups as well as the manager's immediate superior.

The board at the top (1) should include the highest authority (the head of unit 1), his immediate subordinates (e.g., 1.1, 1.2, . . . , and 1.m), representatives of the external stakeholders (e.g., investors, and consumers), and representatives elected by each level of the organization not otherwise represented on that board. The top board then reflects the interests of the corporation's containing system, the corporation itself, and the subsystems and individuals it contains.

Each unit produces a plan for itself. It should be free to take any planning decisions that have no effect on any other unit at the same or a higher level and that require no resources that are not already available to it. Planning decisions that do not meet these conditions should be submitted to the board at the next higher level for approval.

Each board has two major responsibilities. First, it should coordinate the plans made at the level below that of the board. Since the majority of the members of each board except the one at the top consists of the heads of the units from the level below, the coordination that takes place is essentially self-coordination. Second, each board should integrate the plans made at the level of the board with those of the levels immediately above and below. In the case of the top and bottom boards, one of these requirements, of course, is not imposed.

Each board interprets the plans made at its level to the levels immediately above and below it, making clear to these levels the implications of its plans.

If this design of the planning process added to the burdens of already overburdened managers then, no matter how advantageous it is in principle, it would be impractical. Although it may appear to burden them, it has not done so in practice. It is important to understand why.

How much of a manager's time is consumed by boards? This obviously depends on how many boards a manager serves. In general, but not without exception, a manager ought to have fewer than ten people reporting directly to him. As Miller [54] has shown, seven is the average number of distinct activities that a manager can think about simultaneously, hence interdependently. Boards generally meet for no more than four hours per month. Then, if a manager is on, say, ten boards (and most are on fewer) he would spend forty hours per month at board meetings, no more than 25 percent of his time at work. This ordinarily leaves plenty of time for his other activities because many of his most important responsibilities can be fulfilled through participation on these boards. Through them he can coordinate and integrate the work done under him and his own work with that of others. He can also use the boards to inform and motivate his subordinates, and to keep abreast of what is going on above and alongside.

Most managers and other members of an organization who are worth their salt are, in fact, always planning, either consciously or unconsciously. The design presented here organizes this huge informal effort and extracts more of its great potential than is realized from the disorganized way it is usually carried out. Once under way, it actually saves time over the entire enterprise. It taps the energy wasted in worry, complaints, "beefing," and partial (hence abortive) efforts at reform by converting corporate entropy into useful work, play, and learning. Moreover, it provides all those who feel that they are either being served unfairly or are serving inadequately with a chance to "put up or shut up."

This design for participative planning need not be introduced to an entire organization at once. It can be and has been employed independently in a unit, department, or a division. It has also been used at some but not all levels of an organization, the top, middle, or bottom. Such partial applications tend to spread to other parts or levels of the organization.

Participation in unit planning at any level should be required of all managers but should be optional for all other personnel. It should be an opportunity, not an imposition. If nonmanagerial personnel fail to participate, this indicates that they consider it a waste of time. When it becomes apparent to them that planning can affect the quality of their work lives and their personal development, it becomes an opportunity that does not have to knock twice.

A major consequence of participative planning is a reduction of the difficulties normally associated with implementation of plans. People are more inclined to implement plans they have had a hand in producing than those that are handed down to or imposed on them. Through participation, implementation becomes an integral part of the planning process. It is not only an output of planning, but an input as well, as the next operating principle clearly recognizes.

The Principle of Continuity

Most planning is done discontinuously. For example, many companies prepare five-year plans that are updated annually. A designated part of each year, usually months, are used for preparing the plan. Once the plan is approved, planning stops until the return of the designated months in the following year. This on-again, off-again cycle is repeated each year.

Because of events that are not and could not be foreseen, no plan, however carefully it is prepared, works as expected. Therefore, the effects expected from implementing plans and the assumptions on which these expectations are based should be continuously reviewed. When these assumptions and expectations deviate from reality, explanations should be sought and, when found, used to modify the plan appropriately.

In Chapter 7 I describe a design of a management system that makes such continuous monitoring, evaluation, and modification of plans possible. It will be seen that this system requires an explicit formulation of expectations associated with all planning and the assumptions on which they are based. Once they have been formulated, they are monitored. In this way relevant changes in the environment, the corporation as a whole, and its parts that would otherwise have gone undetected are likely to be noticed.

Consider the following example. A company that produces a common heavily consumed food product based its forecasts of sales on population growth, changing age-mix, and per-capita consumption of its product's principal ingredient. Because per-capita consumption of that ingredient had not changed significantly over the last fifteen years, it was assumed that it would continue to be constant. Nevertheless, as part of the company's interactive planning process it formulated this assumption explicitly and checked it as frequently as relevant data became available. In this way a sudden and significant increase in per-capita consumption was detected. An explanation was found through research that indicated that the change would persist. As a result, the company's plans for construction of new plants was considerably accelerated. This change was not detected by any of the company's competitors; therefore, most of them ran out of capacity and were unable to meet the increased demand. The company that had detected the change was able to fill more than four times its share of the increased market.

A second reason for continuous planning derives from the fact that when we pursue something we value, the value we place on it often changes one way or the other as we get closer to it. Therefore, our values change as continuously as do facts, and their changes also require appropriate modification of plans. It is commonplace, for example, to make a detailed plan for a trip to a specific destination only to find a detour or something along the way that is more interesting than the destination. On the other hand, once the destination is reached it may turn out to be disappointing. In such cases plans are commonly changed.

Finally, perhaps the most important reason for continuous planning is the fact that its principal benefit derives from engaging in it. Then why discontinue it?

The Holistic Principles

This principle has two parts: the *principle of coordination* and the *principle of integration*. Each has to do with a different dimension of organization. Organizations are divided into levels, each level is divided into units that are differentiated by either function, output, or market served. Coordination has to do with the interactions between different units at the same level; integration concerns interactions between units at different levels.

The *principle of coordination* states that no part of an organization can be planned for effectively if it is planned for independently of any other unit at the same level. Therefore, all units at the same level should be planned for simultaneously and interdependently.

Why? The answer lies in the fact that a threat or an opportunity that appears in one unit may best be treated in another unit or in several of them simultaneously. This should be as apparent as saying that the best way to treat a headache is not necessarily brain surgery. The producer of a threat or an opportunity may not be located where the symptoms appear. When we label a problem as a production or marketing problem, this does not mean that the appropriate way of treating it is within that function. A production problem may best be solved by a change in marketing, and vice versa. Nevertheless, many managers persist in thinking of problems in terms of the part of the organization in which they appear. This would only make sense if the parts were independent of each other. If they were, they would not be parts of an organization. Therefore, unit problems derive more from the way units interact than from their actions which are not affected by, nor affect, any other unit.

For example, the manager of a factory that produced a high-quality paper observed that his daily output had been decreasing for some time. His examination of the production lines showed no reduction in their output when they were operating. This led him to suspect maintenance problems, but a study of the records showed no increase in down-time for maintenance. Then he examined the records of running times of the lines and found them to be decreasing. The reason for this, he discovered, was an increase in the time required to set up the lines for production. This was found to be the consequence of an increase in the number of different products that had to be produced. At this point the manager called on a research team to find out how to schedule his production lines so as to minimize the set-up time required.

The team knew of a mathematical procedure for doing so. Since the improvement this procedure could yield depended on how accurately demand for each product could be predicted, the team first calculated how much improvement could be obtained with a perfect forecast. This was done by rescheduling the plant over the last five years using hindsight to provide perfect forecasts. The researchers found that a significant improvement could have been obtained with the appropriate scheduling procedure and a perfect forecast. While doing the work the team also found that if 4 percent of the products—those with the least demand, all of which were unprofitable—were dropped from the product line, the same improvement could be obtained as that yielded by their scheduling procedure and a perfect forecast; and this would require no change in forecasting or scheduling.

When the team suggested dropping these products to the production manager, he pointed out that this was not in his area of responsibility but in marketing. He went on to say that he did not want to involve the marketing department in his internal problems and, therefore, wanted the team to confine itself to operations that were under his control.

The team members persisted and eventually obtained the manager's reluctant permission to speak to the relevant marketing manager. When they did, he pointed out that almost all of the unprofitable products were bought by major consumers of profitable products. He expressed great concern over the possibility of losing these customers by failing to provide them with the low-volume unprofitable products. When the team asked him how he knew he would lose these accounts, he said he was not sure, but he was unwilling to run the risk involved in finding out.

The team then addressed itself to finding a riskless way of doing so. It found one that consisted of changing the way salespeople were compensated. They were paid a base salary plus a commission on the dollar value of their sales. The new system that was proposed by the team based their commission on the profitability of sales. The salespeople were to receive no commission for selling unprofitable items, but the commissions on profitable items were set in such a way that if they continued to sell what they had in the past, their earnings would be unaffected. The idea behind the system was that the salespeople would no longer have any reason to sell unprofitable items other than the customer's demand for them.

The marketing manager accepted and installed this system on a trial basis in one region. Its performance exceeded all expectations. The salespeople earned more, company profits increased, and a sufficient number of unprofitable products were not sold in that one region alone to yield a greater increase in production output than could have been obtained with an optimal production schedule and a perfect forecast.

To have treated this problem as a production problem would have been to commit a white-collar crime.

Problems, no matter where they appear, should be attacked simultaneously and cooperatively from as many different points of view as possible. This is what the principle of coordination tries to assure.

The *principle of integration* states that planning done independently at any level of a system cannot be as effective as planning carried out interdependently at all levels. It is common knowledge, for example, that a policy or practice established at one level of a corporation often creates problems at other levels. Therefore, the solution to a problem that appears at one level may best be obtained by changing a policy or practice at another.

Conflict between levels of an organization is as common as conflict between units at the same level. Such conflicts are usually the result of a lack of awareness of the effects of what one level or unit does on other levels or units. If plans are to be implemented effectively, such conflict must be removed. This can only be done by planning in a coordinated and integrated way.

When the principles of coordination and integration are combined, we obtain the *holistic principle*, which states that the more parts of a system and levels of it that plan simultaneously and interdependently the better. This concept of all-over-at-once planning stands in opposition to sequential planning, either top-down or bottom-up.

Now I turn briefly to the phases of interactive planning. This will provide a preview of the structure of Part 2, which is organized around these phases.

THE PHASES OF INTERACTIVE PLANNING

Planning is much like the orange used in discussing alternative views of the universe. It can be sliced in many different ways, each yielding a different view. Identifing the phases of planning is slicing it in a particular way. The way I do so has evolved over time, guided by what managers and planners with whom I have worked, and students who have worked with me, seem to find clear and useful.

There is no way of putting the phases on paper without ordering them. This is unfortunate because there is no necessary order to them. They are interdependent aspects of a systemic process, each feeding and fed by the others, particularly in continous planning. Adjustment of the output of any one phase may be required by the output of any other. The order in which they are presented, therefore, is not the order in which they should be either initiated or terminated. None of them, like the process as a whole, should ever be completed, and they may be started in any order.

I have divided planning into five phases.

1. *Formulating the mess*: the system of threats and opportunities that face the organization.
2. *Ends planning*: specifying the ends to be pursued. It is in this phase of planning that a desirable future is designed.
3. *Means planning*: selecting or creating the means by which the specified ends are to be pursued. It is in this phase of planning that ways of approximating the desirable future are invented.

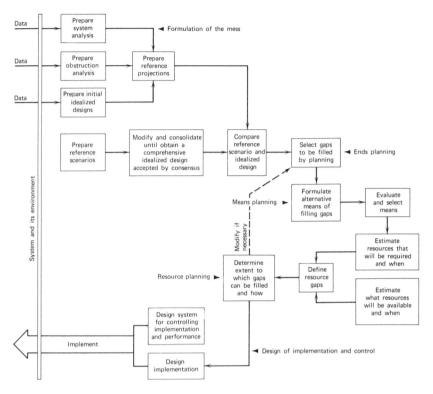

Figure 3.2   An interactive planning cycle.

4. *Resource planning*: determining what resources will be required, when they will be required, and how to obtain those that will not otherwise be available.

5. *Design of implementation and control*: determining who is to do what, when, and where; and how the implementation and its consequences are to be controlled, that is, kept on track.

These phases of planning and their major parts are shown in Figure 3.2. The exposition in Part 2 is organized around this diagram.

CONCLUSION

Interactive planning, as I have characterized it, requires a great deal of time and effort. Therefore, it must be justified by significant improvements in corporate performance. It usually yields such improvements. Nevertheless, few organizations are willing to dive into this pool without first testing the water by gingerly putting one foot into it. Therefore, most corporations initiate the process by trying it in one part of the organization, usually at or near the top. If successful there, it is gradually spread through the rest of the organization.

The formulation of interactive planning that I have provided in this chapter and develop further in what follows, is idealized. It is a description of the kind of planning that I believe a corporation should move toward. It can do this by successive approximations, in small increments. Initially, doing so will be seen as a cost; only through experience with it can its benefits be appreciated.

PART TWO

FOREGROUND

CHAPTER FOUR

FORMULATING THE MESS

Mess, n. *A confused mixture or a disorderly condition of things.*

WESBSTER'S UNIVERSAL DICTIONARY, 1936

The mess that a corporation is in consists of the future that it would have if it were to continue behaving as it does and if its environment were not to change or alter its directions in any significant way. In other words: a corporation's mess is the future implied by its and its environment's current behavior. Every system contains the seeds of its own deterioration and destruction. Therefore, the pupose of formulating the mess is to identify the nature of these often concealed threats and to suggest changes that can increase the corporation's ability to survive and thrive.

Formulating a mess requires three types of study:

1. *A systems analysis*—a detailed description of the state of the corporation, how it operates, those it affects and how it affects them, and how it affects and is affected by its environment.
2. *An obstruction analysis*—identification and definition of the obstructions to corporate development.
3. *Preparation of reference projections*—extrapolations of corporate performance from its recent past into the future assuming no sig-

nificant changes in the behavior of either the corporation or its environment.

The outputs of these studies are synthesized into a picture of the future that the corporation would have if it and its environment were to continue in their current directions. Such a scenario is *not* a forecast of the corporation's future because the assumptions on which it is based— no change of corporate or environmental directions—are known to be false. It is a picture of the future that the corporation currently is in. This future is the mess that confronts a corporation.

SYSTEMS ANALYSIS

Effective corporate planning requires for its foundation a comprehensive and cohesive description of the current state of the corporation and its environment, how the corporation operates, whom and what it affects and is affected by, and how. Much of the information required for this purpose is available in corporations but is usually scattered about; hence, must be collected and organized. The type of picture of a corporation usually appearing in annual reports is painted with too broad a brush and focuses almost exclusively on financial matters; hence is lacking in coverage and depth.

A systems analysis should be directed at answering the following types of question about a corporation and its parts.

1. *How is the system for which planning is to be done to be defined?* A precise formal definition of the system is required. If planning is not to be carried out for all of a corporation but, for example, only for a subsidiary, a division, or a department, the boundaries of that part of the system should be clearly specified.

2. *What business or businesses is the corporation in?* If the corporation is in more than one business, an effort should be made to identify a larger business of which each is a part. What do they have in common, if anything? In the case of a conglomerate it may not be possible to find such an all-inclusive concept of its business.

The point here is to define the business that the corporation or unit thinks it *is* in, not the one it thinks it *ought* to be in. This "ought" is dealt with later in the planning process.

3. *How is the corporation organized?* A detailed organization chart may provide what is needed, but its accuracy and possible obsolescence should be checked.

4. *How does the corporation actually operate?* How do materials, money, orders, and information flow into, through, and out of the corporation? What operations are performed on these inputs and how are they coordinated and controlled? What are the capacities of the people and/ or machines that perform these operations, and how much time do they require?

The answers to these questions can usually be shown on a set of annotated flow charts. The basic flow chart should show how inputs flow from suppliers to the corporation, how they are operated on within the corporation, and how the outputs are distributed and to whom. A first draft of this diagram can show each step in the process. At each location at which something is done to the material or product, the capacity and current level of operation should be noted on the diagram.

The basic flow chart subsequently can be simplified and made more comprehensible by consolidating operations that are subject to the same controls. That is, if a single instruction similarly affects a sequence of steps in a production process, these steps can be combined and given an appropriate name. For example, if all production lots are processed over the same sequence of machines, that sequence can be shown as a single operation with the capacity equal to that of the unit in the sequence that has the lowest capacity.

An overlay should then be prepared to show the sources and flow of instructions that control the operations shown on the basic flow chart. This should then be expanded by showing the information-processing and flow required to support the control system. The finished overlay should reveal the management and information systems that control or otherwise affect corporate operations.

A second overlay (or set of overlays) should be prepared that reveals how each function not directly involved in production operates and ultimately affects the production process. For example, this should be done for marketing, research and development, industrial engineering, personnel, and so on.

Finally, a financial flow chart should be prepared, one that indicates the flow of money from its various sources into and through the corporation, and from it to its various destinations. It should also show where the decisions are made that affect this flow and how they are communicated to others.

In corporations that have two or more relatively independent businesses such an analysis should be made of each. The relationship of each to corporate headquarters can be shown on a separate diagram if necessary.

The set of diagrams produced by a systems analysis are likely to be heavily used for purposes other than planning. Executives and managers frequently find them useful in a number of different ways. They are almost always surprised and enlightened when they see a representation of the system they control that is both comprehensive and comprehensible. For this reason, the application of some artistic talent to preparation of the final versions of the diagrams is not amiss.

Systems analyses usually have valuable side effects. They may reveal operations that are not properly controlled. For example, in one such analysis it was found that make-or-buy decisions affecting about 25,000 parts had not been reviewed for a number of years. By arranging to have this done, considerable savings were realized. In another case, the analysis of a production process suggested a reversal of order of two machine operations which, once made, reduced the generation of scrap by a significant amount.

Such analyses often reveal that much of the paper work in the organization is superfluous and even obstructive. Forms and copies that were once useful have a way of being continued long after their usefulness has ended. Preparation of the information—instruction flow diagram provides an opportunity for reviewing each document that is transmitted from one place to another. For this reason it is desirable to have this particular analysis carried out by those responsible for information systems in the corporation.

Details on how to conduct such analyses can be found in Churchman, Ackoff, and Arnoff [19, Chapters 2 and 4].

5. *What policies, practices, strategies, and tactics are currently in force?* To answer this question is to formulate what might be called the corporate rules of the game. Management may be reluctant to formulate such rules explicitly but they should be encouraged to do so or have it done. The results are not always flattering. For example, the following is part of a formulation of such rules made by several managers in one large corporation.

> We have a commitment to achieving a growth rate and a return on investments exceeding that of the industries in which we operate, and to creating the environment and resources to meet these objectives.

We are not product innovators. We transfer existing products and product concepts, whether ours or derived from other sources, from one country to another.

We market only those products that require similar technology to those we presently produce and that can be produced in high volume through capital intensive operations.

We market for national distribution branded products designed for consumer and institutional markets.

We do not locate manufacturing units in non-Western countries or countries having centrally planned economies.

We do not integrate vertically where such integration would reduce the unit's degree of freedom in choosing suppliers and/or blur the competitive advantages of its products.

The debt to equity ratio is maintained at an annual average of less than or equal to 0.5. At any time it exceeds 0.7, corrective action programs are undertaken.

6. *What are the principal stylistic preferences of management?* Every corporation and unit within it provides a unique working environment, an atmosphere that derives from its style of operation. From what does this uniqueness derive? Relevant factors may include the way people interact (formally or informally), the hours they keep, the amount of company-generated social activity, the number, nature, and duration of meetings, the amount of travel encouraged, and so on. The point here is to put one's finger on the quality of work life for personnel at all levels.

7. *How has the corporation performed in the past and how is it performing now?* This question should be answered with respect to a wide array of commonly used measures of performance such as sales volume, market share, earnings, and return on investment. The answers usually are most easily shown in graph form.

8. *Who are the corporations's stakeholders? How many of each type are there? How dependent on the corporation are they? How dependent is the corporation on them? With respect to consumers or customers, how do they use the corporation's output and for what purposes? What is the distribution of economic, demographic, and personality characteristics among them?*

Most companies have a good deal of information about who their customers and consumers are, and some know the reasons given for using the company's products or services. However, the reasons given by consumers for their consumption seldom provide the explanation. To say, for example, that one consumes a particular product because one likes it, is *not* to explain its use. This comes only from an understanding of *why* it is liked, what purposes its consumption serves. Unfortunately, most consumer research is directed at *describing* the consumer and consumption, and collecting reasons given for it, but not at *explaining* it.

9. *Who are the corporation's competitors? How large are they? How much of their business is competitive with the corporation for which the planning is being done? What are their shares of the market? How are their shares distributed geographically? How have these shares been changing over time?*

10. *What laws and governmental regulations affect the corporation and how? What new laws and regulations are under consideration and what are the chances of their being enacted? Are there any special-interest groups in society—for example, consumerists or ecologists—who are having or can have an effect on what the corporation does? What are these effects? What effects does the corporation's behavior have on the environment?*

The collection of and search for answers to such questions are often facilitated by the use of outsiders who are not biased by corporate prejudices and preconceptions. The answers, once obtained either by insiders or outsiders, should be widely disseminated within the corporation for discussion and criticism. Differences of opinion are particularly important because they indicate possible obstructions to corporate development.

OBSTRUCTIONS TO DEVELOPMENT

As noted earlier, constraints on an organization's growth are primarily found in its environment; but constraints on its development are more likely to be found within the organization itself. The major obstructions to an organization's development are usually self-imposed, often unconsciously, and are of two types: discrepancies and conflicts.

Recognition of the fact that constraints to development are self-imposed is reflected in the common practice of listing corporate weaknesses. Such lists, however, are usually quite superficial because they contain only those weaknesses of which management is aware, and of these only those that they are willing to acknowledge. Such lists seldom touch more than the tips of icebergs.

It is difficult for most organizations to face the truth about themselves. Their unwillingness to do so can be a major deterrent to their development. The reasons for such reluctance become apparent when we consider the nature of the discrepancies and conflicts involved.

Internal Discrepancies

A discrepancy is a difference between what an organization believes about itself and what is actually the case. Discrepancies are of five types: those involving (1) organizational ends, (2) the means employed to pursue these ends, (3) the resources available for such pursuits, (4) the way these pursuits are organized, managed, and carried out, and (5) external stakeholders and other aspects of the environment.

Organizational Ends

The ends—goals, objectives, and ideals—espoused by an organization are not always those that an objective observer sees actually pursued. There is frequently a big difference between what is preached and what is practiced. For example, many corporations proclaim their concern with the quality of the environment, but they protect or conserve it no more than they are forced to by the law and public pressure. Some companies that have propagandized for unrestricted competition and the free-market system run to the government for aid as soon as they feel threatened or suffer somehow from these. Others proclaim equal-opportunity employment but efficiently manage to avoid hiring or promoting minorities or women.

When such inconsistencies are brought to a company's attention it almost invariably responds with internally convincing rationalizations. Such rationalizations usually defend the morality of the company, but morality is not the central issue; development is. An inconsistency, no matter how well rationalized, is an obstruction to development.

In one large company that claimed to be an equal-opportunity employer, about 45 percent of its employees were members of a minority group (blacks) but less than 1 percent of its managers were. Corporate management argued that this was due to the educational deficiencies of its minority employees. An analysis of the company's employees made by an external research team showed that on the average the minority employees had at least a year's more equivalent education than did the whites in the same job. This showed that the lack of upward mobility of minority employees was not due to their educational deficiencies but to discrimination. This finding was rejected by the company's management; the outside researchers were dismissed. About a year later a case was brought against the company but its minority employees. A federal court found the company guilty of discrimination against minorities and imposed a heavy fine.

Again, the point of this story does not lie in morality or immorality, but in the fact that the company deprived itself of a usable source of managers and invited antagonism and hostility from a large part of its work force. This retarded its development.

This last case also shows that an organization may not be pursuing the objective it proclaims. On the other hand, an organization may be pursuing an objective it does not proclaim and of which it is not even aware. For example, a ministry of education in a less than well-developed country prepared a list of objectives for governmentally supported universities. It was a typical "motherhood" list. I asked those who had prepared it what would be the principal social consequences of closing the universities. With some prodding they eventually acknowledged that there would be a significant increase in the number of unemployed young people who in all likelihood would be politically disruptive, to say the least. This revealed that the government was using universities to help keep the lid on the country. To an outsider this objective seemed to have a greater effect than proclaimed objectives on what the country's universities did. Their educational function suffered greatly.

A large number of corporate managers assert that their principal objective is to maximize profit. However, impartial examination of their behavior reveals that such an objective does not dominate their behavior. If it did, executives would work in less luxurious facilities, travel on commercial planes at economy rates, stay in modest hotels, and so on. It is clear that most managements are willing to sacrifice at least some profit in order to provide themselves with an acceptable quality of work life. The point again is not that this objective is inappropriate or immoral; on the contrary, it should be extended to all employees. The truth is perceived by many employees who do not benefit from management's dedication to providing itself with a high quality of work life, and they resent it. Their reduced morale retards corporate development.

In some such cases managers have a considerable sense of guilt. The greater their guilt, the more defensive they usually are; hence the more resistant to change. This too obstructs development.

Organizational Means

This second type of discrepancy involves the means that a corporation claims or believes it is using in pursuit of its ends, and those it actually uses. For example, in the early 1950s I proposed to the executives of a major railroad that the company use a very recently developed mathematical procedure in operating its classification yards. One of the executives told me the company had tried the procedure at least twenty years earlier and that it had not worked. Such self-deception precludes learning and thus reduces the organization's ability to improve itself and others.

One or the divisions of a large corporation is very proud of the elaborate quantitative procedure by which it estimates its future manpower requirements. The estimates are prepared annually for the next five years and are submitted by the divisional vice president to his group vice president. It was widely believed that these estimates were then used to authorize additions of personnel to the division. However, when the group vice president received the estimates he turned them over to his staff with instructions to demonstrate that they were too large. When this had been done, he arranged with the divisional vice president for a confrontation between his staff and the divisional staff that prepared the estimates. The results of the confrontation were always inconclusive. The staffs were then dimissed and the two vice presidents settled down to old-fashioned bargaining with little reference to the estimates.

The chief executive officer of one large corporation believed he had established effective communication with all his employees. They were given an opportunity to attend an annual session at which he made a state-of-the company presentation and invited discussion and questions. These meetings were held at each corporate site on company time. It was only after a prolonged strike had been called just after one of his corporate circuits that the executive came to realize that these meetings were designed to facilitate his communication to the workers, not their communication to him.

Most corporate executives believe that their sales forces spend most of their time selling. Studies of how salesmen actually spend their time, however, usually reveal that more of their time is spent in providing information to headquarters than in selling.

In a study in which I participated many years ago, professionals in corporations were asked how much of their time at work was spent in personal and social activities. The average of their estimates was under 1 percent. Subsequent direct observations of the same professionals revealed that they actually spent about 11 percent of their time in such activities.

In general, there is a great deal of difference between what corporate personnel actually do, believe they do, are believed by others to do, and are supposed to do. The differences are not necessarily bad—in fact, they may be essential for corporate survival. However, if this is the case, the suppositions, beliefs, and specifications should be changed; otherwise what is actually done should be.

Organizational Resources

The third type of discrepancy involves beliefs about the quality, quantity, and use of resources available to the corporation. Such resources are personnel, facilities and equipment, materials and energy, information, and money.

The manager of a plant employing mostly Mexican immigrants complained bitterly about the hostility of the workers to the company ("they are nothing but a bunch of reds") and the fact that most of them could not speak or understand English. A university-based research group was retained to help with this situation. A meeting was set up between those Mexican workers identified by management as the "ring leaders" and the research group. To faciliate communication the researchers took along a young Mexican woman who was part of the university's staff. She was the first to enter the room in which the workers had been gathered; and she introduced herself and the others on the team in Spanish. From then on the workers insisted on speaking in English. They were obviously proud of the fact that they could and they wanted the young lady to know it. When they were asked why they had not let management know of their command of the language, they replied that it was their only protection against mismanagement. Subsequent research showed them to be closer to the truth than management.

In another corporation the executives were very proud of a new plant located in a beautifully scenic countryside. They were particularly proud of the luxurious cafeteria they had provided for the workers. They had also provided themselves with a plush executive dining room. I visited the plant and found the cafeteria to be striking but found that all its windows faced the factory floor, whereas the executive dining room looked out on the countryside. The workers knew this and resented it greatly. They took it as evidence of management's hostility to them.

The managers of most companies that have large computerized data-processing and information systems speak publicly in glowing terms about them. However, I have often found that in private they admit to having little use for them because of the information overload they impose and much irrelevance. These systems are not improved because they are not criticized.

Organizational Structure and Management

The fourth type of discrepancy involves the manner in which the pursuit of objectives is organized and managed. Such discrepancies have been the subject of intensive studies by Argyris and Schön [11 and 12]. It is currently fashionable, for example, to espouse decentralization and participative management. Practice often contradicts such proclamations. Subordinates know this. They correctly view many such organizations as centralized, authoritarian, and nonparticipative.

Students of organization have long differentiated the formal or proclaimed organizational structure and its informal or actual structure. The informal structure may either make it possible for the organization to survive or constitute a major threat to its survival. For example, Hedrick Smith [75] shows clearly the differences between how the Russian economy is supposed to be organized and how it actually is. He argues that it could not function if it were forced to work as it is supposed to.

In a national bank dedicated to rural development in a less than well-developed country I was shown an organization chart of which the relevant portion is shown in Figure 4.1a. Evidence of internal dissension led me and my colleagues to inquire into how the bank actually operated.

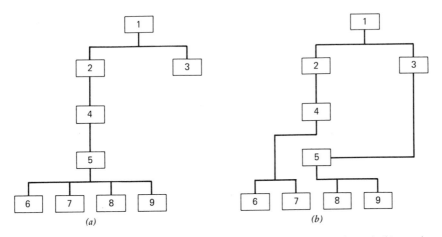

Figure 4.1 Difference between a claimed and actual organization: (a) claimed; (b) actual.

What we found is shown in Figure 4.1*b*. This discrepancy was responsible for serious deficiencies in the bank's operations. More effort went into the war between the factions than into performing the bank's functions.

The Organization's Stakeholders and Environment

The last type of discrepancy involves assumptions about stakeholders, the environment, and others who occupy it. Such assumptions are often used to justify corporate policies and strategies which then cannot be executed because the assumptions are incorrect (see Emshoff and Mitroff [32]).

It is useful to think of a corporate environment as consisting of two parts:

1. *The transactional*, consisting of those individuals, organizations, and institutions with which the corporation interacts directly; for example, consumers or customers, suppliers, investors or creditors, debtors, the government, and competitors.
2. *The contextual*, consisting of everything other than the transactional environment that effects or is affected by the corporation and over which it has no control and, at best, little influence; for example, general economic conditions, the weather, and government expenditures.

Every corporation necessarily makes numerous assumptions about those with whom it interacts; for example, consumers. As I noted above, few companies understand *why* their products are consumed, although they think they do. Companies often believe their own advertising much more than their consumers do. Operating on this belief they conclude, when consumers do not behave as they expect, that their consumers are behaving irrationally. Few companies are willing to consider the alternative possibility: that they are behaving irrationally. Yet experience has shown this to be a much more fruitful assumption. E.H. Vogel, [80] when vice president of marketing at Anheuser-Busch, Inc., put it this way:

> Consumer marketing problems are not solved by assuming the consumer is irrational and the marketer is rational, *but just the opposite.*

> Consumers may behave irrationally in the short run, but not in the long run. They learn fast. Marketers who claim consumers are irrational really mean that they do not understand consumers and either don't know how to acquire such understanding or don't want to. Now mind you, I am not saying consumers are conscious of what they are doing or why. They can be rational even if they

don't understand themselves. It is our job to find out why they do what they do, even if they don't know. . .

One brief and familiar example. Most marketers of gasoline assume consumers buy on the basis of brand preferences. Policies based on this assumption have uniformly failed. Studies have shown that most consumers do not have gasoline brand preferences, and for good reason: they can't tell the difference between the performances of competing brands. And again for good reason: there isn't any significant difference between them. It turns out, however, that consumers pick service stations, not brands, and they do so in such a way as to minimize the amount of time they lose in buying gasoline. This is completely rational behavior under the circumstances. A gasoline marketer who knows and uses this information can select his sites and design his stations so as to give him a significant competitive advantage. In our work we have found that consumer preferences for different kinds of alcoholic beverages are not irrational but are based on different functions that different beverages perform well under different environmental, economic, and physiological conditions.

We must not only develop understanding of the consumer and do so by at least starting with the assumption he is rational, but we must also start with the assumption that most of our marketing errors and failures are due to our own irrationality (pp. 21-22).

I one asked the manager of a packaged food business whose products have a high sugar content, "Why is the British per-capita consumption of sugar higher than ours?" He answered, "Because they like it more than we do." I then asked him how he knew this. He replied impatiently, "What the hell; they consume more of it, don't they?"

At least a partial explanation for the consumption of sugar is available, but most of its consumers and producers are unaware of it. It has to do with the ratio of carbohydrates to protein in the diet and their effects on blood-sugar level. In general, the higher the ratio, the more sugar is consumed. With some understanding of this and related phenomena one can explain many of the dietary differences between countries, and between young and old people; for example, the preference of the former for soft drinks and the latter for bottled water.

When it was suggested to one company that it offer discounts on orders that reflect the amount of time allowed before delivery, that company's lawyers said it would be illegal to do so. An external group of lawyers was then consulted and gave a contradictory opinion on which the company acted successfully. When lawyers, whose task it is to keep a company out of trouble, are asked if it is alright to do something, they usually answer No. They know the company is not in trouble for not doing what is suggested, and they want to keep it that way. However, it they are told the company intends to do something and are asked how to do it so as to keep out of trouble, they often come up with a way.

The government is frequently believed to impose constraints that in fact exist only in management's mind. This is even true of government itself. The Arms Control and Disarmament Agency, ACDA, once negotiated a contract with the university-based research group of which I am a member. After negotiations were complete we were informed about security-clearance requirements that had not been previously mentioned. We refused to comply on the grounds that the work we were supposed to do was not classified. We were told that the law pertaining to the Agency required such clearance on all contracts even if they did not involve classified work. We still refused to go ahead. The Agency told us the contract would have to be cancelled. We did nothing. After several weeks of silence we were informed by the Agency that it had found a way around the requirement. We then went ahead with the work. There is much wisdom in Ambrose Bierce's [15] definition of *self-evident*: "Evident to one's self and to nobody else" (p.318).

Similar examples can be provided of misunderstandings of each type of stakeholder and competitor in the transactional environment, and of parts of the contextual environment as well. The assumptions that a corporation makes about them have a major effect on what it does and how it does it. The validity of these assumptions should be questionned continuously, but this cannot be done unless they are explicitly formulated. Good planning requires such formulations and their evaluation.

Uncovering Discrepancies

It is difficult to raise to consciousness the types of discrepancy I have discussed, and even more difficult to remove them once they are conscious. Their harmful effects on the organization usually must be well documented before any action is likely to be taken.

We are all aware of how difficult it is for us to see inconsistencies and hypocrisy in ourselves. We are also aware of how easy it is to see these defects in others. The difficulties of self-analysis are as great in organizations as they are in individuals. Therefore, such analyses are usually most effectively and painlessly carried out with the help of one or more qualified and objective outsiders.

Effective discrepancy analysis requires an interest in and sensitivity to inconsistencies, and experience with them in a number of corporations. Comparisons between different corporations alert a sensitive observer to discrepancies.

Clues are often revealed during a systems analysis, particularly while working on the rules of the game. Conflicting discriptions of how things are done and of the rules and regulations that apply to them are often symptoms of discrepancies.

In every corporation there are some who are aware of discrepancies and are willing to discuss them with someone who will preserve their anonymity and may get something done about them. Outsiders working inside a corporation are usually flooded with such revelations once their trustworthiness and effectiveness have been established.

Interviews of recent former employees often provide additional clues.

There are several group processes that can be used to bring discrepancies to light. One of these was developed by Argyris and Schön [11]. The other was developed by F. E. Emery [29] and is discussed by M. Emery [39] and T. A. Williams [84]. It is called the search conference.

The essence of the method developed by Argyris and Schön is revealed in their instructions to participants:

Please describe a challenging intervention or interaction with one or more individuals that (1) you have already experienced or (2) you expect to experience in the near future.

If you have difficulty with either of these conditions, try a hypothetical case in which you doubt your effectiveness.

Begin the description with a paragraph about the purpose of your intervention, the setting, the people involved, and other important characteristics.

Next, write a few paragraphs regarding your strategy. What were your objectives, how did you intend to achieve them, and why did you select those goals and strategies?

Next, write a few pages of the dialogue that actually occurred or that you expect to occur. Use the following format.

On this side of the page, write what was going on in your mind while each person in the dialogue (including yourself) is speaking.

On this side of the page, write what each person actually said or what you expected him to say. Continue writing the dialogue until you believe your major points are illustrated. (The dialogue should be at least two pages long.)

Finally, after you reread your case, describe the underlying assumptions that you think you held about effective action.

Once these cases are prepared:

> participants work with a researcher at the task of making explicit the govern-
> ing variables and the strategies for action that seem to determine the partici-
> pant's behavior as it is recorded in the case. Then participants try to assess
> their perception of self and others in the case and what characteristics of the
> behavioral world are manifested in the case. (p.41)

The search conference is a planning conference in the early stages of
which inconsistencies and discrepancies often surfaces. Williams [84] describes this phase of the conference as follows:

> The conference task and program usually take the form of a set of questions
> which participants accept responsibility for answering in collaboration with
> each other. The substance of the questions varies according to the particular
> context, but the general logic is to begin with trends in society as a whole. The
> aggregated answers then compose a picture of changes occurring in the ex-
> tended social field to which the system in question belongs but over which it
> has little or no direct control. Against this background, participants can look at
> the forces that have shaped or are likely to shape the evolution of their own
> organization or community. At this stage participants can make value judg-
> ments about the purpose and aims the system should have. These may be
> objectives that are deemed desirable for the organization or the criteria that
> would set the priorities in future planning. (p.472)

Conflict

In Chapter 2 I argued that the elimination of conflict—the ethical–moral
ideal—is necessary for a continuous increase in one's ability to satisfy
one's own desires and those of others; hence, for development. Conflict
exists when two or more desires interact in such a way that progress
toward one produces retrogression from the other or others. Conflicting
desires may lie *within* an individual or organization, or *between* them.

Where corporate development is concerned, a number of different
types of conflict may be involved:

1. Within individuals who are part of the corporation.
2. Between such individuals.
3. Between individuals and the corporation or parts of it (units).
4. Within units.
5. Between units at the same level of the corporation.
6. Between units at different levels or between units and the
   corporation.
7. Within the corporation as a whole.

8. Between the corporation and external groups, organizations, institutions, and society.

Consider each of these briefly.

Conflicts Within Individuals

There is an increasing awareness in corporations of the harmful effects of inner conflict in employees at all levels. Accumulating evidence shows clearly that alcoholism, drug addiction, and family, financial, and legal problems reduce the ability of individuals to perform effectively. This has led to a proliferation of employee assistance programs designed to provide professional help to employees whose personal problems adversely affect their work.

Conflict Between Individuals

Conflicts are likely to arise in any group whose members interact a great deal. Such conflicts may be caused by differences in personalities or to disagreements over objectives and ways to pursue them. Whatever their origin, they can reduce collective as well as individual performance and the ability to improve it. The higher the corporate level of those involved in interpersonal conflict, the more harm they can do and the more they can obstruct corporate development. Conflicts among executives can have a paralyzing effect on a corporation and can divide governments into hostile armed camps.

Conflicts Between Individuals and the Corporation or Parts of it

Both unionized and nonunionized employees often feel they are being treated unfairly by their unit or the corporation as a whole. Disgruntled employees can be found at all levels of corporations. They often try, consciously or unconsciously, to obstruct the corporation's pursuit of its objectives, and they frequently succeed. Employees so disposed are said to be *alienated*. Alienation is a matter of morale and low morale tends to be contagious.

Conflicts Within Units

Parts of a corporation frequently have conflicting objectives imposed on them by higher authorities. For example, a department that has responsi-

bility for servicing company-made appliances installed in homes in required simultaneously to maximize the number of service calls made per
day, and to minimize the inventory of parts carried in the vans in which
the service calls are made. The less inventory carried, the more frequently
servicemen must return to a central warehouse to obtain parts required
to complete repairs. The resulting conflict is obvious. It frustrates and
alienates members of the unit involved. Unless units thus afficted are
provided with an explicit criterion that enables them to find an acceptable balance between conflicting demands, their performance and their
ability and desire to improve it suffers.

Conflicts Between Units at the Same Level

Conflicting objectives are frequently assigned to different units at the
same level. For example, the purchasing department of one department
store chain was instructed to keep inventories as low as possible. At the
same time, the merchandizing department was told to maximize sales.
These objectives are obviously in conflict.

In a divisionalized electrical manufacturing company one division was
instructed to supply another with motors, and the other was instructed to
use only these motors. Both divisions were profit centers. The supplying
division often preferred to sell to its large regular customers, from whom
it could usually obtain a higher price, than deal with the interdivisional
transfer involved. The division supplied could sometimes obtain equivalent motors from outside sources at lower than the internal transfer
price. The harmful effects on both divisions and the corporation, when
calculated, were considerable.

Conflicts Between Units at Different Levels

Such conflicts are very common. They often involve the way resources
are allocated. One division may see the capital that it generates (and
believes it can invest in itself very profitably) taken from it by a higher
level that invests it in another division that appears to be a "dog." Practices or policies issued from above frequently reduce the ability of a unit
to perform effectively. For example, a blanket order issued to all units
may require reduction of personnel by a specified percentage. I saw this
done in a corporation with a unit in the consulting business that charged
clients on a cost-plus basis. Its profit, which it was supposed to maximize,
was necessarily reduced by the imposed reduction of personnel.

The imposition of reporting, accounting, and administrative practices
that serve one level of an organization well but obstruct at least some
units at a lower level, is commonplace. The compulsion for uniform prac-

tices among bureaucratically-minded administrators often creates major conflicts in lower-level units. I have seen a field-selling force that spent more time filling requests for information from its corporate marketing staff than it did in selling. The same force, however, was under continuous pressure from corporate marketing managers to sell more.

Conflicts Within the Corporation as a Whole

It is not unusual for corporations to have conflicting objectives, even when these are explicitly formulated. For example, most corporations have both a growth objective (e.g., increases in market share, sales volume, or earnings) and a return-on-investment objective. Under many circumstances these objectives are in conflict because growth can only be obtained through investments that cannot yield the desired return. For example, new factories cannot always provide as good a return as older ones built before inflation. There are industries in which each successive plant has yielded a lower return than its predecessor.

Many companies seek simultaneously to maintain good relations with labor and to minimize the number employed. Others want a large share of the minority market but do not want to increase minority representation on the work force, particularly in management. To have such objectives is not unusual, but to fail to face the conflicts they produce and attempt to dissolve them is to obstruct corporate development.

Conflicts Between the Corporation and External Groups

These are the conflicts of which corporate executives are usually most aware, particularly conflicts with special interest groups and governmental agencies and bodies. These conflicts are often used as excuses for poor performance, but poor performance, no matter how well it is excused, does not contribute to corporate development.

Unlike discrepancies between corporate proclamations and practices, or beliefs and facts, that are difficult for personnel within the corporation to identify, conflicts are usually more easily identified by insiders than outsiders. Having identified them, however, it is not it is not always easy to make them public even within the corporate family. To do so is often embarrassing to many, hence they are frequently treated as secrets even though many are aware of them. They cannot be removed unless they are faced openly. In fact, in many cases, such acknowledgment is sufficient to stimulate those involved to eliminate the conflict without intervention by a third party.

Now consider the third type of analysis required to formulate a mess.

REFERENCE PROJECTIONS

A reference projection is an extrapolation of a performance characteristic of a system from its recent past into the future, assuming no significant change in the behavior of either the system or its environment. Such a projection is, in effect, a glimpse of the future that is implied by continuation of the system's recent history.

Reference projections are normally made using the principal measures of performance employed by a corporation; for example, sales volume, market share, earnings, return on investment, and number of employees. Similar projections are also made of related environmental characteristics; for example, the size of the consuming population, its average income, the cost of raw materials, and so on. A comparison of these projections—for example, of total industry sales and company sales—may reveal future relationships that are not possible, for example, obtaining more than 100 percent of the market. I obtained such a result recently when I took the growth objective of one company and projected the sales volume it implied. This volume exceeded the projected size of the relevant market within twenty years. Such an incompatibility of projections shows that either the market in which the company operates must be expanded or its growth objective will not be met.

In the 1960s a projection was made that showed that if American universities continued to turn out scientists at the same increasing rate as they had over the recent past, by the end of the century there would be more scientists in the United States than people. The inevitable reduction in the growth of science programs could, therefore, be foreseen. Unfortunately, it was ignored by many universities whose subsequent financial difficulties are attributable to this oversight.

There is no mechanical way of determining what corporate and environmental characteristics should be used in reference projections. Some trial and error is usually required, but trying often yields clues that reduce the number of fruitless trials. Such clues can often be obtained by preparing a four-quadrant graph as is shown in Figure 4.2. It displays the historical and extrapolated relationships between

1. Sales and time.
2. Market and time.
3. Sales and assets.
4. Earnings and assets.
5. Earnings and time.

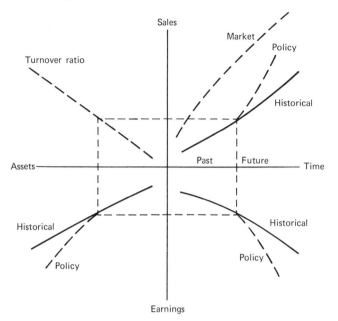

Figure 4.2 A four-quadrant reference projection.

Where possible, at least ten years of past data should be plotted. These plots should then be extrapolated over as many years as there are of past data. Such extrapolations can be made by use of statistical procedures but often the naked eye and bare hand are good enough.

Such plots might show that company sales are increasing more rapidly than industry's; that is, market share is rising. It clearly cannot continue to do so indefinitely. Further projections of industry sales against such things as population size and disposable family income may give some insight into the reasons for declining industry sales and indicate whether this is likely to change.

Using historical data, the following types of measure of performance can be estimated

1. The average annual rate of growth in deflated earnings.
2. The average annual rate of growth in deflated sales.
3. The average annual ratio of sales to assets.
4. The average annual ratio of earnings to sales.

Given the earnings for any specific year, one can estimate (1) the sales required to support those earnings, assuming the continuation of the historical earnings-to-sales ratio; and (2) the assets required to produce those sales, assuming the continuation of the historical assets-to-sales ratio. Therefore, given the evolution of earnings in time, it is possible to derive the curves shown in solid lines in Figure 4.2. In addition, it is useful to show the turnover ratio and the growth objectives (policies) in such a graph.

There are two guiding principles derived from experience that often help in the search for revealing projections. First, the critical assumptions on which corporate expectations of the future are based can often be fruitfully explored with reference projections. Such assumptions are usually buried and, therefore, require digging to get at them. Once exposed they can often be used to prepare a set of projections that test their feasibility.

For example, in 1959 one of the major automobile manufacturing companies in the United States was assuming (1) continuous growth in sales over the rest of the century at the same rate as had occurred in the past, and (2) that the nature of the American automobile would not change in any significant way; for example, with respect to size and shape. These assumptions were tested in the following way.

First, the population of the United States was projected to the year 2000. Then the number of people in this population who would be of driving age was estimated, assuming no changes in the driving laws. Next, the number of cars per person of driving age was projected. Then it was possible to estimate how many cars there would be in the United States in the year 2000 under the company's assumptions. This was followed by projections of (1) the number of miles driven per car per year, and (2) the percentage of these miles that would be driven within cities. An estimate was then prepared of the total number of car miles that would be driven in urban areas if, of course, the assumptions held. Next, a determination was made of the number of additional lane miles of urban streets and highways that would be required to maintain the 1960 level of urban congestion. The cost per lane mile was then projected and used to obtain an estimate of the total cost involved. The cost thus obtained was divided by forty to obtain the average annual cost. This cost exceeded the maximum amount the federal government had ever spent for such purposes by more than twelve times. Moreover, further calculations showed that if this amount were spent, more than 100 percent of the surface of American cities would be covered by streets, highways, and parking areas. (An updated version of this study was published by Sagasti and Ackoff in 1971 [67], a portion of which is provided in Appendix 1.)

Recall that such reference projections are *not* forecasts. The results obtained in the last study could not come about, but they reveal an important characteristic of the mess then faced by the company involved. The projections clearly showed the need to change the corporation's assumptions and to explore other futures than the one its management expected and wanted.

A second fruitful way of looking for projections involves using the supply and consumption of critical resources. For example, assuming a continued increase in the number of checks requiring clearances by one of the Federal Reserve district banks, the space required in the not very distant future to house those who would do the clearing was found to exceed the total amount of space that would be available for such purposes in the bank's headquarters city. This revelation encouraged the bank to explore, and eventually to strongly support, the development and use of an electronic funds transfer system.

An electrical equipment manufacturing company's projected requirements for a certain type of engineer was compared with a similar projection of the number of this type of engineer that would be graduated from universities. The former was found to exceed the latter in about ten years.

REFERENCE SCENARIOS

Those reference projections that turn out to be revealing can be combined with the outputs of the system and obstruction analyses in a scenario of that future the corporation would most likely have if there were no significant changes in its behavior and that of its environment.

It is in such a reference scenario that the corporate mess is best revealed.

An example of such a scenario is given in Appendix 1. This scenario was written historically; that is, retrospectively from a point in the future. Such a format facilitates showing how the transformations that consummate the mess can and might come about. The use of such a format is, of course, optional; but consideration of an appropriate style with which to present the implied future is important. If the scenario is to be effective, it should be interesting and provocative, even shocking. If it is not well written, no matter how good its content is, it will not receive the attention it is intended to attract.

The reference scenario, if well done, will make it apparent that the current mess is at least as much a consequence of what the corporation has done and is doing as of what had been done and is being done *to* it. It should also reveal what changes can be made to evade the mess. For example, in the case of the automobile manufacturer considered above, the reference scenario made it clear that the only way sales volume could be maintained was by significantly reducing the size of the automobile. Subsequent studies of the use of automobiles and the effects of their size on the people-carrying capacity of streets and highways revealed that a two-person vehicle in which the passenger sat behind the driver would increase that capacity by about 500 percent. This would be enough to remove the need for any new urban streets and highways in the United States until after the end of this century. Furthermore, although this automotive scenario was first prepared in 1959, it pointed out that such a vehicle would alleviate the demand for fuel and reduce air pollution, both of which were correctly anticipated as constraints on the industry.

Because the automotive company involved did not believe this particular reference scenario, it ignored it and maintained its inactive posture. About fifteen years later it began to respond to its implications, but largely because of governmental pressure. It waited so long that it lost a great opportunity, one that foreign automobile manufacturers did not miss. The American company could have had a large hand in creating its own future, but now it is having its future created for it by external forces.

A reference scenario should be made as believable as possible. If it reveals a desirable future, then doing nothing would be justified. However, this is very unlikely to occur. In some cases several different scenarios may seem equally likely even under the constraining assumptions used in preparing reference scenarios. In such cases more than one scenario should be prepared.

In preparing a reference scenario it is critical that it not be presented as a forecast of what will happen. The confusion that arises from doing so is apparent in the way that *The Limits to Growth* [53] was received in 1972. The purpose of a reference scenario is to reveal the implications of a corporation's current behavior and assumptions. It is intended to focus attention on the *right* problems and to produce a shared perception of the nature of these problems and their interactions. It is against a background provided by a shared perception of an undesirable future and its sources that the process of redesigning a corporation's future can be initiated. Two examples of reference scenarios are provided in Appendix 1.

SUMMARY

The mess that a corporation faces is the future it will have if it and its environment do not change in any significant way; that is, a corporation's mess is the future it is in. The problems that a corporation would face under such no-change conditions define the problems and opportunities it faces now.

Formulation of its mess by a corporation requires a systems analysis, an analysis of the obstructions to its development, and preparation of reference projections. The outputs of these steps should be synthesized into a reference scenario, a detailed picture of the future it is in.

A systems analysis should define the organization involved; identify its business and the environment in which it operates; and reveal its organization, how it is managed, and how it operates.

The principal obstructions to corporate development are usually self-imposed. Such obstructions consist of discrepancies between that is practiced and what is preached. These are generally more easily identified with outside help. On the other hand, conflict, both internal and with the environment, is usually more easily revealed by insiders.

Reference projections are extrapolations of past corporate performance and conditions. These are based on the assumption of no significant change. Those projections that reveal impossibilities are the key to defining a mess.

The scenario that systhesizes the output of the systems analysis, obstruction analysis, and reference projections should be vividly drawn and designed to provoke. Above all, it should reveal that if the corporation continues to behave as it is, and its environment does as well, it cannot continue to meet its objectives. This discrepancy defines its mess.

CHAPTER FIVE

ENDS PLANNING I: IDEALIZED DESIGN

Every life has its actual blanks, which the
ideal must fill up, or which else remain bare and
profit less forever.

JULIA WARD HOWE

Ends, which are intended outcomes of action taken, are of three types:

1. *Goals*—ends that are expected to be obtained within the period covered by a plan.
2. *Objectives*—ends that are not expected to be obtained until after the period planned for, but toward which progress is expected within that period.
3. *Ideals*—ends that are believed to be unattainable but toward which progress is believed to be possible.

Goals, therefore, can be considered to be means relative to objectives, and objectives can be similarly considered relative to ideals.

The procedure developed here for determining what ends are to be pursued begins with the specification of ideals and works backward through objectives to goals. The next phase of planning involves the choice of means by which the ends selected are to be pursued.

The selection of ideals lies at the very core of interactive planning; it takes place through *idealized design* of a system that does not yet exist, or *idealized redesign* of one that does. Such a design or redesign is a conception of the system that its designers would like to have *right now*, not at some future date. Therefore, the environment in which the system would have to operate need not be forecast; it is the current environment. Nevertheless, assumptions about future environments in which the system might have to operate necessarily enter into the design. I will return to this point.

There are three properties required of an idealized design of a system: it should be (1) technologically feasible, (2) operationally viable, and (3) capable of rapid learning and adaptation. Consider each of these in turn.

1. The requirement for technological feasibility means that the design must not incorporate any technology that is not currently known to be usable. For example, one may not incorporate mental telepathy into an idealized design of a communication system. However, one can innovate using technologies that, although feasible, have not been used in the way conceived in the design. For example, one may design a communication system in which all messages are transmitted by laser beams or in which telephones reveal the identity of the caller before they are answered. In brief, the requirement for technological feasibility is intended to prevent the product of idealized design from being a work of science fiction.

2. The requirement for operational viability means that the system designed must be capable of surviving if it were brought into existence. However, *there is no requirement that it be capable of being brought into existence.* Therefore, the implementability of the design is completely irrelevant. For example, the costs associated with the conversion of an existing corporation into an idealized one should not be considered, but the idealized one should be capable of sustaining itself economically if it were brought into existence. The reason for this disregard of implementability will become apparent when we consider the effects of an idealized design on those who engage in its preparation.

3. The requirement that an idealized system be capable of rapid learning and adaptation can be met if the following three conditions are satisfied.

(a) The system's stakeholders should be able to modify the design whenever they care to. This is desirable because the relevant information, knowledge, understanding, and values of the stakeholders change over time, particularly as a result of their efforts to realize the design. Therefore, this specification assures the possibility of continous improvement

of the design with increasing experience. It also makes it possible for the design to be changed so as to reflect changes in the organization's stakeholders.

(b) The second condition derives from the fact that in any design process questions arise for which objective answers are not available. For example, in preparing an idealized design a national scientific communication and technology transfer system [6] the question arose as to whether refereeing should be required of articles submitted to technical journals. There are two contradictory opinions on this question. One asserts that refereeing should be required because it eliminates poor articles. The other asserts that refereeing should be eliminated because it prevents publication of very good, creative, and unconventional articles. The question that remains is: on balance, which yields the most useful journals? There was no information available that enabled the designers to answer this question objectively.

The requirement that applies to such design issues precludes their arbitrary or subjective resolution; they must be dealt with by *incorporation into the design experimental processes for resolving them.* This endows the system designed with the ability to learn systematically from its own experience and to improve its design over time.

The refereeing question discussed above was handled as follows. (A more detailed description can be found in Ackoff [6].) Initially, the design required that all technical journals publish an equal number of uninvited refereed articles and uninvited unrefereed articles. The latter were to be selected *at random* from those submitted. All articles would appear in journals without identification of their type so that readers would not know which were which. Readers would be asked to evaluate the articles they read for both relevance and usefulness. Using these evaluations a determination would be made separately for each journal as to whether its readers preferred refereed or unrefereed articles. This information would then be used to set a policy for each journal. The policy established would be subject to periodic review by repeating the experiment. In this way not only would better journals be made available, but they could be modified over time as people and conditions changed.

(C) The third requirement is that all decisions made within the system designed should be subject to control. This means that the expected effects of each decision and the assumptions on which these expectations are based should be monitored. When they are found to deviate significantly from the actual effects or conditions, the deviations should be diagnosed and corrective action should be taken where appropriate.

Such a control system should include an environmental surveillance subsystem that can reveal changes in the environment that were not anticipated in the preparation of the idealized design. Adaptation to un-expected types of change is thus made possible.

The American automobile was clearly designed with the assumption that the fuel it required would be plentiful and inexpensive. When these assumed conditions changed they were not detected and, therefore, no adjustments in the design of the automobile were made. Eventually such adjustments were imposed by actions of the government, but this was obviously a matter of too little too late. Had the system that designed and produced the automobile itself been designed with the adaptive capabil-ity described above, the current energy crisis would either have been averted or be very much less serious than it is. An idealized design of a decision-control system is considered in detail in Chapter 7.

In summary, the product of an idealized design is *not an ideal system*, because it is capable of being improved and improving itself. Therefore, it is not a perfect or utopian system. Rather it is the most effective *ideal-seeking system* of which its designers can conceive. It is that system with which its designers would currently replace the system planned for if they were free to replace it with any system they wanted.

Now I turn to the steps involved in the idealized-design process. Al-though I must describe them separately and sequentially, in practice they are taken simultaneously and interact strongly. The three steps involved in idealized design are (1) selecting a mission, (2) specifying desired properties of the design, and (3) designing the system.

SELECTING A MISSION

A mission is a very general purpose that can endow everyone in an or-ganization and all they do with a sense of purpose. A mission can mobi-lize an organization into concerted action. It can be to planning what the Hole Grail was to the Crusades: a vision of something strongly desired accompanied by a commitment to its pursuit. Selection of a mission pro-vides the idealized-design process with a focus that enables it to attain cohesiveness, a complete harmony of its parts.

A mission statement is much more than a specification of a role for a system. Every purposeful system plays a number of roles. A man, for example, may play the roles of father, husband, wage earner, teacher, citizen, and so on. A corporation also plays many roles; for example, consumer, supplier, employer, and taxpayer. A mission is a purpose that integrates the variety of roles that a system plays. Without such an over-riding purpose a corporation, or any purposeful system, lacks cohesiveness and the ability to plan for itself in an integrated way. Thus deprived it can only plan for its various roles independently.

Recall (from Chapter 2) that a corporation or any social system that conceptualizes itself as an organism sees itself as being served by its parts and the larger system of which it is part. They are taken to be instruments of the quest for corporate survival and growth. On the other hand, when a social system conceptualizes itself as an organization, it sees itself as having several functions with respect to its parts and its containing system. Furthermore, its principal function is to contribute to the development of the containing and contained systems. Therefore, a mission statement should make explicit those aspects of development to which the corporation intends to dedicate itself and, in very general terms, how it intends to pursue them.

Corporations often find it difficult to formulate missions for themselves because they usually lack a societal-service orientation. Even when they are in the business of providing service they tend to be self-centered. As a result they usually think of their mission, if at all, in terms of their own growth: to be number one, the largest, the most profitable, and so on. Such a mission seldom inspires more than a few executives and managers who, in most cases, would be the principal, if not the only, beneficiaries of its pursuit. Growth may be a mission of a corporation's management or stockholders, but it is seldom one embraced by most members of the organization and nonstockholding external stakeholders and, therefore, is not an *organizational* mission. A mission should be a purpose to which virtually all of an organization's stakeholders can dedicate themselves.

For example, the following is a mission statement prepared by a corporation here designated as the Eta Corporation.

To be a worldwide integrated manufacturer and marketer of . . . products and related equipment, and to be perceived by all those who have a stake in the Corporation as an organization that is as much concerned with their welfare as it is with its own. More specifically, the Corporation will seek:

a. To satisfy the *STOCKHOLDERS'* financial objectives and to make them proud of the manner in which these objectives are met.

   This statement should be interpreted as follows: given a choice between equal control of equal amounts of Eta stock and other stock with comparable financial performance, the stockholders would prefer Eta because of such nonfinancial aspects of Eta's operations as its community relations and treatment of its employees.

b. To provide *CUSTOMERS* with uniquely valuable products and services that facilitate their use, and to be responsive to their needs and desires, and to be appreciated by them.

Given a choice of products at identical prices, the customer would prefer those of Eta.

c. To be perceived by *SUPPLIERS* as a company that appreciates the products and services rendered and to learn from them.

Eta would relate to its suppliers in the same way as it would like its customers to relate to Eta. If a supplier cannot, at some point, satisfy all demands, it would then give preference to Eta over other customers.

d. To provide a high quality of working life for all its EMPLOYEES regardless of rank or function, including the opportunity for personal development.

If other organizations offered Eta employees equal or better financial compensation, they would choose to remain at Eta. If Eta offered employees of other organizations equal financial compensation, they would choose to work for Eta. Eta employees would enjoy a higher level of prestige in the labor and management communities than employees from other firms.

e. To be considered an outstanding corporate citizen in every *COMMUNITY* in which Eta has operations (including nations, states, counties, and cities).

Eta would carry out its normal corporate activities in such a way as to make significant contributions to the quality of life and development of these communities. Eta would be a corporation for whom communities would actively bid.

It is generally easier to formulate a mission for a public body than for a private organization. The principal function of public bodies is clearly to serve others. Therefore, selection of a mission involves determining what type of service it most wants to provide and to whom it wants to provide it. For example, the idealized redesign and subsequent long-range plan prepared for Paris[61]in the early 1970s was organized around the mission of serving as the informal capital of the world. In similar work done in Mexico City the mission proposed for it was to serve as a development center dedicated to encouraging and facilitating the development of, first, Mexico as a nation; second, Latin America; and, third, of the "third world." The following is a passage from the document in which this mission was proposed.

Mexico City has long been obsessed with the process of *taking in* resources, human, natural, and artificial, from the rest of Mexico, not with the process of *giving out*. Paradoxically, the result of this process is the impoverishment of the quality of life it offers. The City has been preoccupied with its own *growth*, not the *development* of others. As long as it maintains this attitude, it will continue to grow bigger and bigger and to grapple unsuccessfully with the problems such growth entails.

Mexico City should convert itself from a destination to starting-place. We see it as a "development capital" dedicated to encouraging and facilitating the development of others. With this mission before it, it cannot help developing itself.

SPECIFYING DESIRED PROPERTIES OF THE DESIGN

Once a mission is formulated, however tentatively, it is useful to specify the properties with which one would ideally like to endow the system being designed. For example, when someone who wants to build a house first discusses it with an architect, he might say that he would like a single-level modern house with a living room, dining room, kitchen with breakfast nook, three bedrooms, two baths, and utility room. He might also specify that he would like it to be built of wood and have lots of glass. Through discussion with the architect such specifications are usually elaborated and extended.

In a corporation, preparation of a list of specifications is often best done in brainstorming sessions in which all suggestions and proposals are recorded on a large pad or chalkboard so that everyone present can see them.

The process tends to gain momentum after the first few suggestions are made, and there are generally fewer objections to any of them than would be expected beforehand.

In one such session devoted to specifying what properties an ideal telephone system should have there were no disagreements over any of the more than fifty properties that were suggested. Among them were the following.

I would like a system in which there would be no wrong numbers.
I would like to know who is calling before I answer the phone.
I would like to use the phone without hands.
I would like to be able to carry a phone with me around the house rather than have to go to it when a call comes in.
I would like to be able to transfer calls that come to my house when I am away to the number at the place where I happen to be.
When I'm talking on the phone and somebody else is trying to reach

me, I'd like to know this and who it is; and I'd like to be able to give
them a message such as, "Wait a minute, I'll be right with you," without interrupting the call I'm on at the time.

In a corresponding exercise in an American multinational company the
properties suggested included the following.

Allow divisions a designated percentage of the capital they generate
to reinvest themselves at their own discretion.

Each division should, if it so desired, be able to have its own service
units rather than have to use those provided by the corporation.

The corporation should get into at least one entirely new type of
business.

The corporation should become a product-development leader and
depend more on internal developments than on acquisitions.

The corporation should hire more managers and staff members from
the outside so as to provide a continuous influx of new ideas.

The corporation should offer stock options to all its employees.

A substantial portion of each employee's earnings should be a function of his or her performance.

The corporation should provide, or provide access to, personal development programs for personnel at all levels.

In order to assure coverage of all aspects of a corporation's structure,
operations, and relationships with its stakeholders, it is helpful to organize the preparation of specifications around a list of topics that should
be considered. No one list can be prepared that will suit all corporations
because of the wide variety of businesses in which they engage. For
example, a list that is suitable for designing a bank is not likely to be
suitable for designing an industrial equipment manufacturing company.
Nevertheless, it may be helpful to provide one such list because it can be
used as a point of departure in preparing a list that is well suited to the
type of organization at hand.

1. *The business(es).* What types of products or services should the
   corporation provide and what special characteristics, if any,
   should these have?
2. *The markets and marketing.* Where should the products or services be sold, how, by whom, and on what terms? What pricing
   policies should apply?

3. *Distribution.* How should be corporation's products be distributed from their place of production to intermediate and ultimate customers?

4. *Product services.* If appropriate, how should products be serviced, by whom, and where? What arrangements, if any, should be made for returns, trade-ins, salvage, or disposal?

5. *Production.* Where and how should products be manufactured? How should production facilities be designed, how large should they be, and what type of energy should they use? How much vertical integration should there be?

6. *Support Services.* Which support services should be provided internally and which externally? Should internally provided services be paid for by using units or be supported centrally?

7. *Organization and management.* How should the corporation be organized? How would performance of units be measured? What authority and responsibility should be allocated to each level of management? What type of resources would each type of manager at each level control?

8. *Personnel.* What policies and practices should apply to recruiting, hiring, orientation, compensation and incentives, benefits, promotions, career development, retirement, and severance of personnel?

9. *Finance.* How should corporate investments and activities be financed? What policies should apply to debt and credit ratings? What measures of financial performance should be employed?

10. *Ownership.* Who should own the corporation? What kind of board should the corporation have, what responsibilities should it have, and how should it operate?

11. *Environment.* What responsibilities for its social and physical environment should the corporation assume, and how should it handle them? How should the corporation relate to the various levels of government and to relevant special interest groups?

Once a list of specifications has been prepared, the design process can begin. During this process the list will invariably be changed and extended. As the design takes shape and the consequences of the interactions of specifications become apparent, changes in the specifications are often called for. For example, in designing a house it may not be possible to provide a windowed bathroom without sacrificing the desired shape of a bedroom. There is no harm in changing the specifications because their only function is to facilitate the design process.

DESIGNING THE SYSTEM

The conversion of specifications into a design is a difficult task. It requires determining how a specified property should be obtained: what should be done to endow the corporation or its activities with that property. It is not enough to specify, for example, that a corporation should provide a good quality of work life; decisions should be made as to how to bring it about. How should work and the workplace be designed to improve the quality of work life? How much control should employees have over what they do and when they do it? What opportunities for advancement should be provided to them and how? To what extent should they participate in decisions that affect them? To what extent should they share in the benefits to the corporation of any improved performance for which they are responsible?

As an example of the conversion of a specification into a design, consider the way in which the specification of no wrong numbers can be realized in a telephone system.

There are two kinds of wrong numbers: one brought about when the correct number is in mind but is incorrectly entered into the system: the other when an incorrect number is in mind and is correctly or incorrectly entered. Consider these types of error separately.

The first—incorrect entry of the right number—could be eliminated with the following design. One would not lift the receiver before entering the number. The number would be entered by pushing buttons on a touch-tone type of phone. The number entered would appear on a register on the face of a phone, much like the register on a hand calculator. Then this number would be checked by the caller to see if it corresponded to the number wanted. If it did not, the caller would push a clear button and start over. If it did correspond the caller would lift the receiver and the number would automatically be transmitted into the system. This would virtually eliminate wrong numbers of the first type.

Wrong numbers of the second type—correctly or incorrectly entering the wrong number—could be virtually eliminated if, after entering the number as above but before the call is activated, the caller must also enter the last name of the party. Then when the number is transmitted to the system along with the name, the system would first check the match of name and number. If they did not match, a light on the phone would indicate this and the call would not be put through.

Both of these designs are technologically feasible.

Design is a cumulative process. It is usually initiated by using a very broad brush. Therefore, the first version is a rough sketch. Then details are gradually added and revisions are made. The process continues until a sufficiently detailed design is obtained to enable others to carry it out as intended by its designers. For example, the specification of no wrong numbers was transformed into a design sketch in the description of the modified telephone given above. However, to build such a telephone, much more detail is needed.

A detailed design of an organization—one deriving from the specification that it be flexible—is described in Chapter 6. Another design—one growing out of the specification that each manager have a management system that would enable him to learn and adapt rapidly—is described in Chapter 7. Additional examples are provided in Appendix 2.

Once the design elements have been completed they would be checked for their technological feasibility. If their feasibility is not apparent to the designers, experts should be consulted. This was done, for example, for the designs intended to reduce wrong numbers in the telephone system, and they were found to be feasible. They were also found to be very costly to realize, but recall that such costs should be of no concern in idealized design.

Once the technological feasibility of the design elements has been established, they should be assembled and integrated into a comprehensive and coordinated picture, a scenario, of the whole. An example of such a scenario prepared by an American corporation is provided in Appendix 2.

The first comprehensive draft of the idealized scenario should be put through an intensive and extensive review. In particular, it should be checked throughly for its operational viability.

Constrained and Unconstrained Designs

Whether the system being designed is autonomous or subsidiary—corporation or part of one—its design is constrained by the nature of its containing system(s). It is apparent, for example, that what a corporation can do is constrained by at least one government, and what a subsidiary can do is constrained by its parent organization.

Because of these constraints it is desirable to prepare two separate versions of the idealized design, one constrained by the containing system(s) and the other not. The constrained design should assume no changes in any of the relevant containing systems. Even under such constraints, however, most systems can be radically redesigned.

It is preferable to prepare the unconstrained design first. This reduces the chances of assuming that a constraint that is actually self-imposed is externally imposed. There is a strong tendency to make this inversion. When the constrained version is prepared (after the unconstrained version) each constraint on the basis of which a cutback is made should be checked with the appropriate authorities in the containing system to make sure there is such a constraint. If there is, the possibility of getting around it should be thoroughly explored before it is accepted. Most constraints have loopholes, but they are seldom apparent.

For example, a government agency in a developing country incorporated in its idealized redesign of itself the use of a foreign research group. Government regulations, however, precluded the use of foreign consultants by government agencies. Nevertheless, universities in the country completely financed by the government could employ such consultants and government agencies could employ these universities. Therefore, the agency was able to get the foreign assistance it wanted through an appropriate arrangement with a local university.

If the difference between the constrained and unconstrained versions of the idealized design is not great, then it is clear that the system's future is largely in its own hands. If the difference is large, then changes in the containing system should be a major preoccupation of the remainder of the planning process.

The unconstrained idealized design should be accompanied by an explicit statement of the changes in the containing system(s) that are assumed, how they might be brought about, and why they should be. Then both versions of the idealized design of a part of a corporation can be submitted to the corporation. If this is done, differences between the corporation and its parts may be made the subject of a joint design effort. In some cases such a procedure has induced the parent organization to initiate an idealized redesign of itself.

If nested systems—system, subsystem, sub-subsystem, and so on—simultaneously engage in idealized design, their efforts should be integrated and coordinated. This can be done by the use of the planning boards described in Chapter 3.

REASONS FOR IDEALIZED DESIGN

We have now seen enough of the idealized-design process to consider the reasons for and benefits to be derived from engaging in it. These have to do with participation, aesthetic values, consensus, commitment, creativity, and feasibility. I consider each of these in turn.

Participation

Idealized design facilitates participation in the planning process.

Experts are usually considered to be the only ones qualified to plan for a system. Detailed knowledge of the system, its environment, and the planning process itself is generally assumed to be required for effective participation in planning. Because of this assumption, corporate planning is usually carried out by relatively few people—managers, professional planners, and technicians.

The requirement for expertise in conventional planning derives from the fact that it is preoccupied with determining what is wrong with the system planned for, why these deficiencies exist, and how they can be corrected. Such questions require experts for their answering. However, when it comes to considering what a system *ought to be*, no one is an expert at preparing an idealized design of it. Every stakeholder in the planned system can make an important contribution. Their opinions, aspirations, dreams, and preferences are relevant. For example, a person who uses a bank but knows nothing about how to run one or how it operates may nevertheless have relevant ideas about what services it should and how they should be provided. Therefore, anyone who interacts with a system is a potential contributor to its idealized redesign.

Furthermore, because participation in idealized design is usually fun, it is usually easy to obtain. However, it is much more than fun because it provides those who care about a system with an opportunity to think deeply about it, to share their thoughts with others who also care about it, and to affect its future. This encourages the development and exploration of new ideas, and, as we will see, it facilitates personal and corporate development.

Not all who engage in idealized design need concern themselves with the whole system or even the same parts of it. The participants should deal initially with those aspects of the system that most interest them. Eventually different designs of the same aspect of the system, and designs of different aspects, are brought together and synthesized. For example, a group of janitors engaged in idealized design are not likely to consider the same aspects of a corporation as its executives. Executives do not usually concern themselves with the design and servicing of laboratories. Nevertheless, a corporation can no more survive the lack of such facilities than it can the lack of investment capital.

Machine operators who engage in idealized design are likely to concern themselves with the operations, layout, and equipment in their shop, not the corporation as a whole. Janitors in the same shop are likely to consider different aspects of it. When the janitors and operators review each other's work they usually find that each has neglected critical aspects of the shop's activities. This enables them to combine their efforts and produce a more comprehensive and integrated design than either group could produce separately. As this process is repeated with different groups in a corporation, widespread understanding develops of how the parts interact and how these interactions affect overall corporate performance. This enables those who engage in idealized design to learn how the decisions they make and the activities they engage in affect the corporation as a whole. Therefore, there is an immediate and substantial payoff to the corporation: an increased total-system orientation of a large number of its members. This is the principal benefit to be derived from planning.

The learning that takes place in idealized design also increases its participants' ability both to improve the quality of their work lives and that of others and their desire to make such improvements. Therefore, *participation in idealized design produces development.* It takes place in the process, whatever the nature of its product. Its product, however, plays an important role in the subsequent steps of the planning process.

Work, play, and learning are integrated in the idealized-design process. Each is enhanced by its integration with the others. It is in just such a context that development best takes place.

Aesthetics

Participation in idealized design enables the stakeholders of a system to incorporate their aesthetic values into the planning process.

Recall from the earlier discussion of the quality of life (Chapter 2) that one of its critical aspects involves the satisfaction that people derive from what they do and how they do it, independent of why they do it. This involves intrinsic rather than extrinsic value.

Preferences based on intrinsic value make up an individual's *style.*

It is clearly impossible for a small group of corporate planners, however expert they are, to take into account all the relevant stylislic preferences of a corporation's stakeholders, or even determine what they are. Without doing so they cannot plan effectively for improving the quality of the stakeholders' corporately related lives. On the other hand, stylistic preferences are easily taken into account in participative idealized design. The participants cannot avoid inserting such preferences into the designs they work on. Others need not do it for them. Furthermore, such participants cannot avoid incorporating their ideals into their designs, thereby taking care of the other aesthetic need: a sense of progress.

It should also be noted that the design process itself can be a rich and satisfying aesthetic experience. It gives free reign to the creative imaginations of those who participate in it, and, because it is fun, it also has great recreational value.

Consensus

Idealized design generates a consensus among those who participate in it.

Consensus arises in idealized design because it focuses on ultimate values rather than on means for pursuing them. In general, people disagree less about ideals than about shorter-range goals and the means for obtaining them. For example, the constitutions of the United Stated and the Soviet Union are surprisingly alike. Most of the disagreements between these two countries derive from their differences over means, not ultimate ends. This eludes us because we characterize the differences between these two countries as ideological. *Ideologies* have less to do with *ideals* than with means for pursuing them. (The similarity of these two words is misleading.) For example, the ideological question involving who should own the means of production concerns the selection of a means for pursuing the ideal of plenty. Both nations accept this as an ideal.

The idealized redesign of Paris previously referred to was forwarded to the cabinet of France with the support of every one of its large number of political parties. They agreed on what Paris ideally ought to be. This may have been the first time they had agreed unanimously on anything.

In a recent idealized-design exercise conducted in a large American corporation, initial designs were prepared separately by each of the eight members of the corporate executive committee. These executives, who were in frequent disagreement on issues considered by their committee, were amazed at the agreement of their separately prepared designs. This had a major impact on their subsequent behavior. Hostility among them was greatly reduced and their disposition to cooperate was significantly increased.

When agreement is reached on ultimate values, differences over means and short-range goals can often be easily resolved. Furthermore, when such differences cannot be resolved, experiments to resolve them can and should be designed into the system. This property of the idealized-design process tends to stimulate a cooperative atmosphere in which differences come to be treated as minor hurdles rather than as nonnegotiable conflicts. The amount of agreement generated in the process reinforces any inclination to cooperate and accelerates the attainment of consensus.

Commitment

Participation in the preparation of an idealized design and the consensus that emerges from it generate a commitment to the realization of that design.

In general, we develop stronger commitments to ideas and ideals that we have a hand in formulating than to those that we do not. Such commitments considerably reduce the number and difficulty of problems associated with implementation of plans. It is often more difficult to implement conventional plans than it is to produce them. The less developed a corporation is, the harder it is to change; the harder it is to change, the more difficult it is to implement a plan. Therefore, one of the principal objectives of planning should be to overcome resistance to change. Involvement in idealized design often overcomes such resistance.

Recall that a government or a management cannot develop those who are governed or managed. It can only encourage and facilitate their self-development efforts. A corporation cannot do even this, however, unless its members are willing to put their effort into the development process and to change. Therefore, it is important to mobilize the members of a corporation into what might be called a *Crusade for Development*.

Historically, corporate as well as national crusades have been of two types: those directed *against* something—for example, a threatening enemy or competitor—and those directed *toward* something—for example, national or corporate leadership. To put it another way, some crusades are directed at undoing something already done, and others at doing something not yet done. Negatively oriented crusades are more common. Corporations mobilize more frequently and more effectively against an external threat than for an internally generated concept of the desirable.

What brings about positively oriented crusades? The Spanish philosopher José Ortega y Gasset [59] provided an answer:

Man has been able to grow enthusiastic over his vision of . . . unconvincing enterprises. He has put himself to work for the sake of an idea, seeking by magnificent exertions to arrive at the incredible. And in the end, he has arrived there. Beyond all doubt it is one of the vital sources of man's power, to be thus able to kindle enthusiasm from the mere glimmer of something improbable, difficult, remote. (p.1)

Ideas can launch a crusade, and the idealized-design process can generate such ideas.

Creativity

The idealized-design process stimulates creativity and focuses it on organizational and individual development.

In most people creativity is imprisoned behind walls built of self-imposed constraints. Such constraints convert simple problems into unsolvable puzzles. A puzzle is nothing but a problem that cannot be solved because of an assumption incorrectly made. Once the constraining assumption is removed, finding a solution is generally easy. Creativity begins with the removal of such self-imposed constraints.

Several years ago a friend, one of Mexico City's prominent planners, showed me six alternative transportation plans for that city. He asked if I could suggest a way of determining the best one. I responded that such an evaluation would be a waste of time because none would significantly improve mechanically aided movement through the city. He was shocked and offended. After putting himself back together he asked me to support my assertion. I explained that his plans were based on transportation ideas that had been tried many times under more favorable conditions than Mexico City provided, and they had failed.

He said that if this were true, the city's transportation problems were unsolvable. I disagreed and said that he had not yet considered effective alternatives. He challenged me to suggest one. I suggested that most of the federal government of Mexico be moved out of Mexico City and be dispersed throughout the country. Since the government provided almost half the direct and indirect employment in the city, such a move would reduce its population considerably and this, in turn, would reduce the transportation problem more than any additions to the system. I also pointed out a number of other advantages of such a dispersion for the development of Mexico.

My friend reacted by saying, "What you say is true, but the federal government can't be moved." I asked why. He gave some reasons that I challenged. This exchange of reasons and challenges continued until it was clear to both of us that we were getting nowhere. Finally he said I would never understand because I was not a Mexican. That was that!

Then he asked me if I had any other alternatives in mind. I said that I did and suggested changing the working hours in Mexico City. Since most Mexicans employed in that city have a two- to three-hour break for the midday meal, most either return home or go somewhere distant from their places of work. By reducing this interval to no more than one hour the demand for transportation would be considerably reduced.

Again my friend agreed but said that such a change was not possible. When I asked why, it led to another argument that ended with the repetition that I could not understand because I was not a Mexican.

This cycle was repeated several more times. Finally, I pointed out that politics, not planning, was the art of the possible. Few of the things we want most are attainable by means that appear possible. *It is the function of planning to make the impossible possible.*

Shortly after this conversation, when José Lopez Portillo became president of Mexico, he initiated geographic dispersion of the federal government and reduced the length of the midday break for government employees. These changes were obviously not impossible, but they were precluded from my friend's consideration because of the incorrect assumptions that he had made.

Idealized redesign of a system releases creativity because it removes many of the constraints that inhibit it. As the Mexican story illustrates, many of these constraints derive from concern with implementability. Implementability, however, is not a requirement imposed on the product of idealized design. Therefore, it tends to liberate the imagination and stimulate the desire to innovate and invent.

A group of managers and staff members of a major bank were engaged in an unconstrained design of their institution and the system that contained it. They were focusing on the problem created by the rapidly increasing number of checks that had to be cleared and the cost of doing so. Therefore, they agreed that the idealized system should incorporate an electronic funds transfer system.

One of the members of the group suggested that if the banking system required that *all* payments be made in this way there would be a complete record of everyone's income in banks. Another pointed out that records of multiple bank accounts could be assembled if every bank-account number included an identification number assigned to its holder; for example, one's social security number. It was when observed that if this could be done, banks could prepare income tax returns for everybody because they would also have a complete record of expenditures; all expenditures would be withdrawals from banks if all income went into them.

"Wait a minute," one of the participants said. "If the system knew how much we spent and how we spent it, wouldn't it be better to tax expenditures and consumption rather than income?"

This question released a flood of creative ideas. It began with the observation that if a person were taxed only for his consumption, there would be a considerable incentive to leave money in the bank, to save. This would be a larger incentive than interest on savings because the tax rate would be higher than the interest rate for most. Because of this, it was argued, they should not charge interest on loans, only a small service charge for making them. The borrower, however, would have to pay the consumption tax on what he used.

As details of a possible consumption-based tax system were developed the designers became convinced that it would be better than the current system. As a result, the electronic funds transfer system was eventually designed to accommodate such a tax system when it became possible. The point, however, is that in conventional planning the emergence and development of such an innovative idea is very unlikely.

Concern with implementability is a major obstruction to creativity. Idealized design not only reduces such concern but it also significantly effects the participants' conception of what is implementable.

Implementability

The idealized-design process enlarges the designers' conception of what can be implemented.

In conventional planning the implementability of a plan as a whole follows from consideration of the implementability of each of its parts taken separately. Therefore, a plan, like a chain, is believed to be no more implementable than its least implementable link. This belief is both costly and wrong.

A plan is not like a chain. It is a *system* of decisions. This means that the plan as a whole has properties that none of its parts do, and its parts acquire properties by being parts of the plan that they do not have when considered separately. Therefore, it is possible to have an implementable plan whose parts, considered separately, are not implementable. It is also possible to have an unimplementable plan whose parts, considered separately, are implementable.

For example, the plan for Paris included two changes that had they been separately proposed would surely have been dismissed as infeasible. The first was that the capital of France be moved out of Paris, and the second was that Paris be converted into a self-governing open city not subject to the government of France. In view of the mission of Paris that was incorporated into its idealized redesign—that it become the informal capital of the world—these two changes not only became feasible, but they were absolutely necessary. For this reason the government of France has taken significant steps toward their realization.

When a preliminary version of the idealized design of the National Scientific Communication and Technology Transfer System was presented to a large group of its stakeholders for criticism and modification, one of them reacted by saying, "This design is the best thing that ever happened in this field. Its great! But why in the world do you call it *ideal*? We could bring it about tomorrow if we made up our minds to do so."

This stakeholder had responded to what is probably the most important property of an idealized design: it reveals that *the principal obstruction between us and the future we most desire is ourselves.* This obstruction can be removed by a set of mobilizing ideas, and idealized design can provide such a set of ideas.

So much for the reasons for engaging in idealized design. Now consider how the process of producing one can be organized.

ORGANIZATION OF THE IDEALIZED-DESIGN PROCESS

If the planning process as a whole is organized circularly, as suggested in Chapter 3, then, of course, the idealized-design phase of it would be similarly organized. Each unit should prepare both a constrained and an unconstrained version of its design. The planning boards would then have responsibility for coordinating and integrating these designs. These boards and all those engaged in planning should have access to any of the designs that are prepared, and have the opportunity to suggest modifications, additions, and deletions. The flow of these designs up, down, and across the organization should be continued until a complete set of compatible designs, approved by consensus, is obtained.

Many of the corporations initiating an interactive planning process prefer to do so in stages, from the top down. In such cases an idealized redesign of the corporation as viewed from the top is prepared by the executive office or committee. When a first draft is completed, it is submitted to second-level units for comments and suggestions, and they are asked to initiate similar designs for their areas of responsibility. This process is continued until the bottom is reached. When it is, most of the features of the circularly organized planning process are in place.

If unconstrained participation is not possible or permitted, it can be reasonably approximated using a procedure developed for designing the National Scientific Communication and Technology Transfer System. A small group of professional planners serves as the core of the design team. It prepares the first scenario. While doing so one or more advisory groups are set up with as wide a representation of stakeholders as is possible. The initial design is presented to this group or groups. Their comments and suggestions are noted and are subsequently incorporated into a second version of the design which is sent to the members of the advisory group(s) along with a request that each send copies to other stakeholders they think would be willing to react to the work. The comments and suggestions received are pulled together by the team and reviewed with the advisory group(s). Then a third version is prepared. This process is continued until the comments received add little to those received earlier. Then a final version of the design is prepared. Through such a process it is possible to involve several hundred people.

The Role of the Professional Planner in Idealized Design

Recall that the role of the professional planner in interactive planning is not to prepare plans for others but to encourage and facilitate their planning effectively for themselves. This role is no more passive than that of a teacher in a classroom. Among other things, the professional may have to design, plan, and manage the implementation of the planning process.

During the idealized-design phase the professional planner may have to stimulate and instruct those involved to free them from constraints that restrict their imagination and creativity. Initial efforts at idealization are sometimes very self-constrained. The participants may be timid and unwilling to depart much from the current state of affairs. In some cases they confuse forecasting the future with redesigning the present. Therefore, it is often necessary for professional planners to prepare an initial design that liberates the designers and stimulates them to creative work. This may require a design that "blasts" them out of their rut, a deliberately shocking design that forces an appropriate reaction.

In some cases the participants are willing to engage orally in design but want the professionals to do the writing. When this is done the output should be thoroughly reviewed by the other participants.

Once those involved get the idea and have caught the spirit of idealized design, the professional still has a major role to play. He or she must point out to those engaged in the process where they have come up against an issue that cannot be resolved objectively and, therefore, requires incorporation of experimental evaluation into the design. He or she will frequently have to provide assistance in the design of such experiments. In addition, the design process should be monitored to assure inclusion of an adaptive and learning capability in the system designed. How this can be done is the subject of Chapters 6 and 7.

In some cases the members of an idealized-design group prefer to make their first contributions anonymously. They should be permitted to do so. They can submit their designs to the professional planners who can then synthesize them and highlight significant differences among them for discussion by the group as a whole. They should also point out omissions and make suggestions that will provoke further probing of the possibilities. In most such cases, the second version of the design is worked on openly by the group as a whole. Inhibitions and shyness tend to be shed fairly early in the process.

CONCLUSION

An idealized design is a formulation of the ends to which planning should be directed. It is a holistic formulation of a system of ends, not a mere listing of independent elements. It thus provides a target to which the rest of the planning process tries to come as close as possible.

The ideals imbedded in an idealized design are the ultimate values that the design tries to approximate. It is usually worth analyzing the design to extract those ideals. The lists thus obtained are likely to be quite different from lists prepared before such a design is proposed. For one thing, their formulation is usually more operational and less moralistic, more instructive and less like "motherhood statements" than lists prepared beforehand. They are also likely to contain different values than would have appeared on such lists.

The design provides a test of the presence of values. If a value is not embedded in it but is proclaimed, chances are that it is only a proclamation and not a part of practice.

Those characteristics of the design believed to be attainable (and most of them will be) are either objectives or goals, depending on the time required to obtain them. Estimation of these times has to await the selection of means and resource planning. It is in these phases of planning that decisions are made about what is to be done to attain or approximate ends, what resources are required to do so, and whether these resources will be or can be made available.

Before we look at the rest of the planning process, however, there are several very critical aspects of idealized design that require detailed attention. These derive from the requirement that an ideally designed system be capable of rapid and effective learning and adaptation. The next two chapters are devoted to different aspects of this requirement.

CHAPTER SIX

ENDS PLANNING II: DESIGN OF MANAGEMENT SYSTEMS

A man who excels in drive and leadership but is not skilled in the three intellectual functions of management [policy-making, decision-taking, and control] may be compared to a man on a unicycle —the unicyclist gives a virtuoso display over the short term, but a delivery boy on a tricycle will make steadier progress and carry a more useful load.

STAFFORD BEER

The product of an idealized design should be an ideal-seeking system. Such a system must be capable of pursuing its ideals with increasing effectiveness under both constant and changing conditions; it must be capable of *learning* and *adapting*.

To adapt is to respond to an internal or external change in such a way as to maintain or improve performance. The change to which adaptation is a response may present either a threat or an opportunity. For example, the appearance of a new competitor may present a threat; the disappearance of an old one, an opportunity. Both require an ability to detect changes that can or do affect performance and to respond to them with corrective or exploitative action. Such action may consist of a change in either the system itself or its environment. For example, if it suddenly turns cold, one can either put on additional clothing (change oneself) or turn up the heat (change the environment). Furthermore, the change to which adaptation is a response may occur either by choice or without it. The demise of a competitor, for example, may occur independently or because of what a corporation does.

The concept of adaptation used here is much richer than the one used in association with the theory of evolution. In that theory, adaptation refers to only involuntary responses to external changes, and the responses consist of internal changes. This restricted connotation of the concept derives from the fact that the theory of evolution is preoccupied with nonpurposeful systems, and when it deals with purposeful systems it is not concerned with their purposefulness. Here we are preoccupied entirely with purposeful systems and their purposefulness.

To learn is to improve performance under unchanging conditions. We learn from our own experience and that of others. Such experience can be controlled, as in experimentation, or uncontrolled, as in trial and error. For example, if we improve our rifle shooting at a target with repeated tries, we learn. If, after we have done so, a wind comes up that makes us miss the target, adaptation is called for. We can adapt either by adjusting the sight on the rifle or by aiming into the wind.

Because learning and adaptation, as I deal with them, are purposeful activities (i.e., matters of choice) they can themselves be learned. Learning how to learn and adapt is sometimes called double-loop learning. If we did not have such a capability, this chapter would have been written in vain because it is intended to facilitate just such learning.

A system cannot learn and adapt unless its management can. Therefore, an ideal-seeking system must have a management system that can learn how to learn and adapt.

ADAPTIVE-LEARNING MANAGEMENT SYSTEMS

Management is the control of a purposeful system by a part of that system. It involves three functions: (1) identification of actual and potential problems—that is, threats and opportunities, (2) decision making—deciding what to do and doing it or having it done, and (3) maintenance and improvement of performance under changing and unchanging conditions. A continual supply of information is required to carry out these

functions. Therefore, a management system should consist of three interacting subsystems, one for each function, and a management information
(sub)system.

The first design presented here is that of a free-standing management
system, one that does not interact with any other such system. (The
numbers and letters used in describing this system correspond to those
used in the schematic diagram provided in Figure 6.1.) Subsequently,
adjustments are made to this design to incorporate interactions with
other management systems.

The Free-Standing Management System

Management of an organization obviously requires observation of the
organization managed (A) and its *environment* (B). To observe is to generate *data* (1). Data are symbols that represent properties of objects and
events. They are raw material, hence require (data) processing to convert
them into *information* (2). Until they are processed they have little or no
use in decision making. Information also consists of symbols that represent the properties of objects and events, but these are useful in decision
making. Therefore, data processing is a necessary part of the *information
subsystem* (C). For example, a great deal of data must be processed to
produce the information contained in an annual report.

When those responsible for *decision making* (D) receive information
they may find it incomprehensible or unreadable, doubt its validity, or
question its completeness. On the other hand, they may accept it but
want more. For these or other reasons the receipt of information often
leads decision makers to make *requests* (3) for either additional information or reworking of the information already received.

Requests made by decision makers require two additional capabilities
of the information subsystem. It should be able to generate new data;
hence *inquire* (4) into the organization and its environment so that the
necessary data are obtained. It should also be able to reuse data previously obtained. This requires it to store data in a way that makes it possible to retrieve them when desired. A data-storage facility is, of course, a
file whether it is in a drawer or a computer. If in a computer, it is called
a *data bank*.

Once the old or new data have been processed to produce the information required to fill the requests that initiated the process, it is transmitted to the decision makers. This information-request cycle may be
repeated any number of times. Eventually it is stopped because either the
decision makers are satisfied or time has run out. Then a decision is

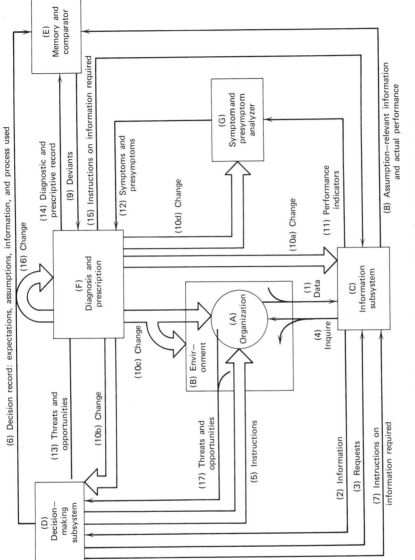

(6) Decision record: expectations, assumptions, information, and process used

(16) Change

(14) Diagnostic and prescriptive record

(9) Deviants

(15) Instructions on information required

(12) Symptoms and presymptoms

(10d) Change

(10a) Change

(11) Performance indicators

(8) Assumption—relevant information and actual performance

(E) Memory and comparator

(G) Symptom and presymptom analyzer

(F) Diagnosis and prescription

(C) Information subsystem

(1) Data

(4) Inquire

(A) Organization

(B) Envir—onment

(10c) Change

(13) Threats and opportunities

(10b) Change

(17) Threats and opportunities

(5) Instructions

(2) Information

(3) Requests

(7) Instructions on information required

(D) Decision—making subsystem

Figure 6.1 Diagrammatic representation of a management system.

made. The output is an *instruction* (5), a message intended to affect the behavior of the managed organization or part of it.

Now consider what is required to monitor and control a decision. Every decision is intended either to make something happen that otherwise would not, or to prevent something from happening that otherwise would. In either case there is an expected outcome and a time by which it is expected. Therefore, control of a decision requires that the expected outcomes and their timing be made explicit. The assumptions on which these expectations are based and the information and decision-making process used in reaching them should also be made explicit. Together these make up the *decision record* (6) which should be stored in an inactive *memory* (E). Human memories are generally much too active for this purpose. They have a way of revising recollections of earlier expectations in light of subsequent experience, as the following case shows.

An industrial equipment manufacturing company initiated a project to determine the level at which its parts inventories should be maintained. In a meeting of the senior managers of the company and the consultant who was to direct the research, the consultant suggested that a little spice be added to the project. What he suggested was that each manager make a guess as to what the effect of the study on the size of the relevant inventories would be, write it on an index card together with his name, place it in an envelope, and seal it. This was done. The envelopes were given to the corporate secretary for storage until the project was over.

After a year, during which the managers played an active role in the study, it was completed. A meeting was called to review the results. After they were presented and discussed, the secretary was called and asked to bring the envelopes down for the "unveiling." He did not appear promptly. Finally, after a few unsuccessful efforts to reach him by phone, he appeared in an apparent state of great distress. He said he could not find the envelopes.

The managers were angry and disappointed, but the consultant said that all was not lost. He suggested that they get a new set of cards and write their original estimates on them. They did so.

The consultant collected the cards and then withdrew the original envelopes from his briefcase. To the embarrassment of the managers he compared the original and the remembered estimates. Their averages differed by a factor of six and, of course, the remembered estimates were much closer to the result obtained.

Without awareness of error, learning is very difficult, if not impossible.

The decision record should be used to *instruct* (7) the information subsystem to provide the information needed to monitor the decision.

The *assumptions* on which a decision is based and the *actual perform-ance* of that decision (8) should be checked periodically. The actual and the assumed conditions and the actual and expected outcomes should be compared (E).

When assumed and actual conditions or expected and actual perform-ance agree, nothing need be done. However, *deviations* (9) of actual from assumed conditions and actual from expected performance should be noted and reported. Such deviations indicate that something has ei-ther gone wrong or is exceptionally right. To determine what has hap-pened and what should be done about it requires *diagnosis* (F).

The purpose of diagnosis is to find what produced the deviations and to *prescribe* (F) corrective or exploitative action. Although the producers of deviations can be difficult to identify, they are only of four types.

1. *The information used in making the decision was in error.* If this is the case, a *change* in the information subsystem (10a) or the symptom and presymptom analyzer (10d) should be prescribed to prevent repeti-tion of the error. For example, if the data collected on competitive pric-ing are found to be inaccurate for the purpose for which they are used, a decision may be made to acquire such data in the future from a commer-cially available service.

2. *The decision-making process may have been faulty.* In such a case, a *change* (10b) in the decision-making subsystem should be made. For example, if a finished-goods inventory is found to exceed expectations but sales are as expected, the decision rules used to set production quan-tities may require modification.

3. *The decision may not have been implemented as intended.* If this is the case, *changes* (10c) are required. Either the communications from the decision makers to the organization should be improved, or the or-ganization should be changed so that it is more likely to carry out instruc-tions as intended. For example, if it takes much longer than expected to carry out a decision, the implementation procedures or the personnel involved may need to be changed.

4. *The environment may change in a way that was not anticipated.* In such cases a way of better anticipating such changes, decreasing sensitiv-ity to them, or reducing their likelihood of occurrence must be found. Doing so may require any one or a combination of the types of change already mentioned, or a change in the environment itself. For example, if the cost of production exceeds expectations because of an unexpected increase in energy costs, the production process might be redesigned to reduce the amount of energy required or the price at which the product is sold might be increased.

The process initiated by the preparation of a decision record (6) and terminated by a change of the system or its environment (10), is what makes it possible for management to learn and adapt rapidly and effectively.

Now let us consider how threats and opportunities can be identified. First we must identify symptoms and then synthesize them into a diagnosis. We normally use the term symptom to denote an indicator of a threat to the health of an organism or organization. However, it may also refer to an indicator of an opportunity. A symptom is one of a range of values of a variable that usually occurs when something is either exceptionally right or wrong, but seldom occurs when things are normal. An unusually high unit cost of production suggests that something is seriously wrong. An unusually low cost suggests that something is exceptionally right. On the other hand, either a low or a high body temperature suggests that something is wrong. A fever is seldom associated with good health.

The techniques of statistical quality control provide effective ways of defining *normal* and *abnormal* behavior.

Variables used as symptoms are properties of the behavior or performance of organisms and organizations. Such variables can also be used dynamically as *presymtoms* or *omens*: indicators of future threats or opportunities. For example, the range of normal body temperature is about one degree Fahrenheit. Suppose that in five consecutive readings of a person's temperature taken a half hour apart, a normal but rising temperature is observed. This would indicate that unless an intervention occurs the person observed will have a fever in the near future. The same would be true if we observed small but repeated increases in the number of defects coming off a production line.

A presymptom is *nonrandom normal behavior.* Nonrandomness can manifest itself in many different ways, the most familiar being trends or cycles. Such nonrandomness is usually easy to detect by statistical tests or even the naked eye.

A complete management system regularly obtains information on a number of *performance indicators* (11) some of whose values are symptoms. In many organizations this is a function of the controller; in a hospital it is the function of the nurses. Controllers and nurses usually obtain and examine a large number of performance indicators in search of symptoms and presymptoms. Therefore, the information subsystem should be responsible for obtaining and providing such observations. These should be supplied to the *symptom and presymptom analyzer* (G). When *symptoms and presymptoms* (12) are found, they should be sent to the diagnostic function. Once a diagnosis is obtained, the *threats* or *opportunities* detected (13) should be reported to the decision-making subsystem.

A *diagnostic and prescriptive record* (14), much like the decision record, should be issued by the diagnostic and prescriptive subsystem. It should be sent to the memory where its elements can subsequently be compared with the facts that are supplied by the information subsystem in response to *instructions on information required* (15). Deviations should subsequently be reported to the diagnostic and prescriptive subsystem where corrective action should be taken. Such corrective action may involve making any of the changes previously referred to (10a–10d) or changes in its own decision-making process (16). Such changes assure double-loop learning and adaptation—learning how to learn and adapt.

Finally, information on *threats and opportunities* (17) may be sent to the decision-making subsystem from a source within the organization or its environment. For example, such information may come from a superior, a subordinate, a customer, or a supplier.

Note that there are three levels of control in this management system. First, the system as a whole controls the organization of which it is a part. Second, the diagnostic and prescriptive subsystem controls the management system. Third, this subsystem controls itself.

The Computer and Management Systems

Each of the functions that is a part of a management system is subject to computerization, in varying degrees. Much of a management information subsystem can be computerized, but inquiry into other than purely mechanical behavior cannot be carried out by a computer at the present time.

Decision making, for which models and explicit procedures for extracting solutions from them are available, can be computerized. Decisions for which models but no solution-procedures are available can be partially computerized; but decisions for which there are no models cannot be computerized.

A model of a decision has two parts. The first is an equation that relates a measure of system performance to those aspects of the decision situation, both controlled and uncontrolled, that can affect it. The performance equation has the following form:

performance of the system = a specified relationship between controlled variables and uncontrolled variables

Measurements of performance may include such quantities as the number of units produced per year, cost of a product or project, and net profit. Controlled variables may include such factors as the number of people employed, the amount of money spent on material, the kind of material used, and the location and size of a facility to be built. Uncontrolled variables may include such things as the weather, national economic conditions, the cost of labor, competitive behavior, and consumer preferences.

The second part of the model expresses the limits within which each of the controlled variables can be manipulated. For example, suppose that a specified amount of money is available and it must be allocated to several activities. Then the sum of the amounts cannot exceed the amount available, and the amount allocated to each cannot be less than zero. Such constraints and the performance equation can often be expressed in symbolic form.

The solution to a modeled problem consists of those values of the controlled variables that, within the specified constraints and under the relevant uncontrolled conditions, yield the best performance of the system. A solution that does so is said to be *optimal*.

A procedure for manipulating the symbols in a model to yield an optimal, or approximately optimal, solution is called an *algorithm*. When we have a model of a problem and an algorithm for extracting a solution from it, the decision process can be either automated or carried out by researchers serving the decision makers. Clearly, the availability of a model and an algorithm reduces or eliminates the need for reliance on experience (trial and error) in the real world, hence greatly accelerates the process of learning.

Models and algorithms are usually developed and applied by operations researchers and management scientists. Their development often requires a considerable amount of research—research that usually provides new and deeper understanding of the operations of the system. Model building also reveals and makes explicit what generally is not, but should be, understood about the system's operations. Hence it directs an important learning process. Because the models developed are explicitly formulated, they are open to examination and criticism by the decision makers and other researchers. This also accelerates the improvement of decision making.

In many cases models are constructed for which algorithms cannot be found; that is, no systematic way of extracting optimal solutions from them is available. Such models, however, can be put to effective use. They can be used to *compare* alternative solutions proposed by the decision maker. This process is often facilitated when the model is in a computer and decision makers engage in a dialogue with it. Through such a dialogue the decision makers can systematically improve a proposed solution to a problem even if they cannot find the best one possible. They can experiment using the model rather than the real world, thereby accelerating and reducing the cost of the learning process.

Models of different problems can be linked together to make explicit the relationships between the problems they represent. Therefore, by forming systems of models, a mess or a major portion of it can sometimes be modeled. Such model systems can be used in the planning process.

For example, a model can be constructed to determine the minimal cost of shipping finished products from a factory or warehouse to dispersed customers who have different requirements. However, there is no algorithm available for determining the best location for such a facility. Nevertheless, a decision maker can propose several widely separate locations to the model and it can calculate the minimum cost of transportation associated with each. The decision maker can then select the best of these, propose a new set of sites closer to it, and repeat the process. This bracketing process can be continued until the decision maker gets as close to a best location as the model and his patience permit.

The problems for which both models and algorithms are available, or can easily be produced, tend to be ones that are repetitive, routine, and operations-oriented. They are usually ones in which human behavior is not important, and means rather than ends are to be selected. Strategic problems are more difficult to model and solve than tactical or operational. However, the use of models and algorithms on simpler problems frees decision makers so they can spend more time on more important, more complex, and longer-range problems that normally are put aside under the pressure of daily short-run crises.

Models are simplifications of reality; they seldom contain *all* the relevant variables and interactions between them. Therefore, the solutions they yield—however they are obtained—usually require adjustment by decision makers so as to take into account what is missing from the model. For example, in locating a factory or a warehouse there are many relevant variables that do not lend themselves to quantification, such as, the quality and attitudes of the work force available in the area the quality of life the location offers to those moving into it, and accessibility from other locations.

Therefore, even when there are algorithms associated with models, the so-called optimal solutions they yield can seldom be implemented automatically. They usually require review by managers who understand the models and know what important considerations they do not include.

Automation of decision making does not diminish the manager's job; on the contrary, it enlarges it and makes it more difficult. The number of problems confronting him is not reduced because the solutions to most problems create several new and more important ones. If a management system is to learn how to be more effective, then the managers within it must also learn how to cope effectively with problems of increasing complexity.

Now let us return to the other parts of a management system and the extent to which they can be automated.

The memory and comparator and the symptom and presymptom analyzer can be completely computerized, but the diagnostic and prescriptive subsystem can be to only a very limited extent. However, recent developments of diagnostic routines applicable to machines and, to a lesser extent, organisms indicate that development of computerized diagnosis of organizations is not impossible.

There is nothing about a management system that requires any part of it to be computerized. Furthermore, the entire system can reside within one mind, a manager's. At the other end of the spectrum, each function can be performed by different groups or individuals. Where more than one person is involved in such a system (and this is the case in all but very small organizations) they should be managed by the manager whose system it is.

An Example of a Management System

The system described here was developed for a marketing department of a company that produces a high-volume, low-unit cost consumer good. When the system was installed the company had the largest share of its market, about 9 percent. It marketed approximately forty product–package combinations in all of the United States which it divided into 200 market areas. The decision-making component of the management system contained models of each market area. These enabled marketing management, through dialogue with the computer, to set values for variables of five types:

1. Prices.
2. Advertising (levels, media mix, timing, and message).
3. Amount of sales effort.
4. Number and type of sales promotions.
5. Amount and type of point-of-sales materials to be distributed to retailers.

Values of these variables were set monthly by management with the intention of maximizing market share in each area. Its expectations were determined with the help of the computerized models and were fed into the memory and comparator which already had relevant aspects of the decision-making procedure stored in it.

In its first month of operation this system generated forty-two deviants which were sent to the diagnostic and prescriptive team. This team consisted of operations and marketing researchers who had participated in the design of the system. The average error of the expectations was large.

The deviants required varying amounts of time to diagnose. Some took several months. Where appropriate, corrective action was taken. The number of deviants decreased from month to month. By the twelfth month there were only six deviants and the average error had been decreased to one-quarter of what it had been in the first month. By the eighteenth month the system stabilized at an average of two deviants per month and an average error or less than one-sixteenth of what it had been in the first month.

Armed with this system, marketing management more than doubled the company's market share within a decade.

Shortly after this marketing–management system was installed a similar system was requested by production management. One was developed and it eventually reduced operating costs by about $35 million per year. Yet the system had cost only about $300,000 to design and install.

Now consider how a number of such systems can be designed to interact in a corporate environment.

The Embedded Management System

Every corporation has a hierarchical network of management units. If some or all of these units have the type of system I have described, these systems require coordination and integration in order to serve the corporation effectively as a whole. Such coordination and integration can be obtained by use of decision-allocation boards organized and operated very much like the planning boards described in Chapter 3. If the chief planner in each unit is also made responsible for diagnosis and prescription, one board can serve both purposes.

Each unit except those at the lowest level has a decision-allocation board. These boards consist of (1) the person or persons responsible for diagnosis and prescription in that unit, (2) the corresponding person(s) from the level immediately above, and (3) those with the same functions from the units immediately below. Therefore each board except the one at the top has three levels represented on it. The one at the top has only two.

Referring again to Figure 6.1, members of each board receive copies of those reports of threats and opportunities (13) from the management system at the next level below. These derive from changes that have occurred or are anticipated outside the system in which the reports are prepared. The members also receive the reports of deviants (9) and symptoms and presymptoms (12) on which identification of these threats and opportunities is based. This means that copies of these reports are received by those responsible for decision making and diagnosis in each unit at the same level of the unit in which the report was prepared, and by the corresponding persons at the next two higher levels.

Each board has responsibility for determining where and how problems thus identified should be handled. They may be assigned to a higher-level unit, to a combination of lower-level units, or to one of them, including the originating unit. Such a procedure reduces the likelihood of trying to solve problems only where their symptoms appear. (See the discussion of the principle of coordination in Chapter 3.)

Solutions to problems afflicting units at levels other than the one at which the problem appears can be discussed in these boards. Doing so assures awareness in the solving unit of the effects its solutions have on units at levels immediately above and below it, and it alerts these levels to the impending decision and its possible effects. This makes anticipatory adaptation possible.

One other aspect of creating a system of management systems merits attention. Economies of scale can often be obtained; one individual or group can often perform the same function for a number of different management systems. Each of the functions shown in Figure 6.1, except that of decision making, is subject to partial or complete consolidation across units.

The management system described here was designed to provide management with an ability to learn how to learn and adapt. The design is schematic and general; hence it permits many variations. Some such design should be incorporated into the idealized design of every system. No organization can effectively pursue the future it desires if its management is not capable of continually improving its performance in turbulent as well as stable environments.

THE INFORMATION SUBSYSTEM

The preoccupation of managers and information scientists with management information systems (MISs) is apparent. In fact, more than a few consider such systems to be a panacea for every type of management problem. Enthusiasm for such systems is understandable. They involve managers and information-system designers in a romantic relationship with the most glamorous instrument of our time, the computer. Although such enthusiasm is understandable, some of the excesses to which it has led are not.

Contrary to the impression produced by a large volume of propaganda about MISs, relatively few have met the expectations of the managers who authorized or use them. Many of the near and far misses could have been avoided if some commonly made, false, and usually implicit assumptions underlying their design had been avoided. There seem to be five such assumptions.

Managers Critically Need More Relevant Information

Most MISs are designed on the assumption that one of the most critical handicaps under which managers operate is the *lack of relevant information*. It is obvious that managers lack relevant information. It is not so obvious that if they had it they would perform better or that they need it critically. My experience suggests that many would not perform better because they suffer from an *overabundance of irrelevant information*. This requires explanation.

First note that the consequences of changing the emphasis of management information systems from increasing relevant information to decreasing irrelevant information are considerable. If one is preoccupied with supplying relevant information, as is usually the case, attention is given almost exclusively to the generation, storage, retrieval, and processing of data. The ideal that has emerged from this orientation is that of an infinite pool of data into which a manager may dip and pull out whatever information he wants. The fact is that he is more likely to drown in such a pool than be saved by it.

If, on the other hand, one sees a manager's information problem primarily, but not exclusively, as one arising out of an overabundance of irrelevant information, then the two most important functions of an MIS become *filtration* and *condensation* of information. The MIS literature seldom refers to these functions, or how to carry them out.

Most managers receive more data and information than they can possibly absorb even if they spend all their time trying to do so. They already suffer from an information overload. This makes it necessary for them to separate the relevant from the irrelevant and to search for the kernels in the relevant documents. I receive an average of more than sixty hours of reading material each week, and most managers I know receive at least as much. Of this amount more than half is unsolicited. Despite this very few MISs make any provision for the treatment of such documents.

I have seen a daily stock-status report of approximately 600 pages of computer printout circulated daily to a number of managers. I have also seen book-size requests for major capital expenditures accumulate on managers' desks. Most managers additionally receive at least one journal and two newspapers per day.

Most of us who have suffered from an information overload are aware of the fact that when the amount of information exceeds a certain amount, a supersaturation point, both the amount and percentage of it that we try to absorb decreases. We give up hope of being able to keep up and abandon our efforts to do so. The more we get beyond this point the less we use. Richard L. Meier [54] has shown that social institutions behave in the same way.

Unless the information overload to which managers are subjected is reduced, any additional information made available by an MIS cannot be expected to be used effectively. The need for filtration should be obvious, but it is almost universally ignored in MIS design. Nevertheless, there are profile-based computerized filtration procedures available and in use. For a detailed description of one such system see Ackoff, Cowan, et al. [6].

Even relevant documents are usually too long. Most of them can be considerably reduced without loss of content. This is illustrated by a small experiment that a few of my colleagues and I conducted on the operations research literature a number of years ago. By using an panel of well-known experts we identified four recently published articles that every member of the panel independently evaluated as above average, and four articles that every member took to be below average. The authors of the eight articles thus selected were asked (without being informed of the evaluation of their work) to prepare objective examinations of thirty minutes' duration and to provide answers to their questions. The authors were told that graduate students would be given their papers to read and we wanted to test their ability to understand what the authors intended. The examinations were prepared. Then several professional science writers were asked to reduce each article to two-thirds and then one-third of its original length only by eliminating parts of it. They also prepared a brief abstract of each article. These writers were not shown the examinations prepared by the authors.

A group of graduate students who had not previously read the articles were then selected. Each one was given a random selection of four articles, one in its original length, one reduced by one-third, one reduced by two thirds, and one in abstract form. Each version of the article was read by two students. All were given the same examinations. The average scores on the examinations were then compared.

For the above-average articles there was no significant difference between average test scores for the 100, 67, and 33 percent versions, but there was a significant decrease in the average test scores of those who had read only the abstract. This result suggests that even well-written material can be reduced by at least two-thirds without significant loss of content.

For the below-average articles there was also no significant difference between average test scores among those who had read the 100, 67, and 33 percent versions, but there was a significant *increase* in the average test scores of those who had read only the abstract. This suggested that the optimal length of inferior material is zero.

It seems clear, then, that filtration to select relevant information and condensation of what is selected should be an essential part of an MIS, and that such a system should be capable of handling unsolicited as well as solicited information.

Managers Need the Information They Want

Most designers of MISs determine what information managers need by asking them what they want. Doing so is based on the assumption that managers know what information they need.

For managers to know what information they need (1) they must be aware of each type of decision they should make and (2) they must have an adequate model of each. The second condition, if not the first, is seldom satisfied. The genius of a good manager lies in his ability to manage effectively a system that he does not understand completely. A system that is completely understood does not require the skills of a manager, those of a scientist who understands it or of a clerk who has been programmed by the scientist are sufficient.

It has long been known in science that the less we understand something, the more variables we require to explain it. Therefore, the manager who is asked what information he needs to control something he does not fully understand usually plays it safe and says he wants as much information as he can get. The MIS designer, who understands the system involved even less than the manager does, adds another safety factor and tries to provide everything. The result is an overload of information, most of which is irrelevant. The greater this overload, the less likely a manager is to extract and use whatever relevant information it contains.

The moral is simple: one cannot specify what information is needed for decision making until a valid explanatory model of the decision process and the behavior of the system involved has been constructed. Information systems are subsystems of management systems and, therefore, cannot be adequately designed without understanding the nature of the system managed and the management of it. Such understanding is not likely to be found in those who normally design MISs.

If Managers are Given the Information They Need, Their Decision Making Will Improve

Even if we grant that managers may not know what information they need surely they would do better if they had the information than they would without it. The following example shows that this assumption is not necessarily true. It involves about as simple a production problem as one can imagine. There are ten products to be made, each requiring time on two machines, M_1 and M_2. Each product must first go to M_1 and then to M_2. The problem consists of finding the order in which to produce the ten items so that the least possible time is required to complete them. Simple enough. All the information required to solve this problem is given in Table 6.1.

Despite the facts that this problem is much simpler than most real production-management problems and all the data needed to solve it are provided, very few managers can solve it. They cannot do it by trying the alternatives because there are more than 3.5 million of them. Yet the problem can be solved in less than a minute *if one knows how*.

Take the product with the lowest entry in Table 6.1, number 9. Since the entry, 1, appears in the right-hand column, place product 9 last in the sequence and cross out line 9 in the table. Take the product with the lowest remaining entry, number 7, with entry 2. Since 2 appears in the

Table 6.1   A Production-Sequencing Problem

Product Number	Time Required on Machine	
	M_1	M_2
1	7	18
2	3	13
3	12	9
4	14	5
5	20	8
6	4	16
7	2	20
8	9	15
9	19	1
10	6	13

left-hand column, place this product first in the sequence and cross out line 7. Take the product with the lowest remaining entry, number 2, with entry 3. Since this entry appears in the left-hand column, place this product second in the sequence and cross out line 2. Continue to come in from the left for left-hand column entries and from the right for right-hand column entries until all the products have been placed in order. In case of a tie, either may be selected.

The point of this example is that if we know how to use the information needed to solve a problem, we can either program a computer or instruct a clerk how to solve it. We need not waste a manager's time. If we do not know how to solve a problem there is no assurance that having the information required to solve it will help.

In most management problems there are too many possible solutions to expect judgment or intuition to select the best one even if provided with perfect information. Furthermore, when probabilities are involved, as they usually are, the unguided mind has difficulty in aggregating them in a valid way. There are many simple problems involving probabilities in which untutored intuition usually does very badly; for example, what are the correct odds that at least two out of twenty-five people selected at random will have their birthdays on the same day of the year? They are better than even.

The moral: if managers do not know how to use the information they need, then giving it to them will only increase their information overload. If they know how to use it they can instruct someone else to use it for them. This does not mean that managers who do not know how to use the information needed to solve a problem do not need any information. What information managers need to deal with problems is whatever information enables them to do better with it than without it. To identify such information, experimentation may be required. Therefore, in order to obtain an information system that is capable of improvement it must be embedded in a management system that can enable a manager to *learn* what he needs. Without such learning he is bound to ask for and receive more information than he needs.

More Communication Means Better Performance

One characteristic of most MISs is that they provide managers with more information about what other managers and their units are doing. Better flow of information between parts of an organization is generally thought to be desirable because, it is argued, it enables managers to coordinate their activities better and thus improve overall performance. Not only is this not necessarily so, but it seldom is. One hardly expects two competing companies to become more cooperative if each is provided with more and better information about the other. This analogy is not as far fetched as one might suppose. Competition between parts of a corporation is often more intense than between corporations and, as has been observed, less ethical. A possible consequence of providing corporate parts with more information about each other is revealed by the following example, which is a simplification of a real case, involving a department store and its two principal functions, buying and selling. Buying and selling are handled by the purchasing and merchandising departments respectively. The purchasing department controls the quantity of each item purchased but little else, because competitive conditions largely control selection of brands. It usually buys in quantities that yield maximum quantity discounts, hence has little control over purchase price. This department was given the objective of minimizing the average value of inventory while meeting expected demand.

The merchandising department's main controllable variable was the selling price. This price, of course, affected the amount sold. The department's objective was to maximize gross profit. The manager of this department was assisted by a statistical staff that recorded previous prices and associated amounts sold. From this data the staff put together a price–demand curve for each class of products. The staff provided estimates of the expected (average) demand supplemented by optimistic and pessimistic estimates (Figure 6.2).

In planning ahead the merchandising manager had to select a price at which to sell a product. Call this P_1. He then used the price–demand curve to estimate how much of the product he would need. Naturally, he used the optimistic estimate (Q_1) because he wanted to guard against running out. If he were short his performance would suffer.

Once the merchandising manager had determined this quantity he notified the purchasing manager. The purchasing manager, who had previously worked in the merchandising department, also had access to the price–demand curves. Knowing the merchandising manager's practices, he read over from the quantity Q_1 (in Figure 6.2) and down to the *average* demand curve. His measure of performance required that he stock no more than the quantity Q_2. He so informed the merchandising manager who promptly adjusted his price so as to maximize gross sales, given that only Q_2 would be available. He reset the price at P_2. The purchasing manager got word of this and adjusted the order quantity to Q_3. As can easily be seen, if this process were to have continued nothing would have been bought, hence nothing sold. Such a state was not reached because the executive office intervened and prohibited communication between the two managers. This did not remove the cause of the prob-

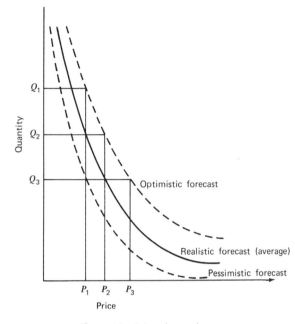

Figure 6.2 Price-demand curve.

lem, faulty measures of performance, but it did alleviate the consequences.

When organizational units have inappropriate measures of performance that put them in conflict with each other (and this is commonplace), communication between them may hurt overall performance, not help it.

The moral: organizational structure and performance measures should be put right before opening the flood gates and permitting free flow of information between parts of an organization.

A Manager Does Not Have to Know How an Information System Works, Only How to Use It

Most designers of MISs try to make their systems innocuous and unobstructive to managers to avoid frightening them. The designers try to provide managers with easy access to the system and to assure them they need know nothing more about the system than how to use it. The designers usually succeed in keeping managers from knowing any more about the system than this. This leaves managers incapable of evaluating the system as a whole. It often makes them afraid of trying to do so because they do not want to display ignorance. In failing to evaluate their MISs managers delegate much of their control of the organization to the system's designers who, whatever else they are, are seldom competent managers. Let me cite a case in point.

The chief executive of an equipment manufacturing company asked for help with the following problem. One of his larger divisions had installed a computerized production-inventory control system about a year earlier. About $2 million worth of computing equipment had been purchased for the system. The executive had just received a request from the division for permission to replace the original equipment with new equipment that was considerably more costly (and advanced). The division had provided an extensive justification for the request. The executive wanted to know whether the request was really justified. He said that he did not know enough about the system and the relevant equipment to make such an evaluation himself.

A meeting was arranged at the division's headquarters during which I was given an extended and detailed briefing. The system was large but relatively simple. At the heart of it was a computer program for determining a reorder point for each item and its maximum allowable stock level. The computer kept track of stock, ordered items when required, and generated numerous reports on the status of the inventory.

When the briefing was over I was asked if I had any questions. I did. I asked whether, when the system had been installed, there had been many parts whose stock level exceeded the maximum allowable under the new system. I was told there had been many. I asked for a list of about thirty of them and for some graph paper. With the help of the system coordinator and many old reports I began to plot the stock level of the first item on the list over time. When this item came down to the maximum allowable stock level for the first time, much to the surprise of those in attendance, it had been reordered. Continued plotting showed that the item had been reordered every time it approached this maximum level. Clearly, the computer program was confusing the maximum allowable stock level and the reorder point. This turned out to be the case for more than half the items on the list.

Next I asked if they had many paired parts, ones that were used only with each other but were separately numbered; for example, matched nuts and bolts. They had many. A list was produced and I began to check the withdrawals from stock reported for the previous day. For many of the pairs the differences in the numbers recorded were very large. No explanation could be provided.

The system was clearly out of control. To determine this I had asked only simple and obvious questions, ones managers would have asked of a hand-operated system. However, they were ashamed to ask the same questions of a computerized system.

The moral: no MIS should ever be installed unless the managers it serves understand it well enough to evaluate its performance. Managers should control their MISs, not be controlled by them.

ON THE APPROPRIATE DESIGN OF AN MIS

Most of the deficiencies in MISs that I have cited can be avoided if such systems are designed as integral parts of management systems. Unfortunately, this is seldom done. The difference between how MISs are commonly designed and how they should be is illustrated in Table 6.2.

MISs are usually designed as independent systems that are intended to serve all managers (the bottom row of Table 6.2). It is better to design a complete management system for a part of management (the first column). Such a system can be extended relatively easily by adding similar systems for other parts of management. Because of overlapping requirements among such systems, each successive system (column) tends to be

Table 6.2 Alternative Approaches to the Design of Management Systems

Subsystems of a Management System	Organizational Units			
	O_1	O_2	$\cdots$	O_n
1. Problem formulation and identification				
2. Decision making		Way it should be done		
3. Control			Way it is usually done	
4. Management information system				

easier to design and can share parts of the earlier ones. Furthermore, the ultimate outcome is a comprehensive and completely integrated management system.

When an MIS is designed as an independent system much of its content is irrelevant to the needs of the other subsystems, which are seldom analyzed for their informational requirements. Once an independently designed MIS is installed it often generates so many problems requiring attention from its designers that they never get a chance to get to the other subsystems of management. Most MIS specialists are disinclined under even the best of conditions to deal with other subsystems. They need little excuse to ignore the need for them.

If and when MIS designers do turn to other subsystems their designs of them are forced to accommodate to the completed MIS. It should be the other way around; the MIS's function should be to serve them. Therefore, if subsystems (rows in Table 6.2) are to be designed in sequence— and it is preferable that they not be—the MIS should come last, not first. In my experience the simplest, most rewarding, and subsequently least restrictive subsystem to develop first is the control subsystem.

Independently designed MISs are seldom endowed with a capability of learning and adapting. They tend to be devoid of either internal or external controls; hence they are not responsive to either their own experience or that or management. Over time they are more likely to deteriorate than improve. This can be avoided by designing an MIS as an integral part of a management system.

CHAPTER SEVEN

ENDS PLANNING III: ORGANIZATIONAL DESIGN

Anergy. *The negative of energy. . . . The amount of energy it would take to clean up some situation you don't like. Anergy resides within messy situations as energy resides within a coiled spring. A coiled spring is full of energy. When fully uncoiled, it is full of anergy.*

JOHN GALL

The idealized redesign of a system necessarily involves consideration of its structure, the way it is organized. The way it is organized affects an organization's ability to learn and adapt, hence develop. Just as an individual's learning and adaptation require an ability to change oneself and what one does, so do an organization's. Organizations, however, are well known to resist change, particularly change in the way they are organized. Therefore, an idealized design of a system should consider how to structure a system to make it one that is ready, willing, and able to modify itself when necessary in order to make progress toward its ideals.

An organization's structure is the way its work is divided (how *responsibilities* are assigned) and how these separate activities are coordinated and integrated (how *authority* is allocated). Conventional structures are usually represented in familiar treelike diagrams consisting of boxes and connecting lines. They show who has responsibility for what and who has authority over whom.

The structures of conventionally organized corporations require frequent modification in turbulent environments. Nevertheless, such corporations tend to resist this type of change. It is important to understand both the need to change and the resistance to it.

THE NEED TO REORGANIZE

The need to reorganize derives from either external or internal sources. First consider the external.

Changing Priorities

In designing an organization three different criteria are commonly (and almost exclusively) used in dividing the necessary work. These are:

1. *Product or service*, the type of *output*—for example, the creation by General Motors of Cadillac, Buick, Oldsmobile, Pontiac, and Chevrolet divisions.
2. *Functions*, the types of *inputs* required to produce the outputs—for example, purchasing, manufacturing, marketing, finance, and personnel.
3. *Markets*, the classes of customers or consumers of the organization's output defined either geographically (e.g., America, Europe, Asia) or by type of customer (e.g., industrial, governmental, commercial, residential).

In conventionally structured corporations the division of responsibility at each level below the chief executive is usually based on one or some combination of these three criteria. Where a combination is used, one tends to dominate. Therefore, the levels at which these criteria are used give them a rank order. If, for example, the second level of a corporation is organized along product lines, this places product considerations above those of function and market.

Changes outside a corporation frequently require the reordering of criteria. For example, a corporation organized at the top along product lines and expanding its foreign operations may find it necessary to begin manufacturing its products abroad. This in turn, may require expansion of its foreign marketing efforts. Both of these may require more emphasis on geography and less on products. This may lead the corporation to reorganize itself geographically.

A series of recent changes by the Federal Trade Commission has completely changed the environment in which AT&T must operate. This corporation, once a protected monopoly, finds itself in an increasingly competitive environment. Therefore, it recently reorganized itself to be more effectively oriented to its markets, subordinating its previous preoccupation with products and services.

Clearly, it would be desirable to change priorities among the criteria used in dividing work without changing an organization's structure. But this is not possible as long as we assume that such structure must be representable by a two-dimensional treelike diagram in which levels and criteria for dividing work tend to be matched. This self-imposed constraint precludes a structure that does not have to be changed when the relative importance of the criteria changes.

By changing the dimensionality of an organization it becomes possible to change the priorities or prominence of the criteria used in structuring an organization *without changing its structure.* An organizational design that incorporates this idea is given below.

Now consider the principal internally generated pressure that promotes organizational change.

Centralization–Decentralization

Many corporations go through regular oscillations between centralization and decentralization in what appears to be a persistent tug-of-war. The pressure to decentralize derives from (1) the desire to facilitate rapid and effective initiatives and responses to changes where needs, threats, and opportunities are first recognized; and (2) to enrich the jobs of lower-level managers and units by increasing their responsibilities. The pressure to centralize derives from (1) the desire to coordinate the activities of lower-level units and exploit their potential synergy; and (2) to prevent serious errors from being made below where effects on the rest of the corporation are not always seen or appreciated.

The larger, the more dispersed, and the more varied the businesses of a corporation, the greater is the pressure to decentralize. This pressure has had the upper hand for a while largely because of corporate growth and the movement toward more humane working conditions. Decentralization, however, is proclaimed a good deal more than it is practiced.

It is clear that in most organizations some decisions are better centralized and others decentralized. In a conventionally structured organization, however, it is almost impossible to mix these modes of management to obtain a satisfactory balance between them. Unless one or the other mode dominates there is usually a great deal of ambiguity and, therefore, overlap of authority and responsibility. Such overlap creates areas like those between two outfielders in baseball in which both go after the ball and collide, the ball falling between them.

The centralization–decentralization issue involves the amount and kind of authority each manager has. The issue arises because in corporations that are neither holding companies nor conglomorates managers require coordination and integration. Even in corporations that are aggregations of independently managed businesses, some coordination and integration is required, and a great deal is required within their parts. Therefore, the problem is one of designing corporations to simultaneously minimize the interdependence of their parts and maximize their inclination to interact cooperatively. To do this it takes an unconventional concept of organizational structure.

Resistance to Change

There are two principal ways by which an organization or an organizational unit can resist externally imposed change or develop immunity to it. The first is based on the fact that the more essential an activity, the less likely it is to be eliminated or changed. Therefore, an organization or organizational unit that correctly perceives a diminishing need for its services must, if it is to preserve itself intact, create the impression that it is essential. This is done by making unneccessary work appear to be necessary.

A unit that has more people than it needs to do what is required of it is usually reluctant to contract, let alone dissolve, because the importance and status of the unit and its manager is normally taken by others to be proportional to its size and the size of its budget. Therefore, growth, not contraction, is desired even if it is not justified. When growth or survival becomes the objective pursued for its own sake, even though this obstructs performance of the function for which the organization or the unit was created, bureaucracy results. Bureaucracies are organizations or organizational units for which growth and survival take precedence over performance of their societal or organizational function. Bureaucracies tend to become maladaptive organizational dinosaurs that take a long time to become extinct.

When a survival- or growth-oriented unit has more people than it needs, it must busy them with "made work" if it is to avoid contraction or elimination. This can be done in several ways. A task that can easily be done by one person can be magnified into one requiring several. For example, a form that can be processed efficiently by one person can be converted into one that is inefficiently processed by several; or new forms can be created and be made to appear essential. Unfortunately, the work thus made obstructs or delays the essential work of others. It is often correctly perceived by them as red tape, but red tape is as difficult to eliminate as the parasites who produce it.

A second way an organization or organizational unit can resist change is by precluding measurement of its performance. It can then substitute propaganda for performance.

This alternative is made easy by the fact that the performance of many units in conventionally organized corporations is very difficult to measure; for example, in advertising, employee relations, public relations, accounting, personnel, and so on. Their costs can be measured but their outputs and their value are difficult to quantify, particularly when efforts to do so are resisted by the units involved.

It is desirable to have one type of measurement of performance, applied to every organizational unit and to the organization as a whole, that would promote willingness to change and expose efforts to resist it. Such measurement is virtually impossible in conventionally structured organizations, but is possible in the type of organization to which we now turn.

THE MULTIDIMENSIONAL ORGANIZATION

The idealized design of an organization that follows, like some of the preceding designs, should be taken as a theme around which many variations can and should be written to suit the conditions that prevail in any particular application of it. Some variations are presented after the basic design has been developed.

The most important self-imposed constraint that is broken in the development of this design is the assumption that an organization's structure can have only two dimensions—up and down, and across. For this reason I refer to designs that reject this assumption as *multidimensional*. This term was used in 1974 by William C. Goggin [36], then board chairman and chief executive officer of Dow Corning, to describe his company's structure. The design presented here differs significantly from his, but both are multidimensional.

This design has three fundamental dimensions, one corresponding to each of the criteria that are commonly used in dividing work:

1. *Outputs*, products or services provided.
2. *Inputs*, activities required.
3. *Markets*, types or classes of customers and consumers.

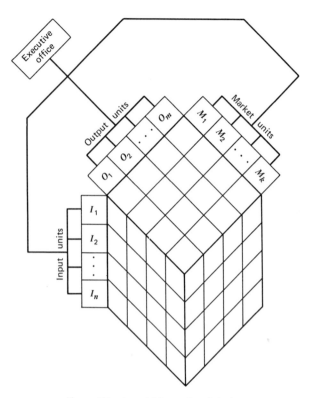

Figure 7.1 A multidimensional design.

These dimensions can be represented by a boxlike diagram as shown in Figure 7.1.

Output Units

Output units are defined by the product(s) and/or service(s) for which they are responsible. They consist of a management and a supporting staff, but no other personnel. They have no facilities other than what is required to house this small number of people. They rent the space required from the corporation or some other source. Therefore, they have no fixed assets, but they have operating capital.

Output units are responsible for all the activities required to make available and sell their products to customers. They must buy all the goods and services they require, but they can do so from either internal or external sources. Before an outside supplier is used, internal suppliers must be given a chance to meet the outside price. But even if the internal price is competitive, the output unit is free to make the purchase as it sees fit unless the executive office intervenes. When such an intervention takes place the unit must be compensated for any demonstrable increase in cost or decrease in income resulting from it. The executive office might intervene for good reason; for example, because it wants to nurture a new internal supplying unit.

An output unit can pay a supplier, internal or external, on any basis it negotiates; for example, cost-per-unit, commission, fixed fee, or cost-plus. It can exercise no authority over internal suppliers, but it can partially control both internal and external suppliers through its purchasing power and its ability to change sources of supply at will.

These units receive income from sale of their products or services. If they require additional operating capital, they must apply for it from the executive office. They are expected to treat such funds as loans. Output units are profit centers; they are evaluated with respect to their profitability.

The profit that an output unit generates is subject to a corporate tax levied by the executive office. The tax rate is designated in advance of the period in which it applies. It should not be so large as to deprive profitable units of discretionary funds. Profitable units should have funds to use as they see fit, subject to the same kind of executive intervention described above. They may use these funds, for example, to improve old products, develop new ones, or open new markets.

Output units are easy to add or subtract because they have no fixed assets and they involve only a relatively small number of people. Their organization is considered under "Unit Design."

Input Units

Input units provide goods or services to both internal units and external customers. They provide such services as manufacturing, transportation, warehousing, personnel, legal, accounting, and all market functions except selling. Selling is handled separately in a way described below.

Input units such as manufacturing and data processing have facilities and equipment as well as the personnel required to manage and operate them. Therefore, these units may require investment as well as operating capital. They can apply for such capital only from the executive office. Such investments or loans must be treated as though they were externally provided.

Like output units, input units are profit centers; hence are evaluated by the amount of profit they generate and the return they provide on the investment in them. They, too, are subject to the corporately imposed profit tax.

As with output units, input units are free to purchase whatever they need or to sell whatever they produce either internally or externally. These decisions are subject to executive intervention as considered above, and to compensation for them when appropriate. They receive the income that the sale of their services generates, and they pay the cost of whatever goods or services they purchase.

If a product or service provided by an input unit attains a sufficient volume of external sales, and the executive office believes this volume is expandable, it may create an output unit to promote such sales. The executive office must purchase the right to do so from the input unit involved. For example, if an internal data-processing unit develops a large external business, the executive office may decide to create a data-processing output unit. Unless constrained from doing so by the executive office, the old data-processing input unit can continue to service external customers, and the new output unit may or may not use its services.

If the executive office observes that a product or service not provided internally is consumed heavily within the organization, it can create an appropriate input unit or extend an existing one to provide an internal source of supply. An input unit may extend itself if it can do so without subsidy.

If an input unit is used heavily by external but not internal consumers, the executive office should want to know why. Either other internal units are not purchasing wisely or they no longer need the goods or services provided by that input unit. In the latter case, the input unit might either be augmented a by new output unit or be sold or discontinued. On the other hand, if an input unit has little or no external sales, and if it has the ability to satisfy an external demand that is known to exist, the executive office should also want know why. Poor management might be the answer.

Although input units are more difficult to delete than output units, it is much easier than with a normal business unit. Getting rid of an input unit need not affect the business that a corporation is in, and its equipment and facilities can either be converted or sold. Addition of input units creates no significant problems. Their internal organization is also considered under "Unit Design."

Market Units

Market units have two functions: first, to act as selling agents for any internal unit that wants to use this service. (They are also free to sell their

services externally, subject to the same type of executive exception applying to other types of unit.) Second, they serve as representatives of the
markets in which they operate. They not only represent the company in
the market, they also represent the market in the company. They serve as
advocates of the relevant interests of those in the markets in which they
operate.

In their advocacy role market units evaluate the activities of input and
output units from the point of view of those outside the corporation who
are, or can be, affected by them. By calling together the heads of market
units, the executive office or heads of other types of unit can obtain an
evaluation of their performance over all the areas served, or in particular
areas. This can help them perceive unexploited opportunities and actual
or potential threats.

In their function as advocates, market units can operate as consultants
to the executive office and unit heads. They should be paid for such
service and be free to provide it to external organizations.

In their function as selling agents, market units operate as input units
do. They are profit centers that can generate discretionary funds. They
can initiate old-product improvements or new-product development.
These developments may be sold internally or externally, subject to the
previously cited executive exception.

Because market units involve no fixed assets or investments by the
corporation, they can easily be added, subtracted or otherwise modified.

The Executive Office

The executive function is performed by one or a group of managers
equipped with staff and support personnel. This office is a profit center.
It is distinct from the corporation as a whole, which, of course, is also a
profit center. The executive office invests in or lends funds to units from
which it expects a return or repayment with interest. It also charges for
any services or facilities that it provides to units, and collects a tax on unit
profits. It must pay for funds borrowed or otherwise received from external sources, and it also pays for (1) any cost-increasing or profit-reducing
constraints it imposes on units, and (2) any services it requests from the
units other than those specified in unit charters; for example, information
not normally provided by units. Because such constraints and services
involve a cost to the executive office, it must evaluate their effects on
unit performance and, therefore, its own income.

If the number of units is too large to report directly to the chief executive, one or more coordinating executives can be used for each dimension (see Figure 7.2). If the number of units in any one dimension is large,
more than one such coordinator can be used. For example, input units

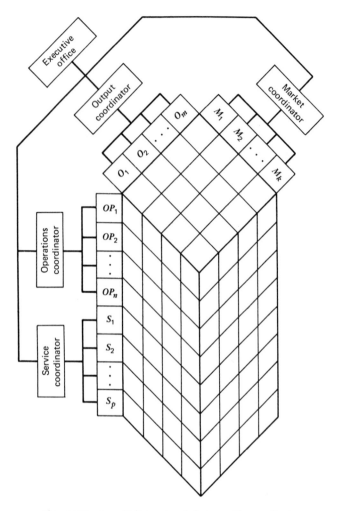

Figure 7.2 A multidimensional design with coordinators.

can be divided into two groups, operations and services. Output units can be divided into broad product categories such as automobiles, trucks, buses, and tractors. Markets can be grouped geographically. Coordinating executives can be incorporated into the executive office.

The executive office can establish policies and practices that affect some or all units. These, however, should be restricted to ones that demonstrably affect corporate performance and should not intrude on unit management for any other reason.

Unit Design

Each unit can be organized in the same way as the corporation as a whole. This is most apparent for the input units, particularly for manufacturing units. Their output subunits might include purchasing, stores, maintenance, quality control, and so on. It can also use market subunits to sell its services. Whichever of these it does not desire to provide itself, it can purchase from either internal units or external sources.

Output units can be divided into output subunits using, for example, brands or models to define them. If large enough, an output unit can use one or a group of persons to take charge of acquiring and controlling each input it requires; for example, manufacturing, transportation, sales, and so on.

A market unit's subunits can be defined by subdivisions of the total area or class of customers called on by the unit. It also requires some inputs for which it can have people in charge. Finally, it has a need to market its own services. It would normally do so itself, but it could use outside agents for this purpose.

The multidimensional structure can be applied right down to the smallest unit of a corporation. The smaller a unit, the less staff and more different responsibilities its manager has. This type of organization enables even the smallest units to be as autonomous as possible within a corporate structure. In sum, a multidimensional design creates as near a free market *within* a corporation as is possible, but it does not exclude opportunities for synergy and economies of scale.

Recalling the obstructions to flexibility discussed at the beginning of this chapter, we can see that each of them is either removed or significantly diminished in a multidimensional organization. First, there is no need to reorganize in order to change priorities of criteria used in dividing work. Emphasis can be changed by reallocation of resources and by the exercise of exceptions by the executive office.

Second, units can be added, subtracted, or modified without serious dislocation of other units. The more internal units a unit serves or is served by, the less it is affected by the removal of one of them.

Third, on the centralization–decentralization issue, lower-level managers are given as much autonomy as is feasible. Nevertheless, the role of the executive office remains a major one. Because it is a profit center, it must take full responsibility for the effects of its decisions on unit performance.

Last, a uniform, explicit, and operationally unambiguous measure of performance—a function of the amount of profit generated—is applied to every unit at every level, including the executive office. This prevents "made work" and bureaucracy from arising. Profit, however, is not the only performance characteristic of importance. Recall that in an interactive organization, *development* of the organization and its stakeholders is its overriding objective. Although profit is necessary for corporate development, it is not sufficient.

On Divided Responsibility

Those familiar with matrix organizations will recognize their superficial resemblance to the multidimensional design presented here. It is not appropriate to dwell on these differences, but it is worth the time of those concerned with organizational design to familiarize themselves with this alternative concept. Davis and Lawrence [21] provide a comprehensive review of the subject.

One comment about matrix organizations is appropriate. The essential characteristic of such an organization is that those in what I have called input units work for two bosses. One is the head of the input (service or staff) unit of which they are a part, the other is the head of the output (line) unit to which they are assigned. This is the most frequently criticized property of the design. It has been accused of producing what might be called "organizational schizophrenia." The multidimensional design creates no such problem.

In a multidimensional organization, members of an input (or market) unit whose activities have been purchased by an output-unit director, are related to that director no differently then if he or she were an external customer. They are responsible to the input-unit director who, naturally, uses the output-unit director's evaluation of the services received. Those who head an input unit working for an output unit are in much the same position as are project directors in construction or consulting firms. Those who work in such units know who their boss is.

Program Budgeting

The concept of program budgeting also intersects with that of multidimensional organization. Program budgeting, as usually proposed or practiced, is a way of preparing a budget for input and output units; it is not necessarily associated with giving resources and choice to output units and requiring input units to earn their way in an internal and external marketplace. In a multidimensional organization the corporation does not prepare unit budgets; the units do. The corporation only invests in or lends money to them.

Program budgeting normally does not affect organizational design (although it is more compatible with matrix organizations than with traditional ones), and it has no effect on organizational flexibility. It is a way of allocating resources to input activities providing greater assurance that the desired output activities will be carried out. In addition, it provides a more effective way than is usually available for determining what the costs of an output are. A multidimensional design accomplishes all this and much more.

Now consider a few variations on the basic multidimensional design and see just how varied they can be.

Some Variations

In a corporation whose businesses are relatively independent of, and different from, each other and whose facilities are geographically dispersed, it is sometimes desirable to organize the business multidimensionally, but not the corporation (see Figure 7.3).

Shortly before the recent revolution in Iran its national health ministry was organized in this way. (It was one of the few branches of the government that was not reorganized after the revolution.) The country was divided into regions, and each was given a multidimensional organization of the type described above. However, the minister, his deputly ministers, and the regional directors were organized conventionally.

A Multidimensional design can be introduced at any level of an organization or in any part of it taken separately. A division, department, or section can be organized in this way. Furthermore, if a division is organized multidimensionally, the departments within it need not be; they can be organized conventionally.

Two or more multidimensional units can share all or some of their subunits along one dimension (see Figure 7.4). It is also possible for a multidimensionally organized unit to buy services from an input subunit of another multidimensional unit of the same corporation.

If two output units were to share all input and market units, they would not be separately multidimensional but would be output units of the same multidimensional organization.

The multidimensional design can be diluted in other ways. For example, the manufacturing (or some other) function can be incorporated into an output unit. If this is done the output unit would have assets. This makes it more difficult to add or subtract output and input units, but, because it is closer to a conventional structure, it may be easier to implement. Such dilutions can be used to ease the transition from a conventional structure to one that is completely multidimensional.

Note that if the selling function is organized as an input unit rather than on a third dimension, the result is a two-dimensional organization. However, if the other features of the multidimensional design are re-

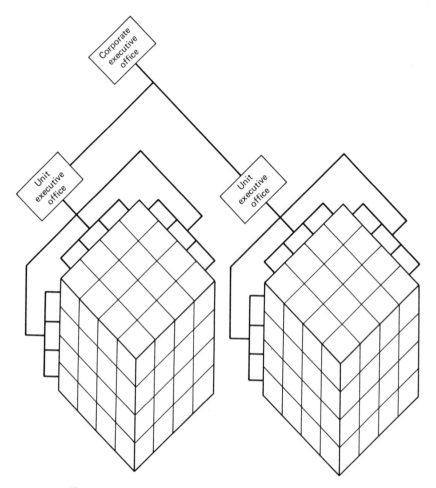

Figure 7.3 Multidimensional units from the second level down.

tained, this does not become a matrix organization because employees do not have two bosses. The principal effect of reducing the dimensions in this way is that it makes it more difficult to change emphasis between two of the criteria for dividing work, inputs and the market.

A minimal step toward multidimensionality consists of converting service units in a conventionally organized corporation into profit centers that operate as input units do in a multidimensional organization. This requires no change of structure. For example, one major oil company converted its corporate computing center into a profit center. It required

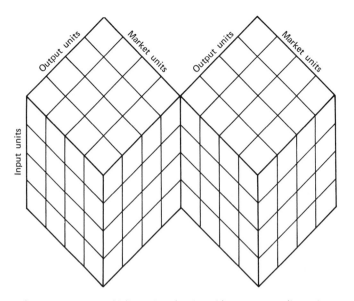

Figure 7.4   Two multidimensional units with a common dimension.

all other units to pay for services from this center but gave them the option of buying such services from external sources. On the other hand, the computing center was free to sell its services externally. Not only did this center become very profitable, but its internal users felt that they received better service from it. Moreover, less equipment was used to turn out a larger volume of work.

No corporation can be given a structure that its members cannot sabotage. Therefore, it is critical to motivate members of an organization to make it function well. No stronger motivation has yet been found than providing members of an organization with an opportunity to participate in making decisions that affect their work. We now turn to a design for such participation.

A DESIGN FOR PARTICIPATION: THE CIRCULAR ORGANIZATION

Good will and cooperation are difficult if not impossible to obtain from employees who derive little or no satisfaction from their work. For this reason there have been numerous efforts since World War II to redesign work. Work structuring, job rotation, job enrichment, and autonomous work groups are some of the better-known efforts. In most of these, however, the work to be done is not designed by those who are to do it, but by managers or the experts they employ.

Unless employees are given a continuing opportunity to redesign their work to make and keep it challenging, they are unlikely to retain their dedication. This is precisely what most managers can do and is what makes their work so attractive. Therefore, the work of nonmanagerial personnel can be significantly enriched by enabling them to participate in management. This need not raise an insurmountable practical difficulty.

Corporations must be organized hierarchically because only by doing so can their divided work be coordinated and integrated. Hierarchy means, among other things, that managers have authority over nonmanagerial personnel and that some managers have authority over others. But participation of lower-level personnel in higher-level management appears to diminish or destroy such authority. Democracy and hierarchy seem incompatible. Democracy requires that anyone who has control over others be subject to their collective control. If those who are managed control their managers, then hierarchy seems to be destroyed.

This appears to be the case because we assume that authority can flow in only one direction. Then, since hierarchy is required by divided work, organizations that require such work—even government agencies in a democratic socity—are hierarchically and nondemocratically organized.

The incompatibility of hierarchy and democracy lies in our minds, not in the nature of things. Once we deny the assumption that authority must flow in only one direction it becomes possible to design a completely democratic organization in which hierachy is preserved. It is just such a design that I offer here.

This design is a generalization of the one that enables planning to be completely participative (Chapter 3). Therefore, as we will see, it can absorb both the planning boards used in that design and the decision-allocation boards used in the network of management systems (Chapter 6). I call this generalized board a *management board.*

Each manager is given a management board (see Figure 7.5). These boards are composed much as they are for the planning system. Each board, except the ones at the top and bottom of the hierarchy, consist of (1) the manager of the unit whose board it is (see board 1.1 in Figure 7.5), (2) his or her immediate superior, and (3) his or her immediate subordinates.

The top board (1) contains the chief executive officer, his or her immediate subordinates, representatives of the external stakeholders, and representatives of each level of managerial and nonmanagerial personnel,

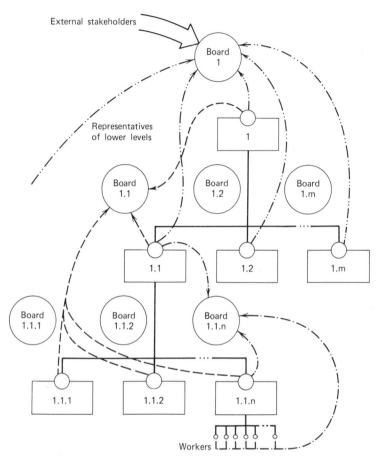

Figure 7.5 A democratic hierarchy: the circular organization.

including those at the bottom. Ideally, these representatives would be elected by their respective constituencies for a specified term. The terms should be staggered so that a complete turnover of the personnel on the board is avoided.

The lowest-level boards (e.g., 1.1.n) do not contain lower-level managers because there are none, but they do contain *all* the nonmanagerial personnel who report to the lowest-level manager. If the size of the lowest-level units is large, the board will be too large to operate effectively. Therefore, the basic work unit should be small, in general no more than ten people. Reducing the size of these units need not increase the number of lowest-level managers required. If the work teams are set up as autonomous work groups, they can select and rotate their own leadership. If this is done, no additional managers are needed, and each work group can have its own board in which all of its members participate along with the manager to whom the group reports. The board of the lowest-level manager then contains the leaders of the autonomous work groups as well as his or her immediate superior.

Now consider the functions of these boards. First, each board has responsibility for coordinating the activities of the units reporting to the manager whose board it is. Since the managers of the units whose activities are to be coordinated constitute a majority of each board (except the one at the top), to a large extent they coordinate themselves. They are assisted in doing so by the two immediately superior managers.

Second, each board has responsibility for integrating the activities of the units represented on it with the activities of two levels above and two below (if there are this many, otherwise as many as there are). Recall that the highest ranking member or each board is a member of two higher-level boards, and the lowest ranking members participate in two lower-level boards (again if there are this many).

Third, the board has policy-making responsibility for the unit reporting to it. A policy is a *rule* that governs decision making; it is not a decision in the ordinary sense. For example, a board might establish a policy of promotion from within, but the decision to promote a particular individual remains the responsibility of the manager. Responsibility for making policy is *not* responsibility for making decisions.

The policies made by any board must be consistent with those of higher-level boards. However, a board can appeal a policy made by a higher-level board through its senior members or, if it is a policy of the top board, through its representatives on that board. Note that each board contains managers of those units that are most affected by the policies it makes. Therefore, the impacts of these policies on other levels are not likely to escape its attention.

The policies made by any board other than the one at the top should not deal with contracts between management and organized labor. Labor–management negotiations should remain a function of a special unit, and approval should remain in the hands of the corporate board. Obviously, many of the problems that can come up in such negotiations can be avoided by board activities.

The question of whether union officials should be permitted to serve as representatives of the workers on the corporate board is one that cannot be answered in general. It depends on the characteristics of each particular case.

The fourth and most controversial responsibility of each board is evaluation and approval of the performance of the manager reporting to it. This is similar to the responsibility that corporate boards currently have with respect to the chief executive officer. Under these conditions *no* manager can hold the position without the approval of his or her board, or immediate subordinates who constitute a majority of that board. However, the board of any manager except that of the chief executive officer cannot fire that individual—only his or her boss can do this—but it can remove the manager from the position he or she holds. Therefore, a manager can hold the position only with the support of both his or her immediate superior and immediate subordinates.

This set of conditions is what makes the design democratic: every person in the system who has control over others is subject to their collective control. It eliminates the arbitrary imposition of authority on any member of the organization by any higher authority.

A manager's staff members require special attention. They are provided with an opportunity to participate in management in the following way. All managers who have staffs either designate chiefs of staff or fill these roles themselves. A board is then formed for each chief of staff. It includes the chief, the manager (unless this role is filled by the manager), and the staff members. The board operates just as other boards do but its domain is the work of the staff, not management. It controls the occupancy of the position of chief of staff, not the managerial position. It sets policy for staff work and coordinates and integrates with other staff units. The chief of staff may be a member of the manager's board.

Now consider a few of the more important operating characteristics of the circular organization.

How much of a manager's time is consumed by boards? This obviously depends on how many boards he or she serves. In general, but not without exception, a manager ought to have fewer than ten people reporting directly to him or her. Most boards meet for no more than four hours per month. Then, if a manager is on ten boards (and most are on fewer) at most forty hours per month would be spent at board meetings, no more than 25 percent of the total time at work.

Although this leaves a good deal of time for other activities, this is not the point. The point is that many of a manager's must important responsibilities can be fulfilled through participation on these boards. They enable the manager to coordinate and integrate the work done under him or her, to evaluate subordinates and their subordinates, to inform and motivate them, and to keep abreast of what is going on above, below, and on his or her level.

Each management board should develop its own rules of procedure.

Some, for example, have the highest ranking member serve as chairman; others rotate this position. Some meet regularly; others on call. Most set up a procedure by which anyone or a subset of board members can call for a session. A great deal depends on how dispersed the members of a board are.

It is important to reemphasize that these boards are *not* management committees. They do not make decisions for the units reporting to them. However, managers may use them in an advisory capacity although they are under no obligation to do so.

As with the previous designs, many variations of the circular organization are possible. This enables the design to be fitted to the characteristics of the organization involved.

This design has been used in a number of private and public organizations, some very large, others small. It has been used in divisions of corporations—that is, from a certain level down—without going to the top. It has also been used at the top without going down. Its implementation has usually been gradual and sequential, taking one level at a time. I know of no application of the design in which those affected do not feel that morale and productivity have improved significantly. In no case of which I am aware has the design been implemented and subsequently abandoned.

CONCLUSION

The designs of a management system and multidimensional and circular organizations can be used either separately or combined into one design. They are completely compatible. Separately and together they are addressed to increasing the capability for learning and adaptation in organizations, their units, and their individual members. Without this capability development is not possible.

Learning arises out of experience, one's own and others'. Experience presupposes choice. Therefore, increasing the capability of learning necessarily involves enlarging experience, increasing the range of available choices.

All three designs are directed at increasing choice, hence at enriching experience. Not only does this increase the chances of learning and adapting, but it also increases both its intrinsic and extrinsic value. It provides greater opportunity for satisfying one's stylistic objectives and for pursuing one's ideals. Therefore, all three designs are directed at improving the quality of work life and the productivity of the organizations within which this life takes place.

CHAPTER EIGHT

MEANS PLANNING I: FORMULATING ALTERNATIVES

Future, n. *That period of time in which our affairs prosper, our friends are true and our happiness is assured.*

AMBROSE BIERCE

Once a comprehensive version of an idealized design has been completed and accepted by consensus, it should be compared with the reference scenario. The differences between the two constitute the gaps that subsequent steps in the planning process should try to fill.

The end at the far side of a gap is an ideal if the gap cannot be filled in principle, or an objective or goal if it can be. It is an objective if the gap cannot be filled in the period covered by planning, a goal if it can be. Such a classification of ends depends on the current state of our information, knowledge, and understanding, and our estimates of the resources required to fill the gaps and the future availability of these resources. Therefore, changes in our information, knowledge, and understanding can require reclassification of the ends. What appears to be attainable at one moment might appear not to be at another, and what appears not to be attainable might subsequently appear to be. Furthermore, our estimates of the time and resources required to reach an end might be significantly affected by what we learn on the way to it.

Once the gaps have been identified and classified, those in each class should be assigned tentative priorities. Such assignments should take the interactions of the gaps into account; the closing of some will have little value unless others are also closed. In such cases the interdependent gaps should be clustered into subsequently undivided sets. When this is completed, means planning can begin.

A means is behavior that either produces a desired outcome or brings one closer to its attainment. Like ends, means are of different types; the most common are the following:

Acts: behavior that takes relatively little time—for example, standing up, sitting down, making a phone call, or writing a letter.

Courses of action, procedures, or *processes*: a sequence of acts directed at producing a desired outcome—for example, taking a trip, negotiating a contract, installing a new piece of equipment, or assembling an automobile.

Practices: frequently repeated acts or courses of action—for example, filling out travel vouchers, preparing monthly reports, or punching a time-clock.

Projects: systems of simultaneous and/or sequential courses of action directed at desired outcomes—for example, erecting a building, moving from one location to another, or developing a new product.

Programs: systems of projects directed at desired outcomes—for example, developing a new product line, expanding into new markets, or integrating vertically.

In addition to these, means planning is concerned with the selection of the following:

Policies: rules that apply to specified types of means-selection—for example, nondiscriminatory employment, not being undersold, or the preservation of the quality of a product.

These categories are not absolute; they blend into each other.

Ways of Filling Planning Gaps

The selection of a means to fill a planning gap is a planning problem. Like any other problems, those that arise in planning can be treated in three ways: they can be *resolved, solved,* or *dissolved.*

To resolve a problem is to select a means that yields an outcome that is *good enough,* that *satisfices.* I call this approach *clinical* because it relies heavily on past experience and current trial and error for its inputs. It is qualitatively, not quantitatively, oriented; it is rooted deeply in common sense; and it makes extensive use of subjective judgments.

Clinicians do, of course, use research, even quantitative research, but they seldom use it exclusively or allow it to play a decisive role. Its output is seldom the major input to their judgment. The research they use tends to be based on surveys of opinions, attitudes, and characteristics of people. Therefore, tests, questionnaires, and interviews are the principal instruments employed in their inquiries.

Most managers are problem resolvers. They defend this approach by citing the lack of information and the time required to do anything else. Like most clinicians, they argue that real problems are so messy that they render alternative approaches either inapplicable or inappropriate. Furthermore, they claim their methodology minimizes risk, hence maximizes the likelihood of survival. Reactive planners tend to be problem resolvers.

To *solve* a problem is to select a means that is believed to yield the *best possible* outcome, that *optimizes.* I call this the *research* approach because it is largely based on scientific methods, techniques, and tools. It makes extensive use of mathematical models and real or simulated experiments; therefore, it relies heavily on observation and measurement, both of which it aspires to carry out as objectively as possible.

The research approach is used most heavily by management scientists and technologically oriented managers whose principal organizational objective tends to be *thrival* rather than mere survival. They are growth seekers.

Researchers, and particularly the managers who use them, often resort to clinical treatment of those aspects of a problem that cannot be treated quantitatively, hence cannot be included in mathematical models. Researchers more than managers resist the adulteration of optimal solutions with qualitative considerations and often prefer optimal solutions of incompletely formulated problems to less than optimal solutions to problems that are completely formulated*. Preactive planners tend to be problem solvers.

To *dissolve* a problem is to change the nature of either the entity that has it or alter its environment in order to *remove* the problem. Problem dissolvers *idealize* rather than satisfice or optimize because their objective is to change the system involved, or its environment, to bring it closer to an ultimately desired state, one in which the problem cannot or does not arise. I call this the *design* approach.

*For a detailed discussion of the limitations of optimization and objectivity, see Ackoff [5].

Designers make use of the methods, techniques, and tools of both clinicians and researchers, and much more; but they use them synthetically rather than analytically. They try to dissolve problems by changing the characteristics of the system that contains the part with the problem; they look for dissolutions in the containing whole rather than for solutions in the contained parts.

The design approach is used by that minority of managers and management scientists whose principal organizational objective is *development* rather than growth or survival. Interactive planners tend to be problem dissolvers.

An example may help to clarify the differences between resolving, solving, and dissolving problems. A large machine-tool manufacturing company was confronted with frequent, abrupt, and large changes in demand for its products. Reactions to these fluctuations were both disruptive and costly. Among other things, the company alternated in a short cycle between hiring and firing personnel, many of whom were highly skilled. This made for low morale, and low morale made for low productivity, not to mention hostility between labor and management.

The company's management periodically resolved this problem by drawing on past experience, using "good sound judgment" and common sense. But this approach came to be regarded as inadequate because the problem kept reappearing, and it tended to get worse over time. It is not unusual for problems that are treated clinically to reappear and get worse. This failing has plagued psychotherapy and sociotherapy since their inceptions. The treatments of alcoholism and drug addiction now in vogue are cases in point.

Out of desperation, management decided to give research and optimization a try. The researchers who were called in to do the job formulated the problem as one of production smoothing, the solution to which depended critically on the accuracy with which demand could be forecast. Unfortunately, a good forecasting procedure could not be developed. Therefore, the solutions obtained by optimizing the model of the problem were only marginally better than those previously obtained by problem resolving.

A third attack using a design approach was then initiated. It began by reformulating the problem as one requiring the reduction of the fluctuations of demand rather than finding a way to respond to these fluctuations. The business of the company was redesigned to reduce them. A product line was added the demand for which was countercyclical to that for machine tools. Nevertheless, its production required the same technology and it used parts and subassemblies that were interchangeable with those used in machine tools. The product line consisted of road-building equipment. Moreover, such equipment employed virtually the same distribution and marketing system as machine tools.

Subsequent fluctuations of combined demand for the two types of product were about one-fifteenth as large as they had been for machine tools alone.

This dissolution of the problem by redesigning the business moved the company closer to at least one of its ideals, stable emplyment. It also significantly improved its earning stream and reduced its cash-flow and labor-management problems.

Improvements obtained by resolving problems tend to have shorter lives than those obtained by solving them. Solutions, however, tend to have shorter lives than dissolutions. Nevertheless, few if any problems are ever permanently resolved, solved, or dissolved. Every treatment of a problem generates new problems. Because of this the consequences of any type of treatment of a problem should be monitored. Such monitoring, discussed in Chapter 11, is a critical part of the control of plans.

The Need for Creativity

Means planning requires the formulation of alternative ways of completely or partially closing the gaps between the reference scenario and the idealized design. Once formulated, the alternatives should be evaluated and a choice made. In many cases, however, none of the candidates seems to be good enough, and even when one does, there often seems to be room for considerable improvement. In either of these cases better means than were initially formulated should be sought or invented. The success of such a search or inventive effort depends greatly on how creatively it is carried out.

In Chapter 3 it was observed that creativity is largely a matter of identifying self-imposed constraining assumptions. These assumptions are usually made unconsciously, hence are well hidden from those who make them. Therefore, the search for and invention of new means requires the identification of the constraining assumptions. Once identified, they should be denied, reasons for denying them should be found, and the possibilities revealed by removing them should be explored. This process of creatively formulating means is the subject of this chapter. In the next I consider how means once formulated can be evaluated so that a good choice can be made from among them.

THE NATURE OF A DECISION

Our ability to formulate means creatively depends in part on how well we understand the nature of a decision. To decide is to select the quantitative or qualitative values of one or more variables. These are called *decision* or *controlled* variables. Not all the variables that are *controllable* in a decision situation are *controlled*; we attempt to control only those that are believed to be *relevant*, to have an effect on the outcome. For example, the *location* of a factory is a variable that effects the costs of its operation.

The outcome of a decision is coproduced by what is done (the means selected) and the environment in which it is done. For example, the performance of a factory in a new location might depend on local weather conditions, the attitude of the community toward the factory, and proximity to sources of raw material and energy. Those aspects of the situation that affect the outcome but are not controlled by the decision maker constitute the decision environment. This environment is made up of *uncontrolled*, but not necessarily *uncontrollable*, variables. A relevant controllable variable may be believed incorrectly to be either irrelevant or uncontrollable, hence be uncontrolled.

To *control* a variable is to be able to set its value unilaterally; that is, to be sufficient to establish its value, hence to cause it. For example, it is in this sense that we control the lights in our houses; we determine whether they are off or on. To *influence* a variable is to have some but not complete control over it: to be a coproducer of it. For example, the pricing of a product influences its sale but does not control it because other variables are relevant.

The set of relevant variables over which we have influence but not complete control constitutes what is called our *transactional environment*. The set of relevant variables over which we have no control constitutes our *contextual environment*. Thus a corporate executive may be part of his or her subordinate's transactional environment; however, the executives of a competing corporation are part of his or her contextual environment.

Since the amount of control we have over things can change with time, these environments can also change. To the extent that we gain control we move elements of our contextual environment into our transactional environment and convert elements of our transactional environment into controllable variables.

A decision maker may consider the control of some variables to be subject to certain constraints that are either imposed by others or by the nature of things. For example, the amount of money one can pay for something can neither exceed the amount available nor be less than zero. On the other hand, a maximum expenditure less than the amount available may be set by the actual decision maker or by one of his or her superiors.

Uncontrolled variables may also be constrained or be perceived as constrained. For example, the time required to receive a shipment of goods cannot be less than the fastest possible transportation time from its source to its destination.

The outcome of a decision is a function of the values of both the relevant controlled and uncontrolled variables, and the values of these variables are often taken to be constrained. Therefore, a decision maker's conception or model of a choice situation takes the form of an equation:

Outcome = a function of the controlled variables and the uncontrolled variables

This equation may be accompanied by one or more constraints on the controlled and uncontrolled variables. These constraints can often be expressed as equations or inequations—that is, expressions containing "is greater or less than." (Recall that the amount spent for something must be greater than or equal to zero and less than or equal to some specified amount.)

It is very important to be aware of the fact that a decision maker's *conception* of a choice situation may differ significantly from the real situation. It is the discovery of such differences that opens up the possibility of formulating new means. These differences are normally obscured by assumptions that either appear to the decision maker to be so obviously true that they need not be questioned, or they are unconscious.

Unconsciously made assumptions often convert a problem into a puzzle. For example, consider the problem of placing a pen or pencil on one of the nine dots shown in Figure 8.1 and drawing four straight lines, covering all the dots without lifting the pen or pencil. Most who try to solve this problem do not try to extend their lines beyond the perimeter of the square formed by the dots because they incorrectly assume they are not permitted to do so. One of the many solutions to this puzzle is shown in Figure 8.2.

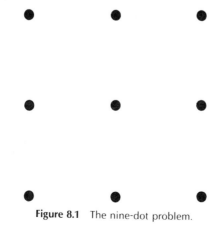

Figure 8.1 The nine-dot problem.

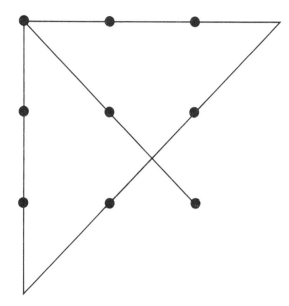

Figure 8.2   A solution to the nine-dot problem.

Formulation of a new means involves either converting an uncontrolled variable into one that is controlled, or using a value of a controlled variable previously taken to be precluded by a constraint. The assumptions that obstruct such formulations are answers to any combination of the following question about a decision situation:

1. What are the relevant variables?
2. Which of these can be controlled and which not?
3. To what constraints are these subject?
4. How do the relevant variables interact to produce the outcome?

Consider each of these in turn.

THE RELEVANCY OF VARIABLES

The variables we perceive as relevant in any particular situation depends on the *frame of reference* or *point of view* with which we come to that situation. Our frame of reference in a specific situation is a part of our more general view of the world. This framework is a product of our culture, education, vocation, and avocations. It is seldom explicitly formulated or, therefore, consciously evaluated or revised. As a result, we are usually quite unaware of the extent to which it excludes variables from consideration in specific decision situations.

On occasion we are made aware of our frame of reference by others who do not share it. For example, I was once part of a group of experts discussing the death of an elderly woman who lived in an urban ghetto. She had died of a heart attack while climbing the stairs to her fourth-floor room. Ironically, she had just returned from a visit to the local free medical clinic for a checkup. The doctor who was present at the meeting pointed out that if the clinic were provided with more doctors some of them could make house calls and such deaths as this woman's might be avoided. The economist who was present said that if such people were provided with larger welfare or retirement payments by the government they could afford either to call a private practitioner or to live in a ground-floor room. An architect pointed out that if multiple-storied dwelling units were required to provide elevators, such problems would not be likely to arise. Finally, a local social worker cited the fact that the woman had an affluent son who lived in a suburban bungalow. Had the mother and son not been alienated from each other she would have been living with him and the problem would not have arisen.

There is an old academic story that illustrates the variety of points of view that can be brought to a problem. Three students—one in physics, one an engineer, and one in business administration—were asked by a professor how they would use a barometer to determine the height of a tall building. The physics student said he would determine the atmospheric pressure at both the base and the top of the building. Then, by using a well-known equation, he would convert the difference between his readings into the height of the building. The engineering student said he would take the barometer to the top of the building and drop it over the side. He would time its descent to the sidewalk and, again using a well-known equation, convert this time to height. The business administration student said he would find the building's caretaker and offer him the barometer as a gift if he would tell him the height of the building.

The participants in both stories had different professional frames of reference within which they conceptualized problems. It is very difficult to escape our points of view, whatever their nature. Therefore, to escape them we often require the help of others who do not share them with us. The more different perspectives brought to bear on a problem, the more alternative ways of dealing with it can be generated. Herein lies one of the important advantages of participative planning: it brings just such a multiplicity of points of view to bear on problems to be dealt with in planning.

Even when groups containing a variety of points of view are organized to formulate alternative means, their members can act in a very constrained way. They might be reluctant to put forward ideas that they think others might consider to be foolish, unconventional, or impractical. Therefore, it is necessary to create a climate that encourages the exercise of imagination and the support of those who do so. There are a number of processes that have been developed and used for just this purpose. These include synectics [37 and 63], brainstorming [60], TKJ [46], and the search conference [31 and 84].

In most group efforts to generate alternative means, many participants feel compelled to show that whatever is suggested cannot be carried out. It is usually easy to find reasons for not doing something innovative but difficult to find even one good reason to do it. This leads to *indecision,* which Ambrose Bierce [15] defines as follows:

> The chief element of success; "for whereas," saith Sir Thomas Brewbold, "there is but one way to do nothing and divers ways to do something, whereof, to a surety, only one is the right way, it followeth that he who from indecision standeth still hath not so many chances of going astray as he who pusheth forwards. (p.159)

Consider a case in which two groups dealt with the same proposed solution to a problem. An organization that processed easily portable and concealable items of very high value was experiencing a number of thefts by its employees. At a meeting of managers and consultants to consider how security might be tightened, one conventional proposal after another was given serious attention. When one participant made a very unconventional proposal, it was dismissed with derision. He had asked how the valuables were removed from the organization's premises and was told it was done on the person, usually concealed in clothing or packages. He then suggested that all employees work in the nude and that they dress and undress for work on the premises and be checked while in the nude.

A subgroup later took this idea and worked on it constructively. Its members found that *working* in the nude was not the essence of the idea, but an inspection in the nude was. Therefore, they suggested that uniforms be designed to facilitate work and that these be required of all employees who would change into when arriving at work. At the end of the work day they would remove their uniforms is an undressing room, go through a shower into an adjoining room in which they would dress to go home. They would be checked when leaving the shower by guard. Furthermore, the valuables being stolen were such that water destroyed them.

To try to solve a problem where it is found—a self-imposed constraint that I discuss in connection with the principle of coordination in Chapter 3—is to impose a restrictive frame of reference on a problem. It limits the kind and number of alternative solutions considered. Therefore, it is important that each planning gap be looked at in the largest possible context, and that this perspective be narrowed incrementally only when satisfactory means are not found in the larger context. Problems and gaps are usually approached the other way around, first in the smallest possible context, and this is broadened only when a satisfactory means cannot be found there. (Recall the production problem that was solved by changing the way salespeople were compensated.) Here is another example with the same point.

A large European city used double-decker buses as its principal means of public transportation. Each bus had a crew of two: a driver who occupied a cab separated from the rest of the bus, and a conductor who had three functions. The conductor signaled the driver when there were passengers who wanted to get off at the next stop, signaled again when to start, and collected fares from those who had boarded. Fares were normally collected when the bus was in motion to make the stops as short as possible. During peak hours this often required the conductor to force his or her way through the crowd on both levels in order to collect fares. Frequently the conductor failed to return to the entrance in time to signal the driver not to stop. (The driver was required to stop unless a signal not to was recieved.) Therefore, the driver often stopped when there were no passengers to discharge or take on board. Such unnecessary stops bred hostility between drivers and conductors, the drivers being on a meet-the-schedule incentive system, and the conductor being penalized for failure to collect fares if spotted by an unidentified inspector.

The hostility became overt and culminated in a "war" between the two relevant unions. A number of efforts to solve the problem by bringing drivers and conductors together into group discussion failed. Most of these meetings ended in violence.

An outsider was brought in to help. He broadened the problem to include the stops as well as the buses. When this was done it was discovered that at peak hours there were more buses operating than there were stops. This led to a solution in which conductors were located at the stops during peak hours, not on the buses. Then they could collect fares from passengers while they were waiting for a bus. Conductors could signal drivers when to start by using a button located at the rear entrance to the bus, and passengers could signal the driver when they wanted to get off by pulling a cord placed around the sides of the bus. Not only did this reduce delays, but it made fare collection easier. When the number of buses in operation was less than the number of stops, at off-peak hours, the conductor could return to the bus.

Summarizing, the range of relevant variables considered in efforts to fill planning gaps can be extended by (1) enlarging participation in the formulation of means to bring as many points of view to bear as possible, (2) creating an atmosphere that encourages and supports unconventional and imaginative proposals, and (3) considering things that can be done to larger influenceable systems containing the system that has the problem.

CONTROLLING THE UNCONTROLLED

Many creative means are developed by finding a way to control or influence variables that were previously considered to be uncontrollable. Such variables can often be brought under partial or complete control by one or some combination of these strategies. First, the effect of an uncontrolled variable may be reduced without affecting the variable itself. This is equivalent to reducing one's sensitivity to the effects of an uncontrolled variable. Second, organizations and individuals whose behavior seems to be out of one's control can frequently be influenced by appropriate incentives. Finally, variables that cannot be controlled by one decision-making individual or group acting alone can be subject to the control of two or more decision makers who collaborate for this purpose. Each of these strategies is considered in turn.

Decreasing Sensitivity to Uncontrolled Variables

The example used earlier in this chapter involving the machine-tool manufacturing company showed how—by taking on an additional product line, road-building equipment—the problems arising from uncontrolled fluctuations of machine-tool sales were significantly reduced.

Here is another case in which the harmful effects of uncontrolled demand were reduced, but in this case by redesign of the product.

A manufacturer of refrigerators had a persistent problem arising from the fact that each model had to be produced in two versions, one with right-hand doors and the other with left-hand doors. The numbers of each version of a model that were bought in different markets varied considerably and significantly from year to year, hence could not be predicted accurately. As a result, stocks were out of balance in many markets, some with too many right-hand doors, and others with too many left-hand doors. this led to both lost sales and excessive inventories.

A research team was called in to develop better forecasting of the sales of the two versions. It occurred to the team that if a refrigerator could be opened from either side, the problem would disappear. The team learned, however, that another manufacturer had built such a door, hinged in the center of its top and bottom, and it had flopped. It was expensive, and ambidexterity had little or no value to the customer.

Nevertheless, the team felt the idea worth pursuing. One day one of its members noted that if the door of the refrigerator made by the company was turned upside down, its outer side looked exactly the same except that the handle was on the other side. Right- and left-hand doors were exactly the same but they were mounted differently. Furthermore, the door and the shelves mounted on the back of the door were so designed that the shelves could be inserted upside down. This led the team to design a refrigerator door frame that had hinge receptacles on both sides. Those on the side not in use could be covered by a snap-on plate. The hinges themselves were designed to snap into the receptacles. This meant that the same door could be mounted on either side; furthermore, it could be changed at any time before or after purchase. The additional cost of production was very small compared to the cost of additional inventory and lost sales resulting from the traditional design. The new design also offered the customer convertibility, should it be required by a move or remodeling.

The principle involved in such dissolutions of problems is much like the one involved in developing vaccines that produce complete or partial immunity to diseases. In a sense, such desensitizing reduces or eliminates the relevance of the uncontrolled variable.

Influence through Incentives

Many creative means are developed by finding a way to control or influence variables that were previously considered uncontrollable. This is particularly the case when the behavior of others is involved. For example, in a case referred to in Chapter 4, a producer of materials used by industry developed an inventory problem that derived from the fact that its customers bought small amounts at a time. The company could not forecast the aggregate of these amounts well enough, hence it saw itself as having a forecasting problem. Its problem was dissolved, however, by offering a discount to customers that was proportional to the amount of time between placement of their orders and required delivery.

In another company the productivity of a large number of inspectors had been decreasing significantly over several years. In an effort to increase their output the plant manager proposed taking them off a flat salary and putting them on piecework. They threatened to strike if this was done. This problem was dissolved by defining a fair day's work—an amount considerably greater than the current output—and allowing the inspectors to leave the plant when it was completed.

In both these cases *incentives* were used to bring uncontrolled behavior under control. Incentives can play a major role in the implementation of any plan because such implementation requires many decisions and actions independently made either by individuals and units that are part of the organization planned for, or by external stakeholders. The behavior desired of those within the organization can seldom be obtained exclusively by the imposition of authority, even in an autocratically run organization. The cooperation of outsiders almost always has to be induced. Furthermore, even if cooperative behavior could be imposed, doing so would be contrary to the development objective. Development, it will be recalled, takes place through one's own decision making, not through decisions made for one by others.

Desired behavior by others can be induced by the use of either *incentives*, rewards for doing what is desired, or *disincentives*, punishment for doing what is not. Incentives are preferable not only because they are more humane but because they are more effective. Disincentives are frequently taken as a challenge, something to be evaded, ignored, or otherwise gotten around, as in tax evasion. Disincentives require enforcement. Fines that are not levied and laws that are not enforced have no effect.

Many of the deficiencies in the behavior of a system or its parts derive from incentives or disincentives that currently are in force even though they are not intended to have such consequences. For example, people who serviced a company's appliances in the home were encouraged by a monetary incentive system to complete as many service calls per day as possible. In order to do so these people carried as many different spare parts as they could jam into their service vans. The cost of this mobile inventory became very large but no amount of urging reduced it. The incentive system had to be changed.

Undesirable behavior is often a consequence of depriving individuals of the information they require to behave in a more desirable way. Hidden costs, for example, may prevent people from making rational economic decisions. The fact that the disposal costs of what we use but do not use up—for example, packaging, automobiles, and appliances—are hidden, prevents both producers and consumers from making decisions that are desirable from the point of view of those responsible for collection and disposal of solid waste. People do not tend to make effective use of goods or services that appear to be free and plentiful. Office supplies, to take a common example, are generally misused and wasted because they are usually plentiful and apparently costless. Where employees or units are required to pay for the supplies they use, even if they are given an allowance with which to do so, they generally use what they buy more sensibly.

On the other side of this coin is the fact that any internal supplier of goods or services whose income is independent of performance has little or no incentive to respond well to the needs and desires of those served.

To subsidize a public or private supplier of goods or services is to invite inefficiency and ineffectiveness. It is almost always better to subsidize the users rather than the suppliers. Doing so creates a marketplace in which the supplier must operate. It is for this reason, for example, that voucher systems have been proposed for public education. In such systems parents of school-age children are given a voucher that covers the cost of their childrens' education. They select the schools to which to apply. The schools receive no subsidy; their only income derives from cashing vouchers received. This system not only makes schools more responsive to the needs of children and the desires of their parents, but it also makes them more efficient and varied.*

In the type of multidimensional organization discussed in Chapter 7, all goods and services used by any part of that organization have to be paid for by that part and all internal suppliers have to support themselves by selling their outputs. This design gets the incentives the right way around.

Incentives should be simple and easily understood by those who are supposed to be affected by them. The recipients of an incentive should be made aware of its purpose and they should be able to determine its effect on them without expert advice or complicated calculations. It is well known, for example, that salespeople do not trust incentive schemes that do not enable them to calculate their earnings for themselves. Such schemes have little effect on what they do. For these reasons incentive systems are best designed with the participation of those who are to be affected by them.

It is possible to design incentives that apply to groups as well as individuals. These are intended to affect both individual and collective behavior. However, they seldom work unless the individuals in the group believe that what they do has a significant impact on group performance, and that what others do cannot detract from their contributions. An effective incentive system must reward those who behave desirably no matter what others do. This means, for example, that a worker whose productivity increases should be rewarded even when the productivity of his or her unit does not. The amount of the reward, however, can be tied to the performance of the unit. By doing so the worker is made attentive to the unit's performance as well as his or her own.

Incentives tend to wear out over time. This was discovered in the workplace many years ago when piecework compensation was found to have decreasing effects on productivity with time. Similarly, bonuses, initially awarded for good performance, have often come to be expected

---

*A more detailed discussion of the voucher system is provide in Ackoff [3, Chapter 5].

independent of performance and thus lose their motivating force. Because incentives tend to lose their effectiveness over time they should be monitored and, when they begin to wear out, should be replaced or modified.

Whenever a means is formulated with the intention of affecting the behavior of others, its effectiveness is clearly dependent on how well the behavior of the relevant others is understood. Such understanding of others has two major components: how well we understand (1) how the others perceive, conceptualize, or model the situation within which we intend to affect their behavior, and (2) how and why they make their choices in such situations. Consider each of these in turn.

It is commonly assumed that others see things much as we do despite a good deal of evidence to the contrary. A classic illustration of this error is found in the field of conflict research. There is an elementary conflict situation called the Prisoner's Dilemma which involves two parties (see [64]). Extensive experimentation with this game reveals that most players play it in a way that most game theorists view as irrational. Nigel Howard [42] found that players had a model of the game that differed significantly from that of the experimenters. The experimenters represent the game by a table that shows the individual moves from which the players must choose in each play of the game, but the players see the game as involving choice of a strategy, a rule for selecting moves, not choice of individual moves. The players' model was better than that of the experimenters and it revealed that the players were indeed rational.

Whenever others are perceived as behaving irrationally, it should be borne in mind that such a perception is based on the perceiver's model of the situation, not necessarily the actors'. Unless the perceiver has the same model as the actors, he or she cannot influence their behavior effectively. Here is another case in point.

In 1957 I spent some time in India at the invitation of its government to review its national development planning procedures. While there I met a number of foreigners who were trying to introduce family planning to India in the hope of bringing its population explosion under control. Most of these serious and dedicated people were distributing contraceptives and information about their use, without success. There was little impact on India's birth rate. They blamed the failure on the ignorance, irrationality, or intransigence of the Indians. Such an explanation of their failure yielded no ideas about how to increase their effectiveness.

I suggested to some of them that they consider the assumption that the Indians were rational and the family planners were not. This, I argued, might yield a more useful explanation of their failure. Furthermore, I pointed out, there was at least some evidence that another of their basic assumptions—that the Indians did not know how to control family size—was wrong. Indian families tended to have considerably less than the twenty to thirty children it was biologically possible for them to have. This suggested that they were already practicing birth control. Granting this, it seemed desirable to determine why they *wanted* as many children as they had. This was quite at odds with assuming, as the family planners did, that the number of children Indians had was out of their control.

None of the family planners to whom I made these suggestions took the bait. Eventually, the Indian demographer T. R. Balakrishnan and my colleague Glen D. Camp [13] did. This is what they found.

After obtaining its independence, India had increased the expected length of life of adults dramatically, but it had not increased the span of *employable* life. The poor Indian—and most of them are poor—could expect to work for only about the first half of the employable years available to him. Therefore, while young and employed, Indians were preoccupied with planning for financial security during the subsequent period of unemployment.

The Indian government provided no unemployment insurance or old-age security. Very few Indians earned enough to insure themselves. Therefore, the only way most Indians could assure survival was by having enough children to support the husband and wife when the husband was unemployable. On the average, one wage earner could provide the minimal support required by one nonwage-earning adult. However, since only males are generally employable in India, this implied a need for an average of four children. Because of the high mortality rate among children, slightly more than four children were required to produce four who could survive. The average family size in India corresponded almost exactly to this requirement.

The average size of families in India could, of course, have been due to other factors. Whether it was, however, could be determined easily. If the security-based explanation of family size was correct, one would expect those couples whose first two or three children were sons to be smaller than those whose first few children were daughters. This was found to be the case.

Balakrishnan and Camp did not claim that concern with advanced-age unemployment was the only factor affecting birth rate in India, but it was a critical factor. Therefore, to ask Indians to have fewer children was to ask them to commit a delayed suicide. To call them irrational because they refused to do so is hardly rational.

Our inability to influence the behavior of others does not derive so much from their lack of susceptibility to influence as from our lack of understanding of their behavior.

Control through Collaboration

It is common knowledge that an obstruction that blocks progress of each of a number of individuals or organizations taken separately can be removed by them if they work together. It is recognition of this fact that has led to so many trade and industrial associations. Members of an industry working together have been able to influence legislation and regulation to an extent that would not have been possible if they had worked independently of each other.

What is not so obvious is that adversaries who obstruct each other can often remove the cause of their conflict if they work together. An outstanding example of this can be found in the recent history of Jamestown, New York [27 and 44], a small city that was going down the drain as industry and its young people deserted it for more attractive places. A collaboration, initiated by its mayor, between labor, management, and government led to a remarkable renaissance of the community.

ON REMOVING CONSTRAINTS

In some choice situations constraints on what can be done and what can happen are explicitly incorporated into the formulation of that situation. These constitute a subset of the class of constraining assumptions, many of which are usually left implicit. Those constraints that are consciously perceived are often ones that appear to be obvious or are assumed to be imposed by a higher authority.

Constraints that appear obvious or self-evident are often worth viewing with great scepticism. Grounds for such doubt can be found in Ambrose Bierce's [15] previously quoted definition of *self-evident*: "evident to one's self and to nobody else" (p.318). *Obvious* has a related but different meaning that is revealed in a story of a professor who was taking a class through the proof of a theorem in geometry. He followed the usual procedure of giving each step and the supporting reasons for it, citing axioms, postulates, definitions, and previously proven theorems. For one step, however, he gave no reasons, saying that it was obvious. He went on to the next step. Half way through it he stopped, contemplated the previous step, turned to the class with a puzzled look on his face and said, "Excuse me, I'll be right back." He left the room and returned after a long absence with a selfsatisfied grin on his face and said, "I was right. That step was obvious."

"Obvious" does not refer to a truth so apparent that it requires no supporting evidence, but to an assertion whose truth one is willing to accept without reason. Obvious assumptions, like the mythical sirens, entice problem solvers and planners to destruction.

Those things that we want to believe we tend to accept without reason. Those things that we do not want to believe we tend to reject no matter what evidence is available to support them. This was the case, for example, in the account given in Chapter 4 of the company that employed a large number of blacks but had very few in its managerial and supervisory ranks. Its managers believed that the lack of upward mobility of the blacks was due to their educational deficiencies. When research revealed that this was not the case and that the problem was management's attitude toward and treatment of the blacks, management refused to accept it.

Constraints are often attributed to a higher authority without evidence. This is reflected in such statements as: "There is no use in trying to do that because by boss would not approve of it." Such assertions may be true but frequently they are not. It is important, therefore, to check their validity before accepting them.

In checking the existence of imposed constraints by questioning the one who is believed to be imposing them, the response received is likely to depend critically on the way the issue is presented. Recall from Chapter 4 the observations of a lawyer who pointed out to me that many corporate executives do not know how to question their lawyers about legal constraints. They usually ask, "Can I do 'so and so'?" The lawyers will almost always reply negatively. They do so because they know the executives will not be in trouble with the law by not doing "so and so." If they do it, trouble, however improbable, might result. Therefore, the lawyers play it safe and say no. However, if an executive tells a lawyer that he or she is going to do "so and so" and asks how to do it without getting into legal trouble, the lawyer will usually tell the executive how it can and should be done.

Consider another kind of constraint, one that involves the incorrect assumption that a familiar technology is necessary for a particular kind of task. For example, a team of faculty members and students from the National Autonomous University of Mexico were working with a group of peasants in a very underdeveloped part of Mexico. They were trying to encourage the peasants to improve themselves. The peasants were very responsive and decided to try to irrigate their fields by digging a large ditch from a water source to their fields, and smaller ditches to distribute the water over the fields. To do this they needed to determine level paths over their hilly fields. The academics said they could help by getting some surveying equipment from their university. The peasants said this would not be necessary. They told the academics that if a burro at one location is shown something he wants at another location, he will take a level path to what he wants. The academics were sceptical but curious. They got their surveying equipment, tested the burro, and found the peasants were right.

We almost always attribute what constraints we are aware of to external sources. Doing so relieves us of any responsibility for them. Nevertheless, many of them are self-imposed, however subtly. If most managers used the same ingenuity to evade apparently externally imposed constraints as they do to legally avoid paying taxes, there would be a great deal more creativity and effectiveness in management.

GETTING THE RELATIONSHIPS RIGHT

Decisions to do something are based on a set of assumed causal or productive relationships between those variables we control, those that we do not control but assume are relevant, and the outcome we desire. The belief that a variable affects the outcome of what we do is what makes us consider it relevant. Therefore, the selection of the variables we try to manipulate is conditioned by what we believe to be the nature of the relationships between them and the outcome we desire.

Our ability to plan effectively depends critically on how well we conceptualize the relationship between what we do and what we want. Many of our failures derive from either assuming a causal relationship where it does not exist or failing to assume one where it does. Perhaps the most common reason for failure to bring about what we want is incorrectly assuming a causal relationship between variables that have only been demonstrated to be *associated*. Variables are associated if they tend to change together in the same or opposite directions.

For example, the weights and heights of persons are clearly associated. This means that if we obtain the weight and height of each of a sample of people and plot these observations on a graph, the points will tend to increase together. Such an association is said to be *positive*. If an increase in one variable is associated with a decrease in the other—for example, income and illness—then the association is said to be *negative*.

Two variables that are associated need not be causally related. Nevertheless, when two variables are associated, either can be used to predict the value of the other. For example, we can use the association of weight and height to predict one if we know the other. However, it is incorrect to *infer* from their association that a change in weight will cause or produce a change in height. Nevertheless, such inferential errors are frequently made. For example, suppose we plot a company's annual sales against its annual advertising expenditures over a number of years. Such plots often show a positive association: sales and advertising expenditures tend to increase together. It does *not* follow, however, that an increase in advertising will produce an increase in sales. Advertising may or may not have an effect on sales; but even if it does, a positive association between them is not proof. Payroll and sales are also positively associated, but it would be incorrect to infer that an increase in payroll will produce an increase in sales.

If two variables are *not* associated we can justifiably infer that they are *not* causally related *under the conditions in which the observations were made*, but not under other conditions. However, if there is an association we should not infer that either is the cause or producer of the other. The most we can infer is that they *might* be so related. Therefore, association can be correctly used to filter a large number of variables to determine which should be studied further for causal relations.

The most commonly used measures of association are *correlation* and *regression* coefficients. The nature of these measures is not important here, but the cautious planner will remember that they are measures of association and, therefore, cannot be used legitimately for inferring causality or production. Caution is required because there are a number of widely used statistical techniques such as factor and cluster analysis that are derived from correlation and regression, but this fact is well concealed, often even from those who use them.

The danger of inferring causality or production from association is revealed by returning to the advertising example. Suppose we plotted annual sales against advertising expenditures in the *following* year. In most cases in which I have done this, I have obtained a stronger positive association than was obtained when advertising in the same year was used. Clearly, we cannot infer that an increase in next year's advertising will increase this year's sales. In fact, the causal connection can be the opposite. Many companies set their advertising budgets as a relatively fixed percentage of forecast sales. Most sales-forecasting procedures are such that if there is an increase in sales one year, a further increase is likely to be forecast for the following year. Now we can see what may be the causal sequence: if sales went up last year the company probably forecast an increase in sales this year. If it forecast such an increase it probably increased advertising expenditures. Therefore, what this shows is that an increase in sales one year tends to produce an increase in advertising in the following year.

One cannot overestimate the frequency with which the erroneous inference of causality and production from association is made. For example, much of the support for the assertion that smoking produces cancer is based on an association of these variables. They may in fact be causally related but an association between them does not prove it. Using the same erroneous logic we could argue from a negative association between smoking and cholera that smoking prevents cholera.

The commitment of many medical researchers to reduce smoking blinds them not only to errors in inferential logic but also to other associations between variables that weaken their case. For example, a study conducted in England showed a strong positive association between discontinuation of smoking and the incidence of mental illness. If we used the same erroneous logic as is used in so much medical research, we would infer that smoking prevents mental illness. Perhaps it does, but a negative association between them does not establish the fact.

Recall that to establish one thing as the cause of another is to show it to be both necessary and sufficient for the other; to establish one thing as the producer of another is to show that it is necessary but not sufficient for the other. It is not easy in general to establish either necessity or sufficiency, but, difficult or not, it is required before we can justifiably assume a causal connection.

Science has developed powerful experimental techniques for determining whether variables are causally connected. It is not much of an exaggeration to say that this is what science is all about. Because of this capability, science is as essential to effective planning as is art. Knowing where, when, and how to use scientific research is part of the art of planning. The planner who is not well versed in science can nevertheless demand an explanation in ordinary English of how proclaimed causal relations were established. He should require the explanation to be complete enough to enable him to judge whether a causal claim is based on an association or a demonstration of either necessity or sufficiency.

The relationship between variables that are causally connected may not be simple. Under some circumstances, for example, demand may increase when prices are increased, or decrease when prices are reduced. The effect of price on demand might depend on other variables; for example, competitive pricing. There are products which, like the Packard automobile, destroyed themselves with reduced pricing. Those who are addicted to simple relationships tend to dismiss such examples as exceptions that prove the rule. Such aberrations, however, can provide valuable insights to complex and subtle relationships from which very creative and effective means can be extracted.

Many effects are the consequences of interacting causes. We know, for example, that water boils at a certain temperature but that this temperature varies with atmospheric pressure. For this reason it takes longer to prepare a hard-boiled egg in Mexico City than it does in New York.

The interactions of causal variables are often overlooked, as the following story shows.

In a conversation about logical thinking among four professionals one asked the others, "If two chimney sweeps climbed down a chimney and one came down with a dirty face and the other with a clean face, which one would go to wash his face?"

The engineer in the group immediately replied, "The fellow with the dirty face."

The scientist in the group disagreed. He said, "The fellow with the clean face would go to wash his face. He would see the other fellow's face is dirty and assume his was also, so he would go to wash his face. But the fellow with the dirty face would see that the other's is clean and would assume his is also, so he would not go to wash his face."

The philosopher in the group came to the defense of the engineer. He argued, "When the fellow with the clean face starts for the washroom, as the scientist correctly reasoned, the fellow with the dirty face would ask him where he was going. The fellow with the clean face would say, 'To wash my face.' 'Why?' the other would ask, 'your face is clean.' The fellow with the clean face would then say, But yours is dirty.' So the fellow with the dirty face would go to wash his face."

A student who overheard this interchange could contain himself no longer and broke in with a question: "How could two fellows climb down a dirty chimney and one come out with a clean face and the other with a dirty face?"

The moral of this story is clear: it is not enough to take reactions into account; *interactions* should be considered.

It should also be borne in mind that the amount of response is not always proportional to the amount of stimulus. For example, some of a drug may be beneficial but more of it may be harmful, in fact lethal. Increases in advertising or sales calls on customers may, beyond a certain point, produce negative responses from the customers. A study showing that this was the case in one company's advertising has been described by Ackoff and Emshoff [8].

Effects are sometimes confused with causes. This is particularly the case in medicine where a good deal of the treatment is directed at removing symptoms, not causes. A patient consulting a doctor begins by listing symptoms of ill health. Then the doctor usually makes some observations of his or her own, taking the patient's temperature, pulse, blood pressure, and so on. In this way the doctor finds additional symptoms and can diagnose. In this process the doctor develops a hypothesis or a conclusion as to what is the cause or producer of the deficiency whose symptoms have been observed. The doctor might check his or her diagnosis by collecting additional information. Once convinced of the validity of his diagnosis, he or she prescribes something to remove the cause. If the cause is removed, the symptoms should disappear.

Unfortunately, it does not always work this way. For example, some patients who complain of stomach pains are eventually diagnosed as having duodenal ulcers. One way of treating such ulcers is by surgery that disconnects the duodenum from the stomach. In many cases after such an operation the patient develops a peptic ulcer. Therefore, the cause of an ulcer that was eliminated was not ultimate enough.

We have a parallel case in the way alcoholism is treated. It is usually treated as a *problem* to be removed rather than as the alcoholic's *solution* to a serious personal problem. This problem is usually left unsolved when the alcoholic is denied alcohol or is induced to abstain. No wonder that, once free to do so, the alcoholic returns to alcohol.

Cause-effect and producer-product relationships usually occur in chains, not simple pairings; that is, if Y is the producer of Z, it is also the product of X. Therefore, the removal of Y may not eliminate Z because X will simply reproduce Y and Z thereafter. To eliminate Z we must intervene early enough in the causal or productive chain to prevent it from reoccurring.

To summarize this discussion of relationships, in planning we try to find a way to change one or more aspects of a mess with the intention of bringing about a desirable change in some other aspect of it. Whether we succeed depends on the relationship between what we manipulate and what we want to change. A change in one thing will bring about a change in another only if they are causally or productively related.

The fact that two variables are associated, that is, tend to change together in the same or opposite direction, does not provide an adequate basis for inferring a causal or productive relationship between them. The lack of such co-related changes, however, does provide a basis for inferring the absence of a causal or productive relationship under the conditions in which the lack of association was observed. Because of this, association between variables can be used as a way of selecting those to be studied further for causal or productive connections. Furthermore, the presence of an association between variables enables us to use one of them to predict, but not explain, the other.

A causal or productive relationship between variables cannot be inferred from data that merely describe their behavior, only from controlled testing of a causal or productive hypothesis about them. Such hypotheses assert the necessity and, in some cases, the sufficiency of changes in one for changes in the other. Experimentation is often the only way of getting at these relationships. One may have to go a long way to gain a little understanding, but a little understanding can carry one a long way.

A change in the value of one variable is seldom a simple reaction to a change in the value of another variable; it is usually the consequence of a complex sequence of interactions between several variables. Therefore, messes confronting an organization can seldom be treated effectively by manipulating only one causal or productive variable. What is required is a mapping of the complex interactions of the critical variables that define the mess. Finally, to suppress symptoms successfully is not to remove the cause or producer of a deficiency but to invite intensification of the problem whose symptoms are treated. Such treatments often exacerbate the problem in hand and create new and more serious ones.

SUMMARY

The gaps between the reference scenario and the idealized redesign of the system planned for are problems to which the remainder of the planning process is devoted. In this chapter we have considered ways by which means of treating these problems can be formulated. Like any type of problem, they may be resolved, solved, or dissolved. To resolve a problem is to produce a satisfactory outcome; to solve it is to produce an optimal outcome; and to dissolve it is to remove or significantly reduce the problem. Resolution is largely based on experience and judgement, solution on experiment and science, and dissolution on redesign of the system involved. Dissolution requires experience and experiment, judgment and science, and, particularly, creativity.

Creativity is largely a matter of identifying self-imposed constraints, removing them, and exploring the consequences of doing so. Such constraints arise in answering, implicitly or explicitly, the four questions that are necessarily involved in formulating an attack on any problem:

1. What are the relevant variables?
2. Which of these can be controlled and which not?
3. To what constraints are these subject?
4. How do the relevant variables interact to produce the outcome?

The range of relevant variables considered in efforts to fill planning gaps can be extended by (1) enlarging participation in the formulation of means to bring as many points of view to bear as possible, (2) creating an atmosphere that encourages and supports unconventional and imaginative proposals, and (3) considering things that can be done to larger influenceable systems that contain the system having the problem.

Apparently uncontrollable variables can often be brought under partial or complete control by one or some combination of three strategies: (1) reducing the system's sensitivity to the effects of the uncontrolled variable, (2) influencing the behavior of individuals and/or organizations by use of appropriate incentives, and (3) by collaboration of decision makers who normally operate independently of each other.

Constraints are often self-imposed but appear to be otherwise. They either appear to be obvious or to be imposed by a higher authority. "Obvious" connotes an unwillingness to question the truth of a statement, not the unquestionability of the statement. Therefore, questioning the obvious is a very fruitful way of generating creative treatments of problems. Attributing the imposition of constraints to higher authority is often just a convenient way of absolving oneself of responsibility for exploring the consequences of their removal.

Finally, our choices are based on the relationships we believe hold between the variables we take to be relevant and the outcomes we desire. In planning, since we try to affect the outcomes we experience, we should be exclusively concerned with cause–effect and producer–product relationships. Unfortunately, these are often incorrectly identified with or inferred from an entirely different type of relationship, association. Association is a descriptive relationship; cause–effect and producer–product are explanatory; therefore, to establish them, some type of controlled experimentation is usually required. Because this is more time-consuming and costly than observing concomitant variations of two or more variables under uncontrolled conditions (from which measurements of association can be extracted) there is a strong tendency to substitute description for explanation. This may well be the single most important cause of planning failures.

CHAPTER NINE

MEANS PLANNING II: EVALUATING ALTERNATIVES

Decide, *v.i.* *To succumb to the preponderance of one set of influences over another set.*

AMBROSE BIERCE

Once a set of alternative means has been formulated one of them can be chosen. Such a choice is always based on a comparative evaluation of the alternatives, but such an evaluation can fall anywhere between the casual and the careful. The amount of effort that should go into the comparison should depend on (1) the potential cost of selecting less than the best of the set, (2) how apparent the relative effectiveness of the alternatives is, and (3) the cost of carrying out a sufficiently careful evaluation.

There are few decisions that arise in the course of planning that do not have a significant cost of error associated with them, and this cost is usually quite large compared to that of a suitable evaluation of the alternatives. However, it is not so rare for one of the means to appear clearly superior. No matter how obvious this superiority may be, a choice should not be based on it unless there is strong evidence to support it.

Perhaps the best way to evaluate a means is by a well-designed experiment, preferably one carried out in all or part of the environment in which it is intended to be implemented; for example, a market test of a new product, or an advertising or pricing experiment in selected markets. Well-designed experiments can accelerate the testing process, reduce its cost, increase the accuracy and reliability of the results obtained, and, perhaps of greatest importance, maximize what is learned about the means tested. Experimental testing can do more than reveal how well a means performs; it can also reveal *why* it does so. Such understanding can often lead to significantly improved reformulation of the means.

Experimentation is not trial and error; it is *designed and controlled experience*. Specialized knowledge is required to design and control effective experiments. Intuition and judgment are not enough. The specialized knowledge required is not widespread, even among scientists. Unfortunately, few of the scientists who lack such knowledge are aware of it. Therefore, the use of a scientist in designing evaluations of means does not assure an effective test; an expert in experimental design is needed.

Evaluation of means before a choice is made requires time and resources, and these may be in short supply or be very costly. Unfortunately, the cost of making less than the best choice, or the best choice if it is not good enough, may also be very high. Ironically, the costs associated with evaluating and not evaluating the alternatives can seldom be estimated accurately without essentially the same research required to carry out the evaluation.

Clearly, the cost of making a poor choice depends on how reversible that choice and its effects are. For example, because the site on which a new plant is built cannot be changed easily, and because a plant's location generally has a large effect on the cost of its use over its entire life, selection of such a site should be carefully evaluated beforehand. However, the selection of a brand of paper clip is very unlikely to merit the investment of time, money, and effort required to evaluate it.

In some cases experimental evaluation of alternative means is not possible, and in others it is impractical. For example, market testing of products that may be harmful to consumers is prohibited by law, and differential pricing of public utilities to different parts of the same market can also be precluded. One can hardly conduct an experimental evaluation of alternative plant sites by comparing the performance of plants built on each of the alternative sites.

Fortunately, experimentation in the real world is not the only way of effectively evaluating alternative means. There is another way, one that involves the use of *models*.

THE USE OF MODELS IN EVALUATING MEANS

Models are simplified representations of reality that can be substituted for it under certain conditions. They are generally easier and less expensive to manipulate than the reality they represent, and they can be used to predict and evaluate the consequences of a choice of means. Models are simplified representations of reality in the sense that, in principle at least, they do not contain aspects of reality that are irrelevant to the inquiry at hand. Furthermore, the better we understand the reality involved, the fewer variables we generally require to represent it.

To explain anything *completely* requires an infinite number of variables, but each of these does not contribute equally to the explanation. Imagine them to be ranked from the one with the largest effect on the phenomenon to be explained to the one with the smallest. Then a small number of the most important variables can usually explain more than all the others put together. Therefore, the better we understand a phenomenon, the more economically, simply, and effectively we can model it. We can effectively increase our understanding of a phenomenon through the research required to model it adequately.

Types of Models

There are three basic types of model: *iconic, analogue,* and *symbolic.* These can be combined in a large variety of ways.

An iconic model is one in which the relevant properties of the reality are represented by those properties, but usually with a change of scale. Therefore, such models look like what they represent; they are images. Examples are photograpshs, drawings, maps, pilot plants, test markets, and model airplanes, automobiles, and ships. Some iconic models are scaled down (for example, those of the solar system), some are scaled up (for example, those of an atom), and some are to same size as what they represent (for example, mannequins).

Iconic models generally represent specific and concrete things and these are usually easy to identify. However, such models are often difficult to change for experimental purposes; for example, the critical properties of a scale model of an airplane or ship may be very difficult to modify.

An analogue model is one in which the relevant properties of the reality are represented by different properties, usually ones that are easier to manipulate. For this reason it is harder to identify what they represent but they are normally easier to change than iconic models. On a map, for example, elevation is represented by contour lines or color. These are easier to change than elevation on a three-dimensional map. There are hydraulic models of electrical systems in which the flow of water represents the flow of electricity. Graphs are perhaps the most familiar and easily manipulated type of analogue model; they use geometric properties to represent a wide variety of variables and the relationships between them.

A symbolic model is one in which symbols are used to represent the properties of the real thing and the relationships between them. For example, in the familiar law of freely falling bodies, $s = \frac{1}{2}gt^2$, s represents the distance fallen, g the gravitational constant, and t the elapsed time of the fall.

Symbolic models that can be used to evaluate means have the same form as a decision model: in the equation $V = f(C,U)$, C represents the controlled variables with respect to which each of the means to be evaluated is defined, U represents the set of relevant uncontrolled variables, V is a measure of the value of the outcome, and f is the relationship that holds between this value and the relevant variables. Although the structure of most such models is quite simple, some of them can be very complex because of the large number of variables involved and the complexity of the relationship between them.

Symbolic models are the most general, abstract, and difficult to construct, but they are the easiest to manipulate and change. They can best be used for evaluating means when all the relevant variables can be quantified. This, of course, is seldom the case and, therefore, there is a limit on their usefulness. There are fewer circumstances in which such quantification is possible than most management scientists realize, but more than most managers believe.

Incomplete models, ones that omit relevant variables because of the difficulty of quantifying them or for other reasons, can have limited use in evaluating means *if* the decision makers are aware of what variables such models do and do not take into account. For example, a model used to evaluate alternative sites for a new plant usually does not include such relevant variables as the labor situation or the quality of life the community offers. Knowing which variables are excluded, decision makers can supplement the output of the model with their judgments about these variables and reach a better decision than they might otherwise. Therefore, it is very important for decision makers to know what is and what is not included in the models whose output they use, or, more generally, just how well these models represent reality.

Before considering how models can be evaluated, consider how they can be used to evaluate means.

How Models Can Be Used to Evaluate Means

The ways in which models can be used to evaluate means fall into two categories: *mathematical* (or anaytical) and *experimental.*

It is possible to manipulate some symbolic models mathematically in order to determine which combination of values of the controlled variables yields the best, or approximately best, performance. Some of the mathematical procedures by which such means are found are deductive in nature, others inductive. An increasing number of both of these types of mathematical procedure is available in the form of computer programs.

The level of mathematical and statistical competence required to construct and use symbolic models is found increasingly among graduates of business schools and, of course, among those who have been educated in the management sciences and operations research.

As was pointed out in Chapter 6, computational procedures are not available for extracting the best, or approximately best, means from some models which, nevertheless, can be useful. They can be used to *compare* alternative means. A decision maker can feed alternative means into such a model which can then be used to estimate the performance of each. These performances can be compared and used to formulate new and hopefully better alternatives that can also be compared with the help of the model. Such a dialogue between a decision maker and a model can be continued until satisfaction is reached or time has run out.

Simulation

The use of models in experimentation as a substitute for reality is called *simulation.* Models represent reality; simulation *imitates* it. It can make use of any of the three types of model: iconic, analogue, or symbolic.

Iconic simulations involve observing the behavior of either a real or iconically modeled entity in an iconically modeled environment, or an iconically modeled entity in a real environment. Such simulation is widely used in testing large complex physical systems and processes. For example, the aerodynamic properties of proposed aircraft are usually tested by use of small iconic models of the aircraft in a wind tunnel which, of course, is an iconic model of the environements in which the aircraft might have to operate. The model aircraft in the wind tunnel is a model of reality; the behavior of the model in the wind tunnel is a simulation of reality. We can conduct experiments by varying the properties of either the model aircraft or the wind tunnel and observing the effects of such changes on the simulated behavior.

Ship models are similarly tested in tow tanks. Pilot plants and test markets are iconically modeled environments in which production and marketing processes can be tested experimentally. Products are also widely tested under iconically modeled conditions of use. For example, estimates of the gasoline consumption of automobiles and the life of automobile tires are often obtained in this way. In both cases treadmills are used to represent the roads on which automobiles and tires are used.

Analogue simulations involve observing the behavior of an analogue model in an analogue model of an environment. For example, a number of years ago a hydraulic model (an analogue) of the British economy, the MONIAC, was constructed by the London School of Economics. It was used to simulate the effects of such changes in the British economy as devaluation of the pound, changes in the money supply, and increases in taxation or interest rates.

Symbolic simulation involves observing the behavior of a symbolically represented entity or process in a symbolically modeled environment. Suppose, for example, that we have a symbolic model of a finished-goods inventory in which the amount in inventory (the outcome variable) depends on the size and frequency of production runs (controlled variables) and on the size of demand (an uncontrolled variable). Suppose further that we know the distribution of demand per unit time; that is, the relative frequency with which any particular demand will occur, but not, of course, the demand in any particular period. Then we can evaluate production policy by taking a sample of demands from the known distribution and using them together with the model to calculate the inventory at the end of each period. From this we can estimate the average size of the finished-goods inventory associated with any such policy. This would be a symbolic simulation.

The technology of symbolic simulations has developed greatly in the last quarter century, largely stimulated by the availability of large computers. For example, urban traffic flows, multiplant operations, railroad car movement, and harbor operations have all been simulated successfully using computers without which our ability to carry out such large-scale simulations would be severely limited.

In addition to evaluating alternative means, simulation can be used in other ways that contribute significantly to the planning process: to study transitional processes, to estimate the values of uncontrolled variables, to determine the nature of the relationship between variables, and to treat variables that cannot be treated quantitatively in models. Consider each of these uses of simulation in turn.

1. *To Study Transitional Processes.* When a model can be solved analytically, the solution usually specifies only the terminal or steady state that eventually results from changing the values of the controlled variables. It does not specify the intermediate transitional states. Simulation can expose the transition to as careful a study as one may care to make. For example, the solution of a complex inventory problem involving the purchase, storage, and use of a large number of items (e.g., spare parts for aircraft) might show that the current stock levels of some items are too high and of others too low. The solution obtained analytically may tell us what the average inventory investment will be after the changes have been made and the system has settled down to a steady state. While the inventory is moving from its current state to its steady state, items that are understocked can usually be brought up to the level indicated by the solution rather quickly by buying more of them. However, items that are overstocked will come down to the appropriate level only with use, and this takes time. Consequently, although the inventory investment may *eventually* decrease if the solution is used, it will increase during the transition. It may be important to know by how much it will increase and how long it will take for the steady state to be reached. Simulation makes it possible to chart this transition and determine its characteristics.

2. *To Estimate Values of the Uncontrolled Variables in a Model, or to Determine the Nature of the Relationship Between Variables and the Outcome.* Sometimes we may be able to construct a model but be unable to evaluate all its uncontrolled variables because of lack of data. We might, however, have plenty of data on the values of outcomes and controlled variables. Then, if there are no more than a few uncontrolled variables whose previous values are not known, we can use simulation to try out a number of their possible values until we obtain one or more sets of values yielding (simulated) outcomes that closely match those known to have occurred. The choice from alternative sets of values of the uncontrolled variables that yield such matching outcomes must be based on judgment, but this judgement can subsequently be tested systematically. This kind of procedure can also be used to explore the functional form of a model; that is, the relationship between the variables and the outcome.

3. *To Treat Aspects of Choice Situations that Cannot be Incorporated into a Model.* When a problem situation involves the behavior of one or more decision makers who are not under our control, we may not be able to identify all their possible choices in advance, or, if we can, we may not know the probability of their selecting each. Furthermore, we may not be able to characterize their behavior quantitatively. If any of these conditions pertain, we cannot model the problem situation completely. Such is often the case, for example, when competition or conflict between two or more parties is involved. Then it is sometimes possible to place the parties involved, or suitable substitutes for them, in a modeled environment in which we can observe their relevant behavior. Such a simulation is called *operational gaming.*

Operational gaming is a simulation in which decision making is performed by one or more real decision makers. This term is sometimes restricted to simulations in which two or more competing decision makers take part, but this restriction is not applied here.

Gaming has come into increasing use in the study of complex military, governmental, and business operations. It is now used in the study of local, state, national, and international problems (for example, see Guetzkow [38]). Gaming, particularly in the military context, has a long history which was described in detail by Young [86] and Thomas [78], but its use as a research tool started after World War II. Hoggatt [40] noted its use as a teaching device. It has also been used to select personnel and to familiarize them with the operations of complex systems (e.g., aircraft, space vehicles, and military units).*

The uses of gaming in problem-solving research† fall into three general classes: to help (1) develop a decision model, (2) find the solution to such a model, and (3) evaluate proposed solutions to problems modeled by the game. Gaming can help in constructing a model by providing a basis for testing the relevance of variables or the functional form of the model. It can also be used to uncover possible courses of action and decision strategies and to compare the alternatives. Where a completely specified course of action or decision procedure cannot be derived analytically from a model, but a partially specified action, procedure, or policy can, its effects can be estimated by gaming.

---

*Gaming has been used in solving municipal problems by Professor Nathan Grundstein when he was at the University of Pittsburgh, and Professor Richard Meier when he was at the University of Michigan. An example of its application to the study of international problems can be found in Guetzkow [38]

†For a discussion of gaming as other than a research tool, see Thomas and Deemer [79], and Cohen and Rhenman [20]. Bibliographies on gaming may be found in [52], [58], [70], [71], and [86] Other uses of gaming can be found in [26], [41], and [65].

Gaming is essentially experimentation in which the behavior of decision makers is observed in a modeled environment.

It differs from most psychological and socio-psychological experimentation in that the conditions under which the play is observed are models of real situations about which knowledge is sought. The experimental situation is deliberately constructed to represent a real situation to which the researcher wants to draw inferences.

For reasons revealed as early as 1957 by Thomas and Deemer, gaming should be used with considerable caution. In many cases it is dangerous to draw inferences from the play of a game to behavior in the real world. This danger derives from the fact that the environment of the game may not be a good model of the real situation because, although it may have the right properties, it may have the wrong structure, that is, the relationship between these properties and the outcomes.

Much of the time we know only that the game and the situation it represents have certain properties in common; we do not know whether the structures of the game and the relevant reality are the same. Therefore, we often do not know if the way the outcome is related to the variables is the same in the game as it is in the relevant reality. Unless we have such knowledge, the game cannot legitimately be taken as a model of reality. Inferences to reality drawn from play of the game of which we do not have such knowledge are dubious at best.

Games are often easy to construct, but to construct one that is a good model of a real situation is often very difficult and time-consuming. Therefore, games that have not been shown to be adequate models of reality are often used as though they were. To do so is to misuse them.

Despite such difficulties, some games have been used effectively to evaluate alternative means. They are generally relatively simple and involve a symbolic model of a major portion of the real situation. The following is an example of such a game developed to help solve a noncompetitive problem.

As is common in many industrial situations, it was necessary in this case to find the order in which items requiring production should be processed on an assembly line. The setup costs associated with each product depended on which items preceded it on the assembly line. The problem, which was to minimize the sum of the setup costs subject to certain inventory requirements, could be represented by a table in which the cost of making any product after any other was shown. (A general solution to this problem was not available at that time. It now is.) Research revealed several decision rules for determining the sequence of the production runs, rules that appeared to yield lower costs than one would expect by using intuitive judgment. However, these rules did not completely specify the decision that should be made in any situation; some judgment was required.

The researchers themselves replanned the production of the last three years using the proposed decision rules and their judgment where required. They compared the resulting costs with those that had actually been incurred during the period. A substantial reduction was shown. However, they did not know whether such improvements could be obtained by the people who actually planned production in the plant.

A game was set up involving the rescheduling of production over a three-year period. The people who actually had scheduled production over that period were taught the new decision rules and were asked to use them along with their judgment in rescheduling the production of that period. They did so, and the results showed a significant improvement over their previous performance. On the strength of these results the rules were adopted and subsequently showed a continuing improvement over previous planning procedures.

Few would argue with the inference that the improvement in performance obtained by the use of the decision rules in this game was a legitimate basis for expecting an improvement if the rules were applied in reality. The confidence one has in such an inference derives from the belief that the model well represented the real production situation.

The use of gaming to identify possible control measures

There is one type of gaming that is particularly useful when the response of one or more competitors or other type of "enemy" must be taken into account in evaluating means. In many planning situations the effectiveness of a choice depends critically on the response to it evoked from one or more other decision makers; for example, a change in pricing policy for a product, or the amount spent on advertising it. Such situations arise in the military where the identity of the enemy and where or when it will be encountered, let alone how it will respond, are not known. Where the responses of others to our behavior cannot be predicted accurately or reliably and we cannot experiment on them, their possible behavior can sometimes be taken into account by the use of a *countermeasure* team.

A countermeasure team is made up of a very few competent planners who are familiar with competition in general or the enemy in particular. Some of them may even be former employees of competitors or members of the enemy's team. The countermeasure team plays the role of the relevant other. It is provided with a perfect intelligence system, that is, it knows exactly what the organization being planned for intends to do. The team's task is to develop counter strategies or tactics directed at minimizing the effectiveness of what the organization plans to do. When the team develops a countermeasure, its effect on activities planned by the organization is determined jointly with the organization's planners. Then the organization modifies its original strategy or tactic to take the countermeasure into account. When such a response to the countermeasure has been formulated, the countermeasure team goes back to work and tries to develop a new response to the reformulated strategy or tactic, and so on. This process continues until the countermeasure team can no longer develop an effective response, or the time required by it to do so is long enough to justify the use of the strategy or tactic by the organization.

The assumption underlying this process is that if, despite the efforts of a highly intelligent and informed (simulated) competitor, a strategy or tactic can be developed that performs well enough over a long enough period of time, it is very likely to do the same under real conditions.

EVALUATION OF MODELS

I have noted several times that the credibility attached to model-based evaluations of means should depend on how well these models represent reality. Therefore, where possible, models should be evaluated before they are used to evaluate means. The most effective techniques for doing so are statistical in character. Therefore, planners should have a considerable knowledge of these techniques. Without this there can be no assurance of the dependability of the models used in evaluating means.

The deficiencies from which a model can suffer are exactly the same as those from which a decision can suffer. This is not suprising, because a model used for evaluating means is a decision model. These deficiencies, it will be recalled, may derive from:

1. The omission of relevant variables and/or the inclusion of ones that are irrelevant.
2. The failure to control a controllable variable.
3. The omission of relevant constraints and/or the inclusion of ones that are irrelevant.
4. The incorrect formulation of the relationship between the variables and the outcomes that can occur.

The construction of models is a generalization of the process of formulating alternative means. (Therefore, all that was said about creativity in connection with means formulation is equally applicable to the construction of decision models.) The controlled variables in a model define the means. The model also represents the environment in which they will be used and specifies how changes in any variable, controlled or uncontrolled, affect the outcome.

Models may be tested either retrospectively (against past performance) or prospectively (against future performance). There is an obvious saving of time associated with retrospective testing. In such testing it is necessary to find or reconstruct the values of the controlled, uncontrolled, and outcome variables that appear in the model, and to do so for each of a sample of periods over which the model is to be tested. Then the values of the controlled and uncontrolled variables are placed in the model and estimates of the outcome variable are generated. The comparison generally takes the form of a test of the hypothesis in which the average difference between model-estimated performance and actual performance should be zero. In addition the reliability of the estimates—that is, their dispersion around actual performance—is also estimated. A good model produces unbiased and reliable estimates of the outcome; the average error is zero and the errors are narrowly distributed around actual performance.

It is not always easy to reconstruct past values of the relevant variables. For example, one might want to know both satisfied and unsatisfied *demand* for a product per unit time, but records may only show *sales* or *shipments* (satisfied demand), thus leaving unspecified the amount of unsatisfied demand. It may be difficult or impossible to determine how much more of a product could have been sold if it had not run out of stock.

In testing a model retrospectively it is critical that the periods covered provide the same variety of situations likely to be encountered in the future. The more the future is likely to differ from the past, the less appropriate retrospective testing is.

Prospective testing employs the same logic as retrospective testing, but the values of the relevant variables are observed in future periods. In both types of testing it is extremely important that the estimates of the actual outcomes be made completely independently of the model; otherwise the test is meaningless.

In some cases it is not possible to test a model, either retrospectively or prospectively. In such cases it may be possible to evaluate it partially by use of *sensitivity analysis.* Such an analysis consists of determining by how much the estimates of the values of the variables used in the evaluation process would have to be in error before the best means specified by the model performs less satisfactorily than an alternative to it. Unfortunately, it is very difficult to include more than a small number of variables in a test of the sensitivity of the outcome to them. If the magnitude of the error indicated by a sensitivity analysis seems small, then some confidence can be placed in the use of the model for evaluating means; otherwise not.

It is very important that the testability of a model be taken into account when it is being constructed. A model that cannot be tested (and many that are constructed cannot be) is no more than a conjecture. To use it is an act of pure faith; it has nothing to do with science.

Managers and planners who are served by management scientists frequently do not understand the technical aspects of the models constructed by these scientists, or of the evaluative procedures applied to them. However, it is always possible for the managers and planners to grasp the logic of the model and the evaluative procedures if they insist on being provided such understanding by the management scientists. A management scientist who cannot reveal this logic in ordinary language does not understand it.

Managers are usually at least as sensitive to the quality of research done for them as management scientists are to the quality of their managers' decision processes. Such scientists should not make the mistake of assuming that managers cannot distinguish between good and bad research because they are not researchers themselves. To do this is like assuming that one cannot tell the difference between a good and a bad egg because one cannot lay one.

DESCRIPTIVE VERSUS EXPLANATORY MODELS

It will be recalled from the discussion of the relationships between decision variables in the preceding chapter that a fundamental distinction is made between associations that are purely *descriptive* relationships and cause–effect and producer–product, both of which are *explanatory* relationships. Therefore, models based on associations are descriptive; only those based on cause–effect or producer–product are explanatory. A descriptive model describes how values of different variables change together; it does *not* describe how changes in one variable affect or produce changes in another.

Descriptive models of a certain type can be used predictively. These are models in which the values of some variables at one point in time are associated with values of other variables at a later moment of time. Econometric models are of this type, but consider a simpler example.

The number of books in children's homes has been found to be correlated with the amount of reading they do when they become adults. Given the number of books in a child's home now, we can predict how much reading he or she will do when grown up. However, we cannot infer from this association that if we change the number of books in the home now, it will change the amount of reading the child will do later. Suppose, as seems to be the case, that it is parents' attitude toward reading that produces the number of books in a home and their child's desire to read. Then, if we were to increase the number of books in the home without changing the parents' reading habits, it would have no significant effect on the child's subsequent reading.

Because implementation of means involves changing the values of controlled variables and determining what effects this has on one or more outcome variables, descriptive models cannot be used to evaluate means. Nevertheless, they are frequently and improperly used for this purpose. Econometric models, for example, are frequently used incorrectly to evaluate alternative economic policies and strategies. Little wonder that so many of the predictions of the effects of manipulating an economy miss the mark.

An explanatory model represents the way one or more variables affect or produce changes in one or more outcome variables. Therefore, they can be used to evaluate means. The difference between these two types of model is illustrated by the following case (referred to previously in Chapter 4 in another context).

In the late 1950s an oil company wanted to evaluate potential service-station sites to avoid placing stations where they would be unprofitable. An internal research group was given the task of predicting the performance of stations at potential sites. The members of this group began by interviewing a wide variety of personnel in the company, collecting opinions of which properties of a service station and its location contributed to its sales. About sixty-five variables were identified. Data were collected on each variable for several hundred stations and a multiple linear regression (an association analysis) of sales was run on these variables. About half the variables turned out to be significantly associated with sales. However, the resulting regression model did not yield predictions sufficiently accurate to avoid most of the unfavorable site selections. It reduced them by about 15 percent.

The reason for this disappointing result is clear. It does not follow, for example, that if the number of pumps at a station is increased, the station will sell more. The fact that better performing stations have more pumps on the average than do poor stations does not tell us that increasing the number of pumps will increase the number of customers or the average amount of a sale. In fact, increases in the number of customers may be responsible for the number of pumps. Furthermore, if the number of pumps is increased but the number of attendants is decreased, sales are also likely go go down.

A second (external) research team was then put to work on the site-selection problem. It was opposed to using a large number of variables because it shared a belief previously expressed in this book: that the better a phenomenon is understood, the fewer variables are required to explain it. Therefore, the team decided to determine how far it could go initially in *explaining* service-station sales using only one variable. It started with the number of vehicles passing the site because, it argued, if no cars pass a station, it can do no business whatever its other characteristics may be.

First, a precise way of describing traffic going by a station was developed. Since there are four ways that a car can either enter or leave a typical intersection, there are (in principle but not necessarily in practice) sixteen ways a car can go through it, including turnarounds through a station. A study of traffic classified by these routes revealed that most customers came out of four of them. A comparison of the percentage of cars in different routes that stopped for service suggested that as the time lost in stopping increased, the percentage of stopping decreased. This hypothesis was then tested experimentally and confirmed. The way in which lost time affected sales was also explained; it involved converting actual time lost (objective time) into *perceived* time lost (subjective time).

The research team then examined the variables that had been found to be significant in the earlier regression analysis and found that most of them were related to sales through lost time. For example, an increased number of pumps would increase sales only if it reduced the time required to obtain service.

The initial regression model was descriptive and, therefore, did not make possible effective evaluation of site selection; it did not explain a site's performance. The subsequent explanatory model made it possible not only to select sites more effectively, but also to design stations to get the most out of the site. It enabled the company to reduce the number of unprofitable stations by eighty-five percent.

SUMMARY

Once a set of alternative means has been formulated, it should be evaluated before a choice is made if the cost of selecting less than the best available means or one that is not good enough can be high. Such an evaluation can be carried out experimentally as, for example, in a well-designed market test. However, experimentation may be costly, time consuming, and, in some circumstances, precluded because of legal or regulatory constraints. In such cases, the use of models can provide an effective way of conducting the necessary evaluations.

Models are simplified representations of reality. They come in three basic forms and combinations thereof: iconic, analogue, and symbolic. An iconic model is one in which the relevant properties of reality are represented by the same properties, usually, but not necessarily, with a change of scale. In analogues the real properties are represented by others that are easier to manipulate. In symbolic models the properties and the relationships between them are represented by symbols.

Some symbolic models can be manipulated mathematically to provide an evaluation of alternative means. This is possible when the alternatives can be characterized by sets of values of quantifiable variables. Many of these evaluative procedures are available in computer programs; others are easily programmable.

It is also possible to conduct experimental evaluations of alternative means by using models of any of the three forms. Such vicarious experimentation is called simulation. Where the relevant phenomenon involves one or more decision makers whose behavior cannot be completely characterized in a model, that decision maker or a surrogate can be incorporated into the experiment. Such simulation is called gaming. Gaming is an experiment carried out in a modeled environment. Therefore, it makes it possible to draw legitimate inferences from the experimental behavior to behavior in the environment represented.

The usefulness of models in evaluating means depends critically on whether they describe or explain the relevant phenomenon. Descriptive models can be used, at best, only to forecast what will happen if there is no planned intervention. But since means are planned interventions, descriptive models have no use in evaluating them.

The design of effective evaluation of means requires technical competence in constructing models, manipulating them mathematically, in designing both natural and simulated experiments, and in carrying out statistical analyses of data obtained from experimentation of both types.

A well-conducted evaluation of means can often suggest how to formulate new means that are better than any previously tested. Moreover, it can also suggest how to formulate means that can be improved with use, thereby facilitating learning and adaptation.

CHAPTER TEN

RESOURCE PLANNING

Money, n. *A blessing that is of no advantage to us*
excepting when we part with it.

AMBROSE BIERCE

Of all the phases of corporate planning, resource planning is probably
the most highly developed. In many organizations resource planning, or a
part of it, financial planning, is virtually all there is to planning. The
pervasiveness of this bias is reflected in the fact that many corporations
locate their planning units in financial departments.

Resource planning is only one aspect of planning, neither more nor
less important than any other part of it. It should affect and be affected
by every other aspect of planning. Moreover, financial planning is only
one aspect of resource planning. Money is not the only or the most
important resource required by a corporation. It is often incorrectly assumed that if enough money were available, all other resources could be
obtained. This is not always the case; for example, no amount of money
can buy energy or skills that are not available. If anything, competent
personnel are more likely to attract money than money is to attract them.
Furthermore, critical shortages of nonfinancial resources are at least as
likely to occur as critical shortages of money.

Four types of resource should be taken into account: (1) *inputs*—materials, supplies, energy, and services; (2) *facilities and equipment*—

capital investments; (3) *personnel*; and (4) *money*. Money can be considered to be a meta-resource since, as Ambrose Bierce observed, its only value lies in its use to obtain other resources.

Information is also a resource, but it requires a different treatment. As discussed in Chapter 6, the idealized design of a corporation should include the design of a management system. This system should, in turn, include a design on an information system that can supply whatever information is required. Ways of creating such a system are selected in means planning. Then the resources required by these means, like those required by any other means, are dealt with in resource planning.

Each type of resource other than money required can and should be divided into relevant categories for planning purposes; for example, facilities can be divided into plants, warehouses, office space, laboratories, and so on. Personnel can be categorized using occupational classes; for example, managerial, technical, clerical, sales, hourly, and so on.

Resource planning should involve asking and answering the following questions about inputs, facilities and equipment, and personnel:

1. How much of each of these types of resource will be required, and when and where will it be required?
2. How much of each will be available at each relevant location at each relevant point in time, assuming no changes in corporate and environmental behavior?
3. What are the gaps between requirements as determined in step (1) and availabilities as determined in step (2)?
4. How should the gaps be filled: by developing or generating resources internally or by acquiring them from external sources?
5. How much will filling the gaps cost?

Once these questions have been answered a related set of questions can be asked about money:

1. What is the total amount required, when and where?
2. How much will be available at each relevant location at each relevant point in time?
3. How large are the gaps?
4a. If the required amount of money will not be available, either how can it be obtained or how should previously-made planning decisions be modified so they can be financed with the funds that will be available?

4b. If more than the required amount of money will be available, how should previously made planning decisions be modified so as to use the excess productively?

Now we consider planning for each type of resource in more detail.

INPUTS—MATERIALS, SUPPLIES, ENERGY, AND SERVICES

The inputs required for those activities planned by a company can create two types of problem. First, their future availability might be in doubt, as is currently the case with oil. Second, even if available, their expected costs may increase at a rate that will create problems. Potential shortages and high costs often go together.

There are three ways by which a corporation may be able to deal with shortages and high costs of resources; substitution, vertical integration, and redesign of products or operations.

1. A corporation might be able to find substitutes for costly or scarce inputs. For example, it might convert from the use of oil to the use of natural gas or coal, or parts made of one material might be replaced with ones made of another. It might also be possible to substitute people for scarce or costly machines, even though the trend has been the other way.

2. A corporation might integrate vertically, thereby supplying itself with all or part of a required input. For example, several brewers now manufacture some of the cans they require. Not only does this make their supply more secure, but it gives them some control over the pricing of their external suppliers. However, they run the risk of making their suppliers' business so unattractive as to drive them from it, thereby requiring complete self-supply. This could create a need for more investment than is either possible or desirable.

"Make-or-buy" decisions should be reviewed periodically with respect to all important inputs, whether goods or services. Internally-provided services tend to become more expensive over time because service departments bureaucratize more rapidly than do line or operating units. This follows from the fact that adequate measures of their performance are seldom applied to them. It is not surprising, therefore, that many companies have found it desirable to contract out such services as security, maintenance, housekeeping, computation, and even research and development.

3. By redesigning products or operations it is sometimes possible for a corporation to reduce the amount of a particular kind of required input.

Currently, for example, many such changes are being made to conserve energy; automobiles are being redesigned to reduce their weight, hence material as well as energy requirements. Processes can often be redesigned to reduce waste and scrap, and even to recycle what waste and scrap there is. The reclamation and recycling of previously discarded products such as cans, bottles, and newspapers have long been used to reduce material costs.

If shortages or high costs are not certain to occur *contingency planning* is called for; that is, planning for each identifiable possibility so it can be responded to quickly and effectively if and when it occurs. Contingency planning is "old hat" to the military; for example, in preparing for an invasion consideration is always given to a wide range of possible outcomes, including the need to retreat, and plans are made for each.

The point to be kept in mind in planning for inputs is that neither the requirements for them generated by previous planning decisions nor their sources of supply should be taken for granted. The assumptions used in estimating input requirements and deciding where to get them should be carefully reviewed to be sure that alleged requirements are real, and that better sources and more effective ways of obtaining them are not available. I have seen companies that have neither reviewed their make-or-buy decisions nor reevaluated their sources of supply in more than a decade.

Too frequently purchasing and contracting departments do not play a significant role in planning; they should. Their productivity should be expected to increase just as that of other functions. To make this possible they must interact with design and operating functions as well as service units, collaborate with them in the exploration of alternative requirements and sources of supply, and do all this within the context of planning.

The output of input planning is a set of cost estimates of the inputs required per unit time over the period covered by the means plan. The assumptions on which these estimates are based should be made explicit so they can be monitored carefully over time.

FACILITIES AND EQUIPMENT

A large number of mathematical techniques are available for use in facilities and equipment planning (see, for example, Ackoff and Sasieni [9]). There are few aspects of such planning for which relevant and useful quantitative procedures are not available.

Once the requirements for additional facilities and equipment have been extracted from previously made planning decisions, models and algorithms can be applied to such questions as the following:

1. *How large should a facility or piece of equipment be?* For example, one may have a choice of building one large plant or several small ones in different locations. The relative advantages of such alternatives can be at least partially determined by use of readily available mathematical techniques.

2. *What location of a facility will minimize the sum of the costs of transporting inputs to it and outputs from it?* These costs are not the only relevant variables in locating such facilities as plants and warehouses, but they are important and can even be overriding.

3. *In view of the uncertainties of demand for the output of a new facility and lack of complete control over its construction time, when should its construction be initiated?*

The techniques for handling equipment-planning questions are also highly developed; for example, when should equipment be replaced? Replacement of equipment and facilities obviously depends on how well they have been maintained. Mathematical procedures for designing effective maintenance policies are also available.

Facility and equipment decisions always depend on estimates of future demand. Because such estimates are almost always subject to errors, it is desirable to hedge against them. One of the most effective ways of doing so is to acquire plant or equipment that can be converted to uses other than the ones for which they are primarily intended. Flexibility, convertibility, expandability, and contractability are obvious hedges against uncertainty. These properties involve a cost, of course, but it can be weighed against the expected cost of error of the estimates of demand.

PERSONNEL

Personnel planning should be addressed to the following questions.

1. For each year, what is the total number of people of each type required to implement the means previously selected?

2. For each year, what is the total number of people of each type expected to be available, given current personnel policies and practices?
3. For each year, what are the gaps between the answers to questions (1) and (2)?
4. How are the positive gaps to be filled and the negative gaps to be eliminated?

Each of these questions except the third requires further examination.

Number of People Required

In order to determine the number of people required to carry out a specified activity it is necessary to use (implicitly or explicitly) a *personnel* (input–output) *function*. Such a function relates the amount of personnel allocated to a specific activity to the amount of output of that activity. Such functions usually take the shape shown in Figure 10.1.

For example, a certain amount of selling effort is usually required before a prospect begins to respond; a call by one salesperson once a year may be unlikely to yield any sales. The amount of effort (number of calls) at which the response (purchases) "take off" is called the *threshold*. In general, the response then increases approximately in proportion to the amount of effort until the customer's response rate begins to decrease at the point of diminishing return. If additional calls are made the customer will reach a point at which he or she cannot or is unwilling to buy more, the saturation point. Increased calls beyond this point eventually become offensive, at the supersaturation point, and the customer's purchases decrease thereafter, often precipitously.

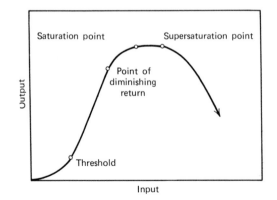

Figure 10.1   A typical resource (input–output) function.

If one had an input-output function for each possible combination of actual and potential customers and salespeople, it would be possible to determine the optimal number of calls to make on each account, hence the number and mix of salespeople that would maximize sales or the return on their cost. If a company has more than a few customers and salespeople it is not feasible to develop all the relevant input-output functions. However, the customers and salespeople can be grouped into a feasible number of classes based on their performance characteristics, and aggregated input-output functions can be obtained for them. Use of such aggregated functions result in decisions that are less efficient than can be obtained with ones that are individualized, but more efficient than can usually be obtained by use of qualitative judgment alone.

Without an explicit input-output function, personnel planning is essentially judgmental, no matter how quantitative the analyses involved. Because of the amount of experimentation (hence time and cost) that their development requires, most personnel planners do not have and do not try to develop such functions. They resort to *implicit* input-output functions, ones that exist only in their heads. The accuracy and reliability of such functions cannot be checked, hence cannot be systematically improved.

Most explicit input-output functions used by personnel planners are linear; they are obtained by fitting a straight line to a set of points representing jointly observed personnel inputs and associated outputs. Such a procedure suffers from serious deficiencies.

First, even if the "correct" line were obtained by sheer luck, it would be valid only between the threshold and point of diminishing return. Therefore, it would incorrectly predict possible changes in output before the threshold and after the point of diminishing return.

Second, even if a significant *association* were found between input and output, it does not follow that the amount of input is causally connected to the amount of output. (Recall the discussion of association and causality in Chapter 8.)

Third, the use of lines fitted to past data in personnel planning can at best ensure only continuation of previously attained levels of productivity. Furthermore, it can do this much only if the activity and the system involved do not change in significant ways over time. Most such activities and systems do change significantly over time; for example, when a buyers' market shifts to a sellers' market or there are relevant new technological developments in the products involved.

Fourth, in comparing the productivity of inputs in different types of account, it is critical that the variability of outputs within each class of account be less than the variability between outputs of different types of account. If this is not the case, differences in the outputs of different classes of account cannot be inferred from even large differences in their average outputs.

Too much effort has been wasted in trying to find easy ways of estimating future personnel requirements. The understanding that is required for the development of effective estimating procedures requires more research than is usually associated with personnel planning. There follows a relatively detailed example of how research can be used fruitfully in the personnel-planning process.

An Example of Research on Personnel Requirements

Although complete knowledge of relevant personnel input–output functions is necessary for completely effective personnel planning, partial knowledge can nevertheless yield results of considerable value. This was shown in a study conducted in support of a long-range planning effort of General Electric's Lamp Division.*

As part of the planning process it was necessary to determine how many additional salespeople would be required in each of the next five years. These estimates were initially prepared by assuming that the average number of accounts covered by salespeople at that time was optimal. The planners did not have time to investigate this assumption. As a result, the plan that was produced specified a large number of additional salespeople in each of the next five years.

The planners felt sufficiently insecure about these estimated requirements to recommend that research be initiated to determine the average number of accounts that should be assigned to salesmen. This recommendation was accepted.

The research began with an analysis of the sales reports prepared by salesmen in the normal course of their work. It revealed that changes over two successive years in the number of calls made on accounts had no association with changes in the amounts sold to these accounts. This finding held for every class of account no matter how complex or sophisticated a classification of accounts was tried.

In order to check this surprising result another type of analysis was carried out. Accounts were classified by whether they had an increase or decrease in the number of sales calls in 1953 as compared with 1952. They were then subclassified according to whether the number of sales calls made on them in 1954 was an increase or decrease relative to 1953. This yielded four classes of account, as seen in Table 10.1.

*A more detailed account of this study is provided in [82], and a discription of the planning process in (35).

Table 10.1   Changes in Number of Calls

Class	1952–1953	1953–1954
1	Increase	Increase
2	Increase	Decrease
3	Decrease	Increase
4	Decrease	Decrease

No significant differences were found in the average changes in amounts sold to accounts in these classes.

Both analyses showed that on the average the number of sales calls being made on accounts fell on the plateau between the saturation and supersaturation points of the relevant input–output function.

How could these results be used for personnel-planning purposes? They suggested that some reduction in number of calls (hence in the number of salespeople) could be made without reducing sales. But how much of a reduction? The maximum reduction that could be justified by available data would result from decreasing the number of sales calls made on each account to the smallest number of calls that had been made on it in an any of the last three years. If, for example, an account had received sixty calls in 1952, forty in 1953, and fifty in 1954, the number of future calls per year could be reduced to forty. In the absence of detailed knowledge of the underlying input–output functions this was a conservative estimate. Larger reductions could probably have been made for many accounts, but the available data could not justify them.

This procedure indicated that a 20 percent reduction in sales calls could be obtained without any effect on sales. However, it raised the question of whether assigning more accounts to salespeople—in order to obtain the reduced number of calls per account and to reduce the sales force—would affect the productivity of individual sales calls. To answer this question an analysis was made of the performance of those salespeople in one district who already carried more accounts than were recommended by the researchers. It revealed that these salespeople had a *higher* average return per call than the other salespeople in their district, and that they had obtained a *higher* total amount of sales. This put the question to rest.

This much had been done using only readily available data. Collection of new data was initiated by conducting a time study of salespeople in one sales district. In addition to their regular sales reports the salespeople provided specially requested information on each call made during a designated month. They recorded the mileage travelled to the account, the time of travel, waiting time, and interview time associated with each call. They also recorded the amount of administrative and preparatory time spent in their offices and at home.

Such data were collected from only nine of over 300 salespeople, and only for one month. Therefore, no general conclusions could be drawn from them. Nevertheless, some of the results were consistent enough over the sample to suggest that they probably held generally. Some of the more important of these results were as follows.

First, travel time was related to distance traveled only within wide limits. The kind of territory appeared to be more important than distance. Calls in metropolitan areas consumed much more travel time than might be expected; those in rural areas much less. The travel time per call in the sample was almost identical for urban and rural territories even though the average distance traveled per call was twice as great in the rural areas. The most stable estimate of travel time turned out to be a percentage of total time, independent of the distance traveled.

Second, a significant portion of total time was spent in waiting to see a buyer. It was not related to the type or size of account.

Third, time with buyers varied for different types of account but not for the four most important ones.

Fourth and finally, administration consumed much more time than had been expected.

Using the time data and information on number of calls made, it was possible to estimate the cost of sales to each type of account. It was also possible to estimate the amount sold per sales call and the profit derived from each type of account. By combining these estimates, estimates were generated of the net return per sales dollar spent on each type of account. Differences among these returns were as great as eight to one among major classes of account, and several hundred to one among minor categories. These results indicated that the practice of allocating sales costs proportionally to sales volume led to serious errors. The appropriate accounting changes were made.

The analysis was further extended to include calls made on prospects. Those that had been converted into accounts were classified in the same way as old accounts had been, and returns per call were determined for both the sum of before-conversion and after-conversion calls per year, and for after-conversion calls alone. It was found that on the average new accounts yielded considerably less return per call (in the first year) than did old accounts. Certain classes of new accounts, however, yielded more return per call in their first year than did certain classes of old accounts. This indicated that a reallocation of calls, reducing the number on certain types of old account and increasing the number on certain types of prospect, would increase the productivity of sales calls.

Table 10.2 Prospect-Call Analysis

Number of Calls	Cumulative Number of Accounts Obtained	Cumulative Number of Prospects Dropped	Cumulative Totals, Number of Calls	Number of Calls per Conversion
1	30	220	500	16.7
2	50	300	750	15.0
3	65	325	900	13.8
4	70	350	1010	14.4
5	72	370	1090	15.1
6	73	380	1148	15.7

Finally, an analysis was carried out to determine how many unsuccessful calls should be made on a prospect before giving up. A table was prepared listing the number of prospects and the number of calls made on them over a two-year period. A similar compilation of modified data is shown in Table 10.2. In the actual data as many as forty calls had been made on a prospect in one year.

An analysis of the modified data in Table 10.2 shows that a maximum of three calls per prospect yields the maximum average number of new accounts obtained per call. If this policy had been followed, assuming that additional prospects of the same type could have been found (a safe assumption in this case), 248 calls (1148-900) would have been made on these prospects. This number of calls would have yielded an expected eighteen (248/13.8) new accounts. The data in this table indicate that the 248 calls actually made produced only eight (73-65) new accounts. Thus the analysis suggested that a policy of a maximum of three calls per prospect could yield a 14 percent increase in the number of new accounts (from seventy-three to eighty-three) with the same number of calls. In the real case an increase of 11 percent was indicated.

On the basis of these analyses several actions were taken, the most important of which was that planned additions to the sales force were curtailed. Nevertheless, planned sales goals were subsequently met. The annual savings obtained by *not* acquiring the additional salespeople originally recommended was approximately twenty-five times the cost of the research.

Some Problems in Personnel-numbers Planning

The personnel-numbers planning procedures that have been discussed are applicable wherever relatively large numbers of people are involved in essentially the same type of activity. In most however, there are usually a large number of tasks in each of which relatively few are engaged but which collectively involve many people. Furthermore, even where large numbers of people are involved in similar tasks, the content or environment of these tasks can change so rapidly that they preclude derivation of relevant input-output functions from history. For example, responsiveness to selling effort devoted to one product may change when the product changes and as the mix of initial, replacement, and expansion sales of a product changes.

Centralized personnel planning is likely to be very difficult or even ineffective in such situations. Even where it is possible, the interactive planner tries to place responsibility for acquiring personnel in the units that will use them and tries to develop measurements of performance that will motivate their managers to seek optimal personnel levels. He or she also provides research assistance to these managers to enable them to better estimate their requirements and evaluate their previous estimates. Then their estimates of unit personnel requirements are sent to higher-level planning groups. These groups may have to modify lower-level estimates in order to take account of changes planned at higher levels. Such adjustments of lower-level estimates should be worked out with those who prepared them so they come to understand the reasons for the changes.

Where small numbers are involved in each of a large number of different tasks, each one cannot be planned for separately. Such tasks must be planned for in the aggregate, seeking as much flexibility in the personnel involved as possible. There is no better protection against errors in personnel planning than personnel who are ready, willing, and able to move from one task to another.

The Numbers Game

As noted earlier, there is a tendency in many organizational units to accumulate as much personnel as possible. This tendency is a consequence of the common practice of assigning status to units proportionally to the number of people they contain. Unless there is a measure of performance applied to units that decreases with overstaffing, the tendency to overstaff can gather momentum and eventually culminate in a bureaucracy whose cost is borne by other units in the organization and the corporation as a whole.

On the other hand, the corporation as a whole and each of its units—which have the societal function of producing and distributing wealth—should employ as many people as they can *productively*. When, despite their best efforts to the contrary, they must let people go, they should make every effort to help them find alternative employment. Such assistance should be planned for as thoroughly as recruitment and hiring.

Determining How Many Will Be Available and Required

Along with estimates of the number of each type of personnel that will be required, estimates of the number that will be available should also be prepared. Preparation of these estimates necessitates determining the number of employees currently in each occupational category and then estimating their movement in and out of these classes, usually for each year covered by the plan. Movement out of a category may be because of firing, quitting, retirement, promotion, or demotion. What is required, therefore, are tables for each year covered by the plan showing the movement of personnel. An example of an appropriate form is shown in Figure 10.2. The changes that should be planned for are entered in the last column of this figure.

Insert Fig. 10.2 W-17

Personnel requirements in each category can be filled either by movement within the organization or by hiring. In determining the number to be hired, it should be borne in mind that the level of recruitment, particularly of professional personnel, cannot be reduced drastically from one year to the next without adversely affecting recruiting efforts in succeeding years. This is particularly true when recruiting fresh college graduates.

Movement of personnel from one category to another may require training. Training may also be required to prevent obsolescence within a category. Therefore, a plan should be prepared for providing what education is required or desirable. It can be provided either internally or externally.

Fair Employment

Equal employment of women and members of minorities (target groups) is being pressed by legislation and an increasing social conscience. The logic often used by corporations in responding to such pressure is as follows.

1. The percentage of target-group members who work in the company is subtracted from the percentage in the labor market from which employees are drawn. The difference is taken as the gap to be closed. Closing this gap is taken to be a fair-share objective.

2. The percentage of target-group workers in each unit and category of personnel in the company is determined and compared with the company's target percentage. The objective here is to approximate the same

Year _____

| Personnel category | Number available at beginning of year (a) | Number leaving during year | | | | Number transferred out to | | | | Number transferred in (d) | Number available at end of year (e) = (a − b − c + d) | Number required at end of year (f) | Number to be acquired (+) or moved out (−) (g)=(f − e) |
		Fired	Quit	Retired	Total (b)	P_1	P_2	P_n	Total (c)				
P_1						▨				(j)			
P_2							▨			(k)			
. . .								▨		(l)			
P_n								▨		(m)			
Total						(j)	(k)	(l)	(m)		▨		

Figure 10.2 A personnel-requirements planning table.

percentage in each organizational unit and personnel category as is intended for the company as a whole. This is sometimes called the balance objective.

3. The target labor market is surveyed for the skills available in it, and, in light of the findings obtained, feasible annual share and balance goals are set.

4. Alternative training programs are evaluated with respect to their ability to reduce the difference between what is estimated to be a *feasible* share and balance and a *fair* share and balance. A selection is made from such programs on the basis of some kind of cost-effectiveness study.

5. Consideration is sometimes given to the problem of integrating target employees into the organization. To assist in doing so, programs are sometimes designed to make other employees more tolerant of and receptive to target employees.

Such planning is a considerable advance over the kind of indifference or antagonism to minorities and women that helped produce the racial and sexual discrimination that prevails in the United States. But the sense of righteousness that often accompanies such planning should not obscure its shortcomings.

First, note that unless *every* employer seeks to employ a fair share of a target group, equal employment of its members cannot be obtained. Not all companies do, nor are they likely to. Furthermore, since a fair share is set as a target (hence is a *maximum* share to be obtained), underachievement is more likely than overachievement. Therefore, unless some companies are willing to hire more than their fair share, corporations collectively must be prepared either to support governmental programs that will care for those not taken care of by private enterprise, or if the government does not provide such programs, to suffer the social turbulence that is very likely to follow.

Second, such equal opportunity programs as are usually conceived and considered in this type of planning are not likely to be effective relative to the hard core of the unemployed in the target groups. Members of this core are usually so alienated from the culture of the majority, hence so uncomfortable in or repelled by it, that they either will not accept work out of their neighborhoods or if they do, will not stick with it. Therefore, there is a great need for increased employment opportunities in or near the neighborhoods in which they reside, employment that can provide a transitional learning experience so that more will become willing and able to work outside their neighborhoods. For this reason, minority personnel planning should consider establishing company-owned or company-operated establishments in urban ghettos that will employ significant numbers of otherwise unemployable members of minority groups. (IBM has done just this.) In designing such half-way operations it is necessary to relax the notion of training people to fit a job, at least initially, and to use ingenuity in designing jobs to fit the people involved and to motivate them to seek new skills and advancement.

Indigenous self-development groups in the ghetto should be invited to participate in the design and operation of such programs. Not only can they contribute conceptually, but they can also apply effective pressure to keep people on the job. Furthermore, such involvement strengthens the indigenous groups and thus further accelerates development of their neighborhoods.

It is difficult for some companies to launch such programs on their own. Therefore, collaboration with other companies is often necessary. Assistance in organizing such collaboration can sometimes be obtained from local universities.

For a corporation to engage successfully in this broader concept of equal-opportunity employment, a senior manager should be made responsible for it. This should be his or her major responsibility. This manager should be an "up and comer," not a down and outer." Equal-opportunity employment is too frequently treated as a pasture into which managers for whom no other use can be found are placed to graze. Such a practice often evokes justifiable minority labeling of company efforts as tokenism.

What appear to be minority personnel problems are often majority personnel problems. Recall the cases involving black and Mexican workers described in Chapter 4.

FINANCIAL PLANNING

Using the output of previous aspects of resource planning it is possible to initiate financial planning. Such planning is considerably facilitated by the use of a corporate financial model. Such a model is a set of interconnected equations that can be used for estimating the financial consequences of a wide variety of planning decisions. These consequences can be estimated for a number of different assumptions about future business conditions.

No one financial model can apply to every corporation nor may one model be applicable to different parts of the same corporation. Nevertheless, the general structure of such models tends to be the same, however varied they may be in detail. This structure is shown in Figures 10.3, 10.4, and 10.5. As can be seen, there are four submodels:

1. The capital-requirements submodel (Figure 10.3).
2. The capital-availability submodel (Figure 10.3).
3. The cost-and-expense submodel (Figure 10.4).
4. The sales submodel (Figure 10.5).

Separate models for all but capital availability are usually required for each product type, geographically defined market, or type of customer. In general, the capital-availability submodel can serve the corporation as a whole, but it can also be subdivided to treat parts of the corporation separately.

The planning decisions that provide inputs to the sales, cost and expense, and capital-requirements submodels are interdependent. For example, the amount of a product that can be sold might depend on the production capacity made available, and the amount of capacity made available might depend on the amount of sales believed to be possible. Similarly, costs of production depend on the amount invested in improving production facilities.

Financial models are normally designed to project *annual* financial reports, but they can be designed for longer or shorter periods. They are also usually designed to project five or ten years, but this is subject to modification.

The usefulness of financial models is greatly enhanced when they are computerized. This facilitates rapid exploration of a large number of alternative means and environmental assumptions. Such explorations obviously have great value in the planning process.

It is possible to use financial models to estimate a wide variety of financial consequences of means and environmental conditions. For example, they can be used to generate projections of such performance measures as:

1. Earnings per share.
2. Dividends per share.
3. Return on investment or assets.
4. Profit per unit sold.
5. Capital availability.
6. Debt-to-equity ratios.
7. Market shares.

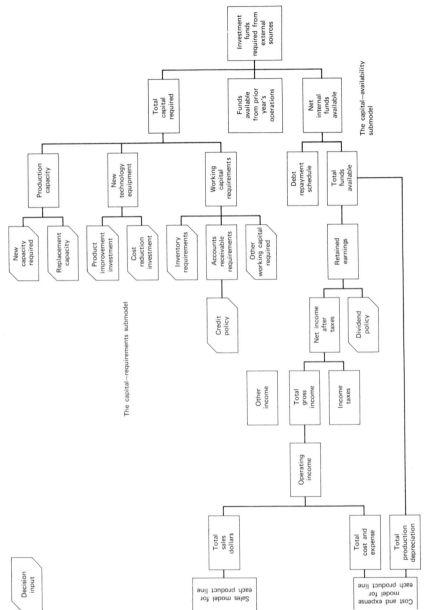

Figure 10.3 An example of a corporate financial model.

228

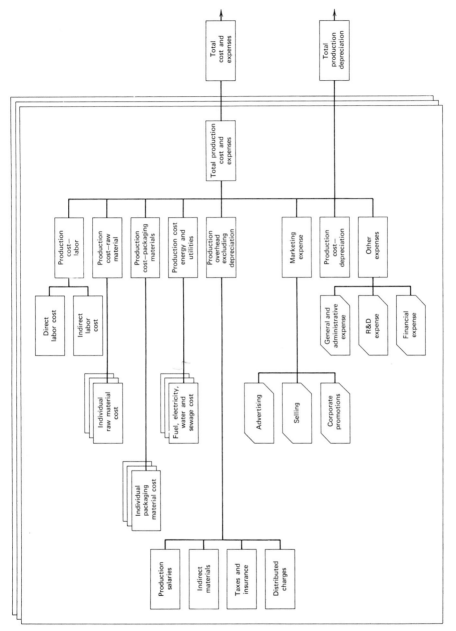

Figure 10.4 A typical cost-and-expense submodel.

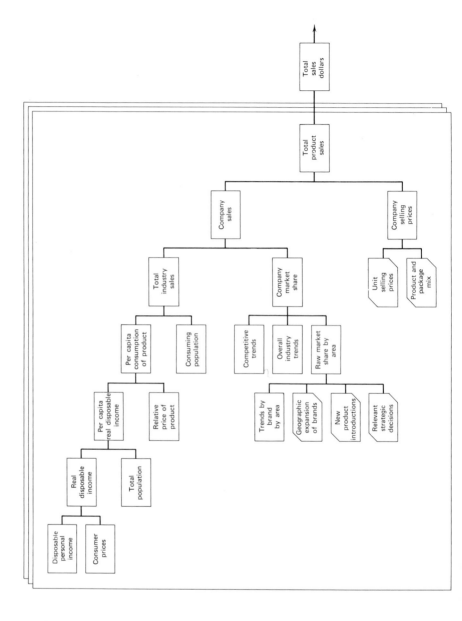

Among the types of alternative means that can be evaluated by using financial models are:

1. Pricing policies.
2. Dividend policies.
3. Borrowing policies.
4. Plant modernization or replacement programs.
5. Process or product modifications.
6. Market-mix strategies.

Finally, among the conditions of the business environment in which sensitivity can be estimated are:

1. Rate of inflation.
2. Cost of money.
3. Tax rates.
4. Depreciation allowances.
5. Wage rates.
6. Costs of energy and materials.

SUMMARY

Resource planning involves determining (1) the amount and kind of each type of resource required by the means plan, (2) how much of each will be available, (3) what the gaps are between requirements and availabilities, and (4) how they are to be filled. Four types of resource are usually relevant: inputs (materials, supplies, energy, and services), facilities and equipment, personnel, and money.

Planning for inputs requires consideration of their potential shortages and high costs. There are three ways these possible deficiencies can be bypassed: by substitution of other inputs, vertical integration, and redesign of products and processes. If shortages and high costs are not certain but there is some significant chance of their occurring, contingency planning is well advised.

Facility and equipment planning can be greatly aided by use of mathematical models and procedures for extracting solutions to problems from them. They enable one to determine such things as the size of future facilities, their location, when they should be made available, the assignment of work to them, and from what sources to supply them. Equipment can be similarly treated, for example, relevant replacement and maintenance policies can be developed by the use of available mathematical procedures. Such procedures are seldom sufficient for making a planning decision because the models employed can seldom include all the relevant variables, particularly qualitative variables. Therefore, some judgment is usually required to temper the output of mathematical procedures.

Personnel planning is in general the least developed aspect of resource planning. It is usually carried out on a piecemeal basis using extrapolations from the past for estimating future requirements. Such procedures can at best only assure continuation of previously attained levels of efficiency. Effective personnel planning requires developing personnel input–output functions that show the causal connection between number and type of personnel assigned to a task and their output. Development of such functions usually requires some experimentation, much of which can be done without serious disruption of normal operations. Even with partial information and understanding obtained in this way, significant improvements in the use of personnel can often be realized.

Effective use of personnel can sometimes result from application of appropriately designed incentive systems.

Minority personnel planning is receiving increasing attention. The search for a fair share and balance of minority employees is not likely to yield a solution to our related social problems. Many organizations are going to have to do more than their fair share because many others cannot or will not do their part.

Corporate planners should be concerned with the humane use of human beings because these free-willed individuals can either destroy a plan or magnify its benefits. What they do depends on how well their own and the organization's objectives are coordinated.

The outputs of the preceding three types of resource planning provide the inputs necessary for financial planning. Such planning is considerably facilitated by the use of a corporate financial model. This kind of model usually has four interdependent submodels: for capital requirements, costs and expenses, sales, and capital availability. Such models can be used to explore the financial feasibility and desirability of alternative plans, indicating where changes may be required to improve them. They can also be used to determine the financial sensitivity of plans to a wide variety of possible changes in the business environment.

However good a corporate plan may be in other respects, it will not be a good plan unless its expected financial consequences are at least satisfactory. Therefore, financial planning is, in effect, the bottom line of corporate planning.

CHAPTER ELEVEN

IMPLEMENTATION AND CONTROL OF PLANS AND PLANNING

To one who, journeying through night and fog,
Is mired neck-deep in an unwholesome bog,
Experience, like the rising of the dawn,
Reveals the path that he should not have gone.

AMBROSE BIERCE

The last phase of interactive planning is concerned with carrying out the decisions made in the prior phases, and controlling their implementation and subsequent performance. It is through implementation and control that continuous feedback is obtained. These, combined with surveillance of the relevant organization and environments, provide the inputs required for continuous planning and make possible the improvement of its output.

IMPLEMENTATION AND CONTROL OF PLANS

In this last phase of the planning cycle, decisions should be made concerning who should be responsible for doing what and when they should do it. Such decisions require the translation of previously made planning

233

decisions into a set of assignments and schedules. These should be developed jointly by those who are to be responsible for carrying them out, those to whom they report, and those who report to them. Responsibility for coordinating the assignments and schedules should rest with the planning boards described in Chapter 3. Information on all assignments and schedules should be given to the corporate planning staff so that it can maintain a comprehensive description and assessment of the plan's implementation.

Planning for implementation can be initiated by preparing a PERT-like flow chart of the activities required by the pursuit of each goal and objective previously designated in the planning. An example of such a chart is shown in Figure 11.1. It is one that was used by a company to cover the first phases of development of a new food product.

Such flow charts should identify the activities required, the relationships between them, and the time allocated to each. If the different activities shown are to be assigned to different individuals or units, these should be designated on the chart. (They have been removed from Figure 11.1 to protect the identity of the company involved).

To facilitate control of the implementation and control of the plan, each flow chart should be transformed into an implementation and control form such as is shown in Figure 11.2. This form should specify the following:

1. The nature of the task to be carried out.
2. The relevant goal or objective.
3. Who is responsible for carrying it out.
4. The steps to be taken.
5. Who is responsible for each step.
6. The timing of each step.
7. The money allocated to each step, if any.
8. The critical assumptions on which the schedule is based.
9. The expected performance and when it is expected.
10. The assumptions on which this expectation is based.

Since each step shown in Figure 11.2 has two rows beside it labeled planned and actual, progress can be recorded on this form and compared with what was intended. This form can also be used to compare actual and planned expenditures, both by step and time period. Such comparisons make it possible to detect quickly the need for corrective action. Explanations of and comments on significant deviations of actual from planned performance should be recorded in the last column along with any corrective action taken.

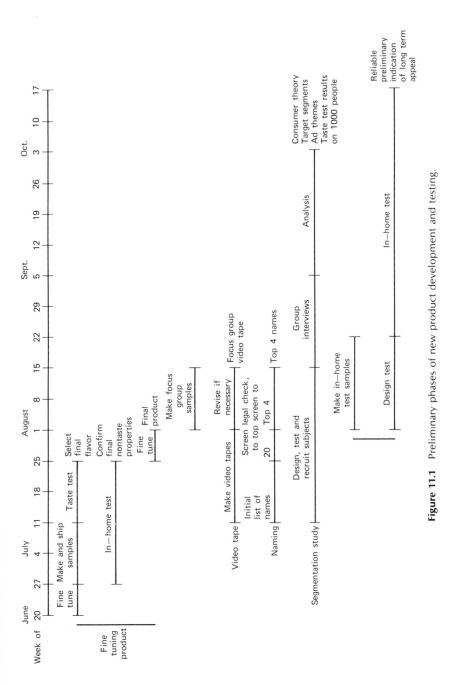

Figure 11.1 Preliminary phases of new product development and testing.

Task:

Goal or objective

Date of issue:

Responsibility of:

Steps	Resposibility of		Percent completed and expenditures: Time periods 1		2		. . .		n		Comments, explanations and corrective actions
			%	$	%	$	%	$	%	$	
		Planned									
		Actual									
		Planned									
		Actual									
		Planned									
		Actual									
		Planned									
		Actual									
	Total expenditures	Planned									
		Actual									

Assumptions on which implementation schedule is based:

Expected performance and when expected:

Assumptions on which expected performance is based:

Figure 11.2 An example of an implementation and control form.

Copies of the updated implementation and control forms should be provided to the appropriate planning boards—the one to which responsibility for implementation has been assigned, and the ones at the levels immediately above and below. In addition, a copy of each such form should be sent to the corporate planning staff. This staff should evaluate continuously the implementation and performance of the plan as a whole, and the controls to which these are subject.

Any part of a task that is assigned to someone other than the one responsibile for implementation of the task as a whole should itself be treated as a task for which an implementation and control form should be prepared.

The assumptions and expectations that appear on implementation and control forms can be collected and summarized on a form such as is shown in Figure 11.3. This form, or one similar to it, can be used to control the control process. It indicates who is responsible for checking what, and when they are to do it. Their results can be entered in the box of the appropriate time period. Every manager and his planning board should maintain a copy of this form and review it regularly.

In the steps described above considerable emphasis is placed on control. This is done for a reason that was well expressed by E. H. Vogel, Jr. [81] when he was Vice President of Marketing of Anheuser-Busch, Inc.:

> We did not try to impose recommendations [derived from research] as though we had suddenly gained possession of ultimate truth. We usually initiated the application of recommendations on a small scale with close controls imposed on them. As confidence in results developed, we extended applications.
>
> No matter how generally management accepted a research result it was never applied without a well-designed control system to tell us whether the recommendation worked as expected. We have learned as much from the feed-back such control provided as we have from the research that produced the initial recommendations.
>
> More important, perhaps, is that we now design controls for evaluating decisions which management reaches without the benefit of research. This enables them to learn more rapidly and accurately from experience, and it has indoctrinated management with an experimental approach to decision making. (p.25)

To put it another way, if an organization's ability to improve its performance continuously is to be developed, the implementation of plans should be undertaken *experimentally*. Experimentation is *controlled experience*; it enables us to learn much more rapidly and effectively than we can from ordinary experience and trial and error.

Unit: Date:

	Task to which related and who is responsible for it	Time periods (* indicates time to check)				Comments
		1	2	. . .	n	
Implementation assumptions						
Performance expectations						
Performance assumptions						

Figure 11.3 Summary of assumptions and expectations to be controlled.

238

IMPLEMENTATION AND CONTROL OF
INTERACTIVE PLANNING

Interactive planning is usually initiated as a result of the efforts of one or several executives or managers. The trial they initiate is usually carried out in parallel with the old planning process used by the corporation. This minimizes the cost of possible failure, and hence overcomes much of the resistance that usually accompanies an effort to start something new.

The "prime mover" of interactive planning often brings an outside expert to the organization to make a presentation of it to the relevant managers and their staffs. Such a presentation should be as exciting and provocative as possible, and it should make liberal use of real examples. If possible, no less than three hours should be devoted to such a presentation and discussion of it.

The question most frequently asked of me by managers who have heard one of my presentations of interactive planning is: Where should it be started? The answer is simple: wherever *you* are. In response, I am often told that the support of a higher level of management is required before they can take such a step; therefore, I should really be addressing that level. My response to this usually consists of the following true story.

The university-based center of which I am a part was doing research for one of the largest corporations in the United States. As a result of conversations I had with several executives of the company about planning, one of them asked me to put on a series of two-day seminars on interactive planning for the top four levels of company management. These were arranged for small groups to encourage and facilitate discussion. First, a set of sessions were held for the fourth-level managers, then a smaller set for the third level, and so on to a final session with the corporation's executive committee.

In each of the sessions before the last I was asked if I was going to make a similar presentation to the next higher level of management because, they explained, without approval and support from above, they could do nothing. In each instance I replied affirmatively. In the process my curiosity mounted: what would be asked in the last session with the top executives?

At the last session the chief executive officer asked me if I was going to present the same material to his subordinates because, he explained, he could do nothing without their support. Q.E.D. The buck-passing circle was closed.

The corporation involved was paralyzed because none of its parts was willing to initiate a change on its own. It is not surprising that the life of that company since the seminars has not been a happy one. It has experienced one financial crisis after another.

In contrast, I know of several fourth-level managers, also in a large corporation, who have unilaterally initiated interactive planning in that part of their organization for which they are responsible. Their success with it subsequently led to its diffusion both to other units at the same level and to higher-level units. For example, E. H. Vogel, Jr., the former vice president of marketing at Anheuser-Busch, Inc. whom I quoted above, introduced interactive planning in his department entirely on his own initiative. It later spread horizontally and vertically. Today the corporation as a whole plans interactively.

There are three reasons often given by managers for their reluctance to initiate a new type of planning, even with approval and support from above. First, they do not have the time it requires of them. All or a large part of conventional planning can be turned over to staff and subordinates, but not in interactive planning. The unwillingness to give such planning the time it requires reflects a willingness to sacrifice the future for the present, and a lack of understanding of the fact that most of the urgent matters requiring attention now are consequences of inadequate planning in the past. Only planning can provide an escape from crisis management, and effective planning does require an investment of some of management's time.

Second, some managers have told me that they have tried interactive planning, and it did not work. I have never found this assertion to be true. What I have found in these cases is that those who make such claims have tried one or a few aspects of interactive planning, but not interactive planning as a whole. Although some of its aspects can be used effectively without all the others, this is not true for many of them. Interactive planning is a *system* of activities, hence is more than the sum of its parts; it is a product of their interactions. The parts, moreover, lose their essential properties when separated from that system.

Third, I am told by some managers that interactive planning may work for others, but their situation is more complex than that of others and therefore makes such planning less applicable. I have met few managers who did not believe their problems were more complex than those of others. This follows from the fact that familiarity breeds complexity. Complexity is less a property of problems than it is of those who face them. A complex problem becomes simple when we have learned how to handle it effectively.

Interactive planning is not a rigidly specified process. It is flexible and adaptable. It is not carried out in exactly the same way in any two places, and it is not carried out exactly as I have described it in any one place. Each of its applications is an adaptation of the version of it presented here, and these have changed over time as the organizations and their environments have changed.

To paraphrase Ambrose Bierce, there are always an infinite number of reasons for not doing something, but only one for doing it: it is right. This, however, is usually difficult to prove. The willingness to try something new is more a matter of personality than it is of proof.

The Planning Department

As previously noted, it is commonplace for corporations to combine planning and development in one department, and incorrectly to take development to mean growth. A corporation develops when it increases its ability and desire to improve the quality of life of its own stakeholders and those of other organizations. Development in this sense takes place *in* the interactive planning process. For this reason corporate development should be combined with interactive planning.

It is also appropriate, indeed desirable, to place responsibility for the design and operation of the corporate management system with corporate planning. This generally assures its being more than financial data processing or a clerical-replacement system. Management and planning systems can benefit from close association. Planners, more than any other type of corporate personnel, know the informational needs of managers and are the most likely to be responsive to them. Furthermore, their own informational needs often completely overlap those of the managers they serve.

The proper function of planners, it will be recalled from Chapter 3, is to encourage and help others to plan for themselves, not to plan for them. This requires that the planning staff have the ability to provide the wide variety of disciplinary inputs required by interactive planning. In addition to expert planners the department should contain people with broad-gauged research capabilities, particularly those with skills in experimental design, applied statistics, and mathematical model building and manipulation. It should also include some who have a deep understanding of management and corporations. In-depth knowledge of corporate finance is also essential.

If a planning department has responsibility for corporate development, then it should also include experts in organizational and human development. If, in addition, it has responsibility for the management system, it requires the wide variety of skills usually associated with design and operation of information and computer-based systems.

The corporate planning department should report directly to the chief executive officer and serve as his or her general staff. If should *not* be placed in any functionally defined department, particularly finance. A planning department so placed inevitably winds up doing financial planning exclusively or predominantly.

Group, divisional, and departmental planning units should report to the senior managers of the parts of the organization for which they are responsible.

Attraction and Retention of Planning Skills

Professional planners at any level of an organization should be encouraged to keep up to date by attending relevant professional meetings and courses. They should also be encouraged to monitor the relevant literature. They should have available funds for acquiring the more important journals and books in their fields. Finally, planners should be encouraged to publish and make presentations to professional meetings, subject, of course, to the usual constraint on revealing competitively useful information. This has a number of advantages for the corporation. First, the reactions of their peers outside the company provide management with information about the quality of work done inside it. Second, such activities of corporate personnel attract good professionals to the company. It also helps the corporation to retain the highly qualified personnel it already has.

There is no better place to train promising young professionals for general management than in a good planning department. Here, more than any other place in a corporation, they can be exposed to and come in contact with every part of the organization. This enables them to develop an understanding of the important interactions and interdependencies within the corporation. Planning also teaches young professionals how to distinguish between what is important and what is not, and how to be sensitive and responsive to changing internal and external needs.

The most effective members of a planning staff are *professionals*. A professional has standards of performance and principles of practice to which he or she gives primary allegiance. Loyalty to the employer is secondary. An employee whose primary loyalty is to the employer rather than the profession has at most limited value to the company. A corporate doctor, for example, whose primary interest in treating the victim of an industrial accident is to protect the company against legal action, is not functioning well *as a doctor*. If the two loyalties come into conflict, the professional will go with the profession. Unless he or she does so the company will receive less than the best professional services.

Corporations that have no planning department or have one that is unfamiliar with interactive planning usually require external assistance in getting such planning started. Varied sources of assistance are available.

It is provided by consulting firms, research organizations, university-based centers and institutes, and individual advisers. All are not equally capable. Therefore, successful planning often depends critically on obtaining the right source of help.

Such a selection should not be based on a reading and evaluation of proposals submitted by competing sources. The ability to write an attractive proposal is not a reliable indicator of an ability to "deliver the goods." A better selection procedure consists of the following two steps. First, have the potential sources of assistance make an oral presentation to management. Allow enough time for discussion in depth. This, better than a proposal, can reveal the competence of the source and its fit with the corporation. Harmony of styles of operation is critical to the success of any joint planning venture.

Second, obtain evaluations of each potential source of help from at least three of its recent clients. More useful information can generally be obtained in this way than by any amount of communication with the source itself.

The company should assure itself that whatever external source of assistance is selected, it will assume responsibility for educating and training company personnel so they can eventually carry on independently. The company should also retain the right to terminate the use of an external source of help within a reasonable amount of time, usually thirty days. Mistaken choices are not uncommon, and they should not have to be lived with. For this reason fixed-fee contracts are less desirable than cost-plus.

It is prudent to contract initially only for a part of the planning process; for example, formulation of the mess and preparation of an idealized design. This can be accompanied by an understanding that if the company is satisfied with the work done, the contract will be extended. This makes it possible to restrict the initial commitment to three to six months.

Internal and external planners should be expected to communicate frequently, briefly, and understandably to managers and their staffs. It is their obligation to communicate in ordinary English, not in jargonese. Those who are not capable of doing so generally do not understand what they are talking or writing about.

Although a single document presenting *the plan* in detail is sometimes desirable, it is seldom necessary if it is a product of interactive planning. There are two reasons for this. First, the more participative planning is, the less the need to inform people about what has been done. Of course, even in highly participative planning few are involved in every part of it. Therefore, it may be helpful to prepare a summarizing document that refers to more detailed descriptions of parts of the plan. These detailed documents should be held in a central file maintained by the corporate planning department.

Second, since interactive planning is a continuous process, records that are made of its output tend to become obsolete while they are being prepared. Therefore, if one comprehensive document is prepared, it should be kept in a looseleaf binder so that additions, deletions, and substitutions can be easily made.

Reasons for Discontinuation Planning

Most discontinuations of conventional planning processes that I have seen resulted from a change of the person or persons who were key to it. Reassignments, departures, and hiring of new personnel can be very disruptive to conventional planning. However, the more participative planning is, the less it is subject to such disruption, and, conversely, the less participative it is, the more it is subject to discontinuation.

The emergence of crises also leads to discontinuation of planning. If crises do not stop planning, they usually disrupt or delay it seriously. This too is more likely to occur in conventional planning than in the interactive variety. Although interactive planning is based on a vision of a desirable future, its choice of means is firmly rooted in the present. Such planning involves deciding what to do *now* to bring about a desired future. Therefore, those engaged in interactive planning do not lose contact with the present and find that it provides guidance in reacting to even the most serious crisis.

SUMMARY AND CONCLUSION

John Gall [34] opened his last chapter of *Systemantics* with some very pertinent questions:

> We have come to the end of our presentation; why not simply stop? Does Euclid bother to round off his *Elements* with a polished little essay on the significance of the whole work? (Of course not.) But lest readers feel they have been left hanging in air, so to speak, this coda is appended. (p.85)

Perhaps I too should simply stop, but I cannot resist a brief review of the key ideas presented in each chapter. I hope the reader finds this useful. If not you can simply stop.

1. A system is a set of elements that cannot be separated into independent parts. From this it follows that (a) the essential properties of a system are lost when it is disassembled physically or conceptually, and (b) the essential properties of the parts are also lost when the parts are separated physically or conceptually from the whole. For these reasons, analysis of a system, which begins by disassembling it, can reveal only its structure and how it works but not its essential properties or why it works the way it does. To obtain such knowledge and understanding one must use synthetic thinking—that is, inquiry into the functions that the system performs both for the larger system of which it is a part and for its parts.

2. Corporations have historically been conceptualized as machines or organisms. Only recently have they come to be understood as organizations. Organizations are purposeful systems that contain purposeful parts and are themselves parts of larger purposeful systems. Corporations are organizations whose primary functions in society are the production and distribution of wealth. It is through these functions that they are expected to contribute to social development. In a free-enterprise system their failure to distribute wealth satisfactorily is more likely to invite government intervention than is their failure to produce it. Corporations are also increasingly held responsible by society for preserving the social and physical environments they share with others. Their purposeful parts, people, are pressuring them to contribute to their personal development and to provide them with a satisfactory quality of work life.

To develop is to increase one's desire and ability to satisfy one's own desires and those of others. Therefore, the most general and appropriate objective of a corporation is to develop its desire and ability to encourage and facilitate the development of the society (or societies) of which it is a part, and its purposeful parts. Thus development is not as much a matter of what one has as what one can do with whatever one has. It is better reflected in the quality of life than the standard of living. Quality of life is a matter of aesthetics—the satisfactions one derives from what one does (a) independently of its outcome, and (b) from the sense of progress derived from doing it.

3. Planning ought not to be an effort to resurrect the past or to prepare for a predicted future. The future of any organization depends more on what it does between now and then than on any of its past. Therefore, planning should consist of the design of a desirable future and the invention of ways to bring it about. The principal (but not the only) benefit to be derived from such (interactive) planning is realized by participating in it. Each participant has an opportunity to increase his understanding of how his behavior affects the performance of the whole, thus leading to improvement of that performance. In addition, participants can imbed their ideals and stylistic preferences into the organization through planning, thus contributing to an improvement in the quality of their work lives. Therefore, the process of planning, as well as its products, contributes to the development of the organization as a whole and of its parts.

Participation in planning should be as widespread among the relevant stakeholders as is possible. Planning should be continous and involve interactions between all parts of an organization. It should have five phases: (1) formulation of the mess, (2) specification of the ends to be pursued, (3) selection of the means by which they are to be pursued, (4) planning the acquisition or generation and allocation of the resources required to implement the means selected, and (5) design of the implementation of these means and control of their implementation and performance.

4.   The mess an organization should confront is the future it will have if both it and its environment do not change their behavior in any significant way. Messes are systems of problems and opportunities that, because they are systems, are not merely the sum of their parts, but a product of their interactions. Therefore, messes must be perceived and understood holistically. Formulation of the mess faced by a system requires a detailed knowledge and understanding of how that system can and does operate and which of its own and its environment's characteristics obstruct improvement of its performance.

The formulation of a mess is best recorded in the form of a scenario of the future that is extrapolated from its and its environment's past and current behavior.

5.   The objective of interactive planning is an effective pursuit of an idealized state. This state is formulated as a design of that system with which the current system's stakeholders would replace it if they were free to do so. Such a design should be technologically feasible and operationally viable, and it should provide the system with an ability to learn and adapt quickly and effectively. Because this system can be improved and can improve itself it is neither utopian nor ideal; it is the best ideal-seeking system of which its designers can conceive.

The idealized-design process facilitates and encourages widespread participation in planning, tends to generate consensus among its participants, extracts commitment from them, stimulates their creativity, and significantly enlarges their concept of what is feasible. It makes those involved aware of the fact that they, not something external to them, are the principal obstructions to the future they most desire.

The differences between the reference scenario and the idealized design constitute the gaps that the remainder of the planning process is dedicated to filling.

6a. A corporation or any organization is capable of developing and contributing to the development of others only if it is flexible and able to learn and adapt rapidly and effectively. Most conventionally structured corporations lack flexibility because their structure imposes a rank ordering on the three principal dimensions along which work is divided: inputs (for example, functions), outputs (for example, products), and markets. Therefore, when the relative importance of these criteria changes, as it frequently does, major restructuring is required. It is usually strongly resisted. The need for structural change can be significantly reduced and the willingness to make such changes significantly increased by the use of a multidimensional structure in which all three dimensions share each level of the organization. Furthermore, by making every unit in such an organization a profit center with a great deal of autonomy, their survival is made dependent on their performance. Such units tend to be more flexible and willing to change than ones whose survival is independent of their performance as, for example, is the case in a bureaucracy.

6b. There is no organizational structure or function that the members of that organization cannot sabotage if they are so inclined. Such an inclination is often a product of their dissatisfaction with work and the lack of an ability to affect it, that is, powerlessness. These conditions are more likely to arise in an organization that is managed autocratically than in one that is managed democratically. In a democratic system members have some direct control over (a) what they do and (b) what is done to them.

There is an apparent contradiction between the desire to make democratic participation possible in an organization and its need for a hierarchical structure to coordinate and integrate the divided labor it contains. This apparent contradiction is resolved in a circular organization, one in which every manager has a board of which he or she is a member together with the immediate superior and immediate subordinates. These boards have responsibility for (1) setting policies subject to the constraint that they be consistent with those emanating from above, (2) coordinating the activities at the level immediately below, and (3) controlling the occupancy of the managerial positions reporting to them. Such a design gives employees some control over those who have direct control over them, hence over their own activities. This enables each employee to do something about sources of dissatisfaction at work.

7. An organization cannot be capable of rapid and effective learning and adaptation unless its management has this capability. Management is the part of an organization that has responsibility for controlling it. To carry out this function, management must identify and anticipate problems and opportunities, decide what to do about them and do it, and monitor and change, if necessary, what is done to assure its effectiveness. Information is required by each of these activities, hence the need for a supporting management information system.

A design of a management system that integrates these functions is presented in Chapter 7. It incorporates three levels of control: control of the organization by management, control of management, and control of the controllers of management. These controls are so designed as to make possible efficient and effective learning and adaptation by the organization as a whole, by its management, and by those who control the managers.

8. The gaps to be filled between the reference scenario and the idealized design present planning problems that require the formulation and selection of means. There are three ways of dealing with these or any other problems; they can be resolved, solved, or dissolved. To resolve a problem is to find a means that does well enough, that satisfices. To solve a problem is to find a means that performs as well as possible, that optimizes. To dissolve a problem is to so redesign the relevant system or its environment that the problem is removed. This idealizes. It is better to solve than resolve, and better to dissolve than solve because few problems stay solved for long. Dissolution requires more creativity than solution, and solution more than resolution. Unfortunately, creativity is a very scarce commodity.

The creative formulation of means requires identification (often unconsciously) of self-imposed constraining assumptions, removing them, and exploring the consequences of doing so. Such assumptions can severely limit (1) the range of variables that are considered to be relevant, and (2) our perception of the extent to which relevant variables can be controlled. They also (3) exaggerate our perception of the number and severity of externally imposed constraints, and (4) lead us to infer causal connections that do not exist and to miss some that do.

A conscious effort to identify and remove self-imposed constraining assumptions (using the procedures I suggest in Chapter 8, or others) can often reveal means that are clearly better than any that have been considered previously.

9. Once a set of alternative means has been formulated, a choice must be made. This requires evaluation. However apparent the superiority of one means over the others might be, some systematic comparative evaluation is desirable. Fortunately, scientific methods, techniques, and tools can be very helpful in making such evaluations. These include experimentation, the use of mathematical models and algorithms, simulation, and operational gaming. It is rarely possible, however, to take all the relevant variables into quantitative account when using such procedures.

Therefore, some human judgment is almost always required to supplement the output of scientific procedures.

However a means is selected and no matter how superior it is believed to be, its use should be controlled; that is, it should be systematically and continously evaluated when in use. This should be done if for no other reason than that the conditions under which means are evaluated are likely to change in significant ways over time. But there is another reason: there is no better way to evaluate a means than when it is in use.

10. Once means are selected, the amount and timing of the resources they require should be determined. These requirements should then be compared with what will be available. Deficiencies will either have to be made up or removed by revision of the means selected. Oversupply of resources should also lead to reconsideration of the means selected and the goals and objectives with which they are associated.

Those aspects of resource planning that involve (1) purchased goods, materials, and services, (2) facilities and equipment, and (3) money are highly developed in the sense that a number of quantitative techniques and tools are available to facilitate them. However, the quality of the results obtained by their use is no better than the quality of the data that go into them. The use of numbers is no assurance of precision; numbers can be very imprecise.

In personnel planning more is often assumed to be better. This is not always the case. The output of an activity into which there is a continued infusion of labor levels off and eventually declines. It is critical, therefore, to uncover the relevant input–output (personnel) functions, even if only approximately. This requires well-designed research, often experimentation. However time-consuming and costly such research may be, it is usually more than justified by the efficient and effective use of human beings that it makes possible.

In bureaucratic organizations the importance of a unit is often taken to be proportional to the number of people in it. This presses for growth. Although maximizing employment is an important social function of corporations, employment is socially useful and individually satisfying only if it is productive and meaningful. The waste of human labor is a product of a bankrupt mind.

A quantitative financial model of a firm can greatly facilitate financial planning. It can make possible a rapid financial exploration and evaluation of the consequence of a wide variety of alternative means and environmental conditions. The usefulness of such models is greatly enhanced when they are programmed into a computer.

11. Implementation and control are parts of planning, not subsequent steps. They are simultaneously the consummation of one planning cycle and the initiation of the next. What is learned in these processes provides the impetus and inputs required for continuous planning. The more carefully implementation and its consequences are controlled, the more can be learned.

The interactive planning process is both demanding and rewarding. It demands time, effort, and resources, but not as much as one might come to believe from reading this book. Because it is participative, the time and effort required are divided among the many involved. Moreover, it takes more time to set up the process and develop the forms and procedures that facilitate it than to maintain them once they are under way.

The rewards of interactive planning are progress towards ideals, the fun in doing it, and personal and organizational development. By providing an opportunity to combine play and learning with work, such planning enables individuals to enjoy a high quality of work life.

Now I am back to where I started, at the end. Having behaved like the apocryphal snake who began to eat its own tail and continued until it consumed itself, I too am about to disappear.

APPENDIX ONE

REFERENCE SCENARIOS

In this appendix two very different styles of reference scenario are provided. The first consists of a set of interrelated reference projections, and the second is a portion of a "history" supposedly written in 1990.

Recall that a reference scenario is an extrapolation from the past into the future assuming that the system involved and its environment will develop without intervention, that is, with no change of the trends experienced over the relevant past. Recall also that such a projection is not a forecast of what will happen but of what *would* happen if there were no interventions. Since some interventions are highly probable, a reference projection is more a forecast of what is not likely to happen than of what will.

The purpose of a reference scenario is to identify when and how a system will break down if there are no interventions. One can plan interventions *now* rather than wait (as is usually the case) until the system is in a state of crisis. Interventions under crisis conditions seldom provide effective solutions to problems. Planned interventions are more likely to be creative and effective.

Moreover, reference projections and scenarios can be used to suggest creative types of intervention, ones that would not normally be considered even in planning prior to a state of crisis. The first scenario provides an example of such solution-generation.

SCENARIO 1

The following set of projections was briefly described in Chapter 4. It was originally prepared in 1960 for an automobile manufacturing company. A later version by Sagasti and Ackoff [67] was published in 1971. This presentation, extracted from the later version, appeared as Chapter 7 in *The Art of Problem Solving.*

The automobile currently accounts for about 85 percent of all urban passenger travel. This percentage has been increasing and will continue to increase unless restrictions are introduced deliberately or are self-generated because of increases in (1) our adult population, (2) the number of automobiles per adult, and (3) the miles per year that vehicles are driven.

The projected growth of our total and adult (over twenty years) population is shown in Table A1.1.

The projected number of automobiles per adult is shown in Table A1.2. These projections assume continued expansion of city streets and highways at a rate that will not reduce recent trends of increasing usage of automobiles; that is, they assume unconstrained growth. They also assume that a "saturation point" is not reached with respect to the number of automobiles per adult.

Table A1.1   Projected Population Growth

Year	Population (in millions)	Percentage over 20
1960	180.6	61.0
1970	206.0	60.9
1980	239.3	61.5
1990	288.6	60.9
2000	321.9	62.4

Source: Landsberg et al. [48], Table A.1.3.

Table A1.2   Projected Number of Automobiles per Adult

Year	Low	Medium	High
1960	0.54	0.54	0.54
1980	0.76	0.79	0.91
2000	1.06	1.19	1.51

Source: Landsberg et al. [48], Tables A.5.1 and A.5.2.

In what follows we do not use the high projection for the number of automobiles per adult, because it appears to go beyond the saturation point. Bottiny [16] suggested that a reasonable saturation point for automobile ownership is one automobile per licensed operator. It is difficult to imagine 1.51 automobiles per adult in the year 2000.

To estimate the future unconstrained volume of automobile traffic, it is also necessary to estimate the average miles per vehicle per year.

Data on past usage are shown in Table A1.3 which also includes data on vehicles other than automobiles.

According to Lansing and Hendricks [49]:

> The relation between family income and thousands of miles travelled is surprisingly close to a straight line. . . It may be a good approximation to say that every dollar of additional income leads to one additional mile of travel.

> As people's income rises, the number of vehicle-miles which they travel may be expected to rise in proportion. . . Over a period of 10, 20, 30 years one should project an increase in average vehicle miles at approximately the same rate as average stability of the relation between income and mileage (p. 23).

Lansing and Hendricks [49] also showed that the average automobile usage per year is higher for those who live in metropolitan areas than for the population as a whole. However, their result, 13,000 miles per family in metropolitan areas, is not directly comparable with the per vehicle data of Table A1.3. They also observed that the average number of miles travelled by suburbanites (14,000 miles per family) is substantially higher than that of urbanites (less than 9000 miles per family).

Unfortunately it is not possible to combine the historical data of Table A1.3 with that obtained by Lansing and Hendricks to obtain a precise

Table A1.3   Average Miles per Vehicle per Year

Year	Automobiles	All Passenger Vehicles[a]	Trucks and Trailers	All Vehicles
1950	9020	9078	10,776	9369
1955	9359	9400	10,697	9615
1960	9446	9474	10,585	9652
1965	9255	9278	11,373	9674

Source: Bureau of Public Roads [17], Table WM-201A.
[a] Includes buses and automobiles.

Table A1.4   Percentage of Total Increase in Population in the United States

Area	1950–1960	1960–1966
SMSAs		
Central Cities	22	9
Fringe	66	75
Outside SMSA	12	16
Total United States	100	100

Source: Department of Housing and Urban Transportation [22].

projection of the average miles per automobile per year. Nevertheless it is possible to use the data they provided in a qualitative way together with expected rises in income and shifts to suburbs and conclude that the average miles per automobile per year will continue to increase slowly under the assumption of unconstrained growth.

Landsberg et al. [48] estimated that the disposable income per household will increase from about $6500 in the early 1960s to nearly $10,000 in 1980 and somewhere between $13,000 and $15,000 by the end of the century. In addition to this, the trend toward increasing suburbanization is indicated by the relative growth of central cities and fringe areas within a Standard Metropolitan Statistical Area (SMSA). As seen in Table A1.4, it is in the urban fringe that the largest percentage increase of population is occurring.

These two factors, increase of family income and suburbanization, combined with the results obtained by Lansing and Hendricks, point in the direction of an increase in the average miles travelled by a family per year. Part of this increase will be because of increasing automobile ownership and part because of extended usage of the automobile. Following the policy of favoring the existing system, we take into consideration only the historical growth and extrapolate it into the future, keeping in mind that further increases in the average miles per automobile per year are not only possible but likely. Table A1.5. gives the constrained growth in average miles per automobile per year, based on the average growth over the period from 1950 to 1965.

Using the information contained in Tables A1.1 to A1.5, estimates of the total number of automobiles and vehicle miles can be prepared using the 59.49 million automobiles of 1960 as a base. This is done as follows:

(population over twenty) × (automobiles/adult) = total number of automobiles

(total number of automobiles) × (average miles per automobile) = total vehicle miles

Table A1.5   Projected Average Miles per Automobile per Year

Year	Miles per Automobile per Year
1960	9,446
1980	9,759
2000	10,072

The results of such calculations for each of the two growth rates of number of automobiles per adult are shown in Table A1.6.

During the past fifteen years approximately 50 percent of the miles travelled in a given year was in urban areas, as indicated in Table A1.7. Using different projection methods, Wilbur Smith and Associates [83, p.36] estimated that by 1980 about 60 percent of the total vehicle miles travelled will be on urban roads and that by 2000 this will increase to about 65 percent. Table A1.7 shows that the historical percentage distribution of urban–rural miles for automobiles and all vehicles has remained practically constant at about 50 percent of the past two decades.

Continuing our policy of being conservative, we assume that urban vehicle miles will account for 50 percent of the automobile vehicle miles in 1980 and 2000 even though the estimates made by Wilbur Smith and Associates are significantly higher.

By applying these percentages to the data shown in Table A1.6 we can estimate unconstrained total urban automobile miles per year. The results are shown in Table A1.8

Thus far we have considered unconstrained growth in traffic volume because of automobile travel, but buses and trucks will also generate their share of traffic volume.

Projections of urban truck traffic are only available in specific studies of cities, and these vary in the amount of detail they provide. The data from different sources are difficult to combine with the aggregated statistics provided by government agencies. Table A1.9 shows historical data and extrapolations to 1975 on the vehicle miles travelled by buses and trucks and their relation to automobile vehicle miles.

Table A1.6   Projections of Total Automobile Miles (in Millions) for Various Growth Rates in Automobiles per Adult Year

Year	Low	Medium
1960	561,943	561,943
1980	1,091,544	1,134,581
2000	2,144,453	2,407,510

Table A1.7   Percentage Distribution for Urban-Rural Miles Travelled[a]

Year	Automobiles		All Vehicles[b]	
	Urban	Rural	Urban	Rural
1950	50.2	49.8	47.6	52.4
1955	47.4	52.6	45.4	54.6
1960	48.4	51.6	46.1	53.9
1965	50.3	49.7	47.8	52.2

[a] Estimated from Table VM-201, Bureau of Public Roads [17].
[b] Includes automobiles, buses, and trucks.

Table A1.9 shows that the volume of traffic generated by buses can be neglected without introducing substantial error and that the ratio of truck vehicle miles to automobile miles has remained, and is expected to remain, stable at a value between one-fourth and one-fifth. Therefore, when analyzing increases in traffic volume—the ratio of projected vehicle miles in 1980 and 2000 to vehicle miles in 1960—it is enough to take into consideration the volume of traffic (vehicle miles) generated by automobiles.

Now to the question: How many additional miles of urban highways would be required to maintain the 1960 level of congestion? To answer this question we use information made available by the National Academy of Sciences [57]. The data apply to 1958, but little error results from using them for 1960. The measures used were explained thus:

In an overall consideration of the problem of road utilization, it is the latter group of highways [major roads] that is approaching capacity. Since the Federal-aid primary highway system roughly approximates the roads most intensively used, a comparison was made of its actual usage and its capacity.

Table A1.8   Urban Automobile Miles per Year (in Millions) for Various Ownership Growth Rates

Year	Low		Medium	
	Miles	Percentage of 1960	Miles	Percentage of 1960
1960	280,972	100.0	280,972	100.0
1980	545,772	194.2	567,291	201.9
2000	1,072,226	381.6	1,203,755	428.4

Table A1.9   Past and Extrapolated Vehicle Miles (in Millions) for Buses and Trucks and Ratios to Automobile Vehicle Miles

Year	Trucks		Buses		Automobiles
	Vehicle Miles	Ratio to Automobile	Vehicle Miles	Ratio to Automobile	Vehicle Miles
1950	90,552	0.25	4081	0.01	363,613
1955	108,817	0.22	4194	0.008	492,635
1960	126,409	0.21	4353	0.007	588,083 [a]
1965	173,659	0.24	4684	0.007	709,800
1970	209,200	0.24	4760	0.005	891,800
1975	249,000	0.23	4890	0.005	1,084,000

Sources: Department of Housing and Urban Development [17] and Bureau of Public Roads [23].
[a] This figure differs from that given in Table A1.6 by 4.5 percent due to differences in the method of calculation.

In order to estimate the degree of utilization of the Federal-aid primary system it was necessary to calculate the practical and the possible capacities of the system. Practical capacity represents the maximum number of vehicles that can pass a given point in one hour under prevailing conditions, without unreasonable delay or restrictions to the driver's freedom to maneuver. Possible capacity, on the other hand, represents the maximum number of vehicles that can pass a given point on a lane or roadway during one hour under the prevailing roadway and traffic conditions. (p. 76, italics ours)

Table A1.10 gives the results obtained.

The National Academy [57] noted, "The urban portions of the Federal-aid primary system are operating at 90 percent of their practical capacity. . . The margin is uncomfortably thin." (p. 77)

If urban traffic congestion is to be maintained at the 1958 level and no major shifts in traffic from the federal-aid highway system to other systems occur, we can estimate the additional highway miles (assuming a standard four-lane highway) in the Federal-aid system as follows. Using the low growth rate of automobiles per adult, for example, there will be about 3.82 times as many urban automobile miles in 2000 as in 1960. We will need about this many more urban highway miles in the Federal-aid primary system to retain the 1958 level of congestion; that is,

$$3.82 \times 20,076 \text{ miles} = 76,690 \text{ miles}.$$

Table A1.10   Relation Between Highway Usage and Capacity of the Federal-Aid Primary System

	Rural	Urban	Total
Extent of system (miles)	261,791	20,076	286,867
Average daily traffic			
(million vehicle miles)			
Actual usage	571	257	828
Practical capacity	897	284	1,181
Possible capacity	2,460	443	2,903
Ratio of capacity to usage			
Practical capacity	1.57	1.10	1.43
Possible capacity	4.31	1.72	3.51
Proportion of capacity used (%)			
Practical capacity	64	90	70
Possible capacity	23	58	29

Source: Reprinted from *U.S. Transportation: Resources Performance, and Problems* [57], page 77, with the permission of the National Academy of Sciences, Washington, D.C.

There were 20,076 miles in this system in 1960.

Table A1.11 shows the miles required in 1980 and 2000 for low and medium growth of automobile ownership.

The Federal-aid system consists of the major roads that are used for the movement of people and goods through an area, as contrasted with movements having origin or destination within one area. These are the roads that carry a heavy traffic load and provide access to residential locations, to the central business district, to industrial areas, to peripheral business areas, and so on, that is, to the main destinations in urban areas. When traffic congestion increases in this system, it also increases on other urban streets and highways not included in the system. For this

Table A1.11   Estimated Miles of Standard Urban Highway Required in the Federal-Aid Primary System to Maintain 1960 Level of Congestion

	Growth Rate	
Year	Low	Medium
1980	38,987	40,533
2000	76,690	86,006

reason a major shift of urban traffic from the Federal-aid primary system to other urban roads is not expected.

Using the low growth rate of automobile ownership, about 55,000 (76,690–20,076) additional miles of urban highways will be required in year 2000 to maintain the 1960 level of congestion. At the very conservative estimate of an average cost of $10 million per mile of standard four-lane urban highway (Lyle Fitch and Associates [50, p.14]) the total investment required over the next thirty years would be approximately $550 billion, or an average of $18.3 billion per year. This constitutes more than a threefold increase in the total expenditure for transportation facilities in 1967 (approximately $5.35 billion). The amount required ($18.3 billion) is more than ten times the amount spent on urban highways in 1967 ($1.4 billion). Such an increase in expenditure is virtually impossible, but it is not the only obstacle to constrained growth of automobile usage.

The amount of land that can be allocated to roads, highways, and parking spaces in urban areas, particularly in the central business district, also limits such growth. Lyle Fitch and Associates [50] quote Senator Harrison Williams on this subject:

> Even if we were to try [to solve urban transportation problems by highways alone] with an urban highway program averaging $10 to $20 million a mile in high density urban areas, there is every possibility that the remedy would only succeed in killing the patient—by replacing valuable tax ratable property with nontaxable concrete and asphalt, by creating huge downtown parking demands which would further remove land for commercial and cultural purposes, and by slowly carving away the activities that created the demand for access in the first place. (p. 14).

In most cities the proportion of land devoted to streets and parking in downtown areas already exceeds 40 percent of the total land available. Table A1.12 shows the relevant percentages for five metropolitan areas.

Table A1.12 Proportion of Central Business District Land Devoted to Streets and Parking

| | | Percentage of CBD Devoted to | | |
CBD	Year	Streets	Parking	Streets and Parking
Los Angeles	1960	35.0	24.0	59.0
Chicago	1956	31.0	9.7	40.7
Detroit	1953	38.5	11.0	49.5
Minneapolis	1958	34.6	13.7	48.3
Dallas	1961	28.5	12.9	41.4

Source: Wilbur Smith and Associates ([83], Table 11, p. 59).

Clearly, these percentages cannot be increased 3.82 times. Many cities, of course, have smaller percentages, and additional highways (for example, ones bypassing the CBD) need not generate additional parking requirements. Nevertheless it is clear that the space constraint would be reached for increases less than twice the current allocations.

Proposals have been made to use two-level highways to avoid the space problem. The costs associated with this are much higher than those for surface-level highways. Thus, if construction of the "required" conventional road is not economically feasible, as we have demonstrated, building elevated highways would be even less feasible.

Therefore, it does not appear to be practical to expand the existing urban road and highway system to cope with the unconstrained growth of traffic volume over the next thirty years because of the expenditures of money and amounts of space such expansion would require.

We have not considered the social costs that might arise from increased accident rates, increased air pollution, and decreased attractiveness of the environment. The consideration of these costs would provide additional support to the conclusion that we will not be able to solve the urban transportation problem by expanding the highway and road system.

(The study that the reference projection presented above is part of went on to consider other changes in the city that might reduce the projected requirement for highways. It showed that these cannot be expected to significantly affect the requirements. It also showed that it is unlikely that mass transit and highway and vehicle technology now under development will significantly reduce this requirement. The study did find several possible directions in which possible solutions might be found. I include only one of these here. It is sufficient to show how reference projections can be used to reveal both the nature of a future problem and creative solutions to it.)

There are no signs that increasing reliance on the automobile will be affected by increasing traffic congestion or the inconveniences derived from the widespread use of the automobile. On the contrary, there is some evidence that urbanites would prefer to relocate their jobs or residences rather than switch from the automobile to another mode of transportation. The Department of Housing and Urban Transportation [23] noted that:

> The experience of recent years contradicts the belief that traffic congestion will itself set a limit to car ownership. If there is to be any chance of coexisting with the automobile in the urban environment, a different sort of automobile is needed with improvements in the supporting systems. (p. 41, italics ours)

The present design of the automobile, the five to six passenger family car, is a compromise intended to satisfy a wide variety of needs. Automobiles are used for inter- and intracity travel, to and from work, recreation, shopping, and so on.

Of considerable importance is the fact that the number of two-car families increased from 7 percent in 1950 to 25 percent in 1966. This and other facts we consider later suggest a functional differentiation between an intra- and intercity automobile. Families that own or use more than one car would obtain distinct advantages by using special-purpose automobiles better suited for specific needs, for example, cars better suited to the characteristics of center-city traffic.

A major improvement in automotive systems is suggested by the figures on automobile occupancy in urban areas. For example, average occupancy rates in metropolitan Philadelphia are approximately 1.5 passengers per car, ranging from 1.2 for commuting trips to 1.6 for non-work trips (*Penn Jersey Transportation Study* [62], p. 91). The average capacity of an automobile, on the other hand, is about five people. It is apparent that substantial reduction in automobile congestion could be obtained if the average occupancy of automobiles, particularly for work trips, were increased. Car pooling, however, reduces the advantages of door-to-door travel by automobile. A less inconveniencing alternative would involve the use of small urban automobiles, referred to by some as "urmobiles."

This alternative has been explored in several studies (for example, *Cars for Cities* [18] and Department of Housing and Urban Development [23]). It is generally acknowledged, however, that at higher speeds and in free-flowing traffic the effect of reduced vehicle length on congestion is very small. For example, at forty miles per hour the majority of the road space can be said to be occupied by safety space between vehicles, and, according to McClenehan and Simkowitz [51] the effect of reducing car length by half on expressway traffic would be an increase in flow of no more than 10–15 percent. Greater increases would occur on heavily used city streets; as much as a 70 percent increase in flow would be achieved when congestion reached the not-uncommon level of fifteen vehicles per light. If only a fraction of long cars is replaced by small ones, the resulting flow is approximately a linear interpolation between the two extremes.

Relatively little is known about the effect of car width on traffic flow. Experiments carried out by the Ministry of Transport in England [18, p.13] showed that a lane width two and one-half to three feet wider than the car itself represents a reasonable minimum for safely purposes. They also showed that in mixed traffic conditions, when small and large cars travel together, the small ones usually travel behind the larger ones. using the same road space.

A considerable increase in passenger density could be obtained by the use of short (less than ten feet) and narrow (three and one-half feet) two-passenger vehicles, one passenger seated behind the other. If traffic were made up exclusively of such vehicles, an increase of at least 2.2 (2.0 $\times$ 1.1* on expressways (two vehicles per normal lane and a 10 percent increase in flow due to shorter cars) and 3.4 (2.0 $\times$ 1.7) on city streets could be obtained. If shoulders of four-lane expressways were used for one lane of such vehicles, their capacity would increase by 2.7 (2.2 + 0.5), and the additional lane would be used for one narrow car which would have half the width of a normal car. Following a similar line of reasoning, city streets with two moving lanes for current automobiles and one for parking, the increase would be 5.1 (3.4 + 1.7). These calculations do not take trucks and buses into account, but they show it is possible to deal even with the 4.28 medium forecasted increase in requirements for the year 2000 if the small car we have described were generally adopted.

Parking requirements would also be greatly reduced. For example, a normal car takes more than twenty feet along the sidewalks. Three ten-foot-long cars could be parked in the linear space required for two normal cars, and additional road space would be left free for vehicular traffic. Parking space requirements could be further reduced if the door or doors were either sliding on the side or placed at the front or back. The latter would permit face-in parking with very high density.

A large variety of small automobiles is under development now (*Mechanics Illustrated*, October, 1969, p. 76 and *Life*, December 11, 1970). In many cases the new designs incorporate changes that will reduce the polluting effects of cars, and, because of their decreased weight and lower speeds, they would greatly reduce fuel consumption. They can be made to hook on to each other in train-like fashion to facilitate towing or taking the family along on a trip (using nonmotorized cabs, for example). Their reduced maximum speed and acceleration capabilities increase their safety.

The advantages of using small cars for intracity traffic depend on the restrictions imposed on the use of large vehicles. During a transitional period, vehicles of different sizes can mix together. Eventually the use of city streets and highways could be limited to small cars from, say, 7:00 a.m. to 7:00 p.m. on weekdays. In some cities trucks are already kept off CBD streets during these hours.

*Using McClenehan and Simkowitz figures for the increase in traffic flow with short cars.

Many benefits could derive from publicly or privately owned fleets of small cars that would be available as drive-it-yourself taxis. Their pick-up and drop-off points could be widely dispersed over the city (see *Minicar Transit System* [56]).

It is clear that a change to small urban automobiles can be accomplished in at least a decade. Furthermore, such a change would require little public cost and would yield economies to the individual without the loss of convenience or comfort. Most important, it could reduce congestion significantly and permit less restricted use of automobiles than would otherwise be possible.

SCENARIO 2

The following portion of a reference scenario has been modified only to protect the identity of the company involved. It is referred to here as "Alpha." This company is a wholly-owned subsidiary of the Beta Corporation which acquired it form its orginal owners in the 1960s. Alpha makes its products in an old plant in which the relations between the management supplied by Beta and the unionized work force have never been good. This scenario was prepared under the direction of George Calhoun in the second half of the 1970s.

Early in 1980 Alpha's management defined the market in which it intended to compete over the next decade. At that time it was competing for about 70 percent of the demand in the market. During the 1970s the industry of which Alpha was a part grew at an average annual rate of 7 percent in dollars and just under 3 percent in volume. Alpha expected its market to grow from $2 billion in 1980 to $3.8 billion in 1990.

During the 1970s Alpha's volume increased by an average of 3.5 percent per year. Extrapolating to 1990, Alpha expected a 10 percent increase in its share of the total market. This expectation was based on the assumption that the part of the market in which it competed would maintain its share of the total market, but this share had been decreasing in the 1970s. Aware of this, Alpha's management decided to make a large investment in efforts to increase demand for its products.

Anticipating a significant rise in demand for its products in response to its planned impetus in advertising and sales promotions, Alpha's management thought it necessary to increase the output of its plant. It decided to speed up its production line by 10–15 percent for a period of two months, but negotiations with the unions for the speed-up ran into a snag. Management argued that it was in the interest of the employees for the unions to permit job rotation and flexible work assignments without requiring the company to pay wages at the rate of the highest-paid job category. The unions argued that the company's only objective was to increase profits. They wanted a substantial share of the benefits of increased productivity.

Management did not communicate with the workers about these negotiations. The unions did. This, combined with the prolongation of the negotiations increased the workers' hostility to management, thus bringing more difficulty to the negotiations. In desperation management decided to go ahead unilaterally and increase the speed of the production line for two months. It instructed the plant supervisors and foremen to this effect but neglected to inform the workers of the temporary nature of the change. As a result, when the speed-up was initiated a small group of workers started a wildcat strike. Their trade unions decided not to support them. Several acts of violence ensued. Management then used its legal right to dismiss those on strike. When the workers in the plant heard of this, they walked out. This forced the unions to reverse their position and support the strike.

The unions formed a coalition and made two demands: reinstatement of all those who had been dismissed, and reduction of the production line's speed to its previous rate. Alpha's management was willing to accept the first demand but not the second.

The strike continued for several weeks. Alpha's sales began to suffer from the lack of production and the "bad press" it was receiving. Thus pressured, management finally reached an agreement with the unions. All workers except those who had been involved in acts of violence were reemployed. Increases in the speed of the production line were restricted to one month per year and no more than 10 percent.

After the strike, sales recovered and reached their previous level by the end of 1980.

The new marketing efforts initiated in the latter part of that year led to significant increases in the demand for Alpha's products in 1981 and 1982. The company operated at capacity with only a few additions to the workforce. However, the production "ceiling" attained was lower than had been expected by management. To a large extent this was because of the unions' refusal to allow flexible work assignments. In addition, at the end of 1981 the productivity of the workers began to decline and absenteeism and tardiness began to increase. Moreover, the old machinery in the plant performed less efficiently than had been hoped.

Alpha's production equipment had been poorly maintained because its management expected Beta to build new facilities for it as soon as its profitability justified doing so. As a result, breakdowns increased in frequency and duration, and maintenance of quality became a major problem.

By the mid 1980s the industry of which Alpha was a part had consolidated considerably through mergers, acquisitions, and bankruptcies. As a result, Alpha was increasingly involved in a cutthroat advertising and promotional war with its major competitors. In order to maintain, let alone expand, its market share, it had to increase its marketing expenditures significantly above the levels planned. This, together with machinery maintenance and replacement and new product development, consumed most of Alpha's profits. Little was left over for improvement of the quality of work life. This confirmed the belief, by then widespread among employees, that the company "didn't give a damn" about anything but squeezing more profit out of them.

Difficulties in operating the plant at near capacity mounted throughout 1985 and 1986. It was widely assumed that poor communications were to blame. For this and other reasons, coordination of plant operations became a major concern of management. It recognized that the first-line supervisors were under great stress, and that some of them were not adequately prepared for dealing with the personnel problems engendered by running the plant full out. Therefore, in order to give these supervisors more time with their subordinates and to enable them to take time off for training in human relations, another supervisory level was installed above them. This second level was intended to take over the increasingly complex problems of coordination. The first-line supervisors were encouraged to become more personnel oriented. As it turned out, however, the new supervisors obstructed the flow of communications both up and down. The failure of their efforts made it apparent that the coordination problems were not rooted in production scheduling but in the growing resentment among workers of the fast pace of production. All this led management to decide that the next labor contract would have to permit flexible job assignments.

In the latter half of 1986 Alpha experienced a significant decrease in sales. This was generally believed by management to be the result of the reduction of the quality of their products. Whatever the cause of the drop in sales, it became clear that a major layoff was necessary. Because management expected to be able to negotiate flexible job assignments in the next labor-contract negotiation, and because Alpha's wholesalers had large stocks of the company's products on hand at the time, management decided to go ahead with the layoffs. To avoid the kind of adverse publicity previously experienced, only a small number of workers were laid off at one time. The intention was to continue making such layoffs until the large reduction desired was realized.

The layoffs increased the insecurity of the workers who remained and led to a further deterioration of the already poor labor relations. Productivity decreased; fights and threats became commonplace. What was left of the workers' commitment to the company evaporated as they came to believe that they had no future there. Initial discussions with the unions made it apparent that they would strike again rather than agree to increased flexibility in work assignments.

Sales continued to decline and costs to increase. Meanwhile, Alpha's major competitors were installing significantly more efficient production equipment. With reduced production costs they increased their investment in marketing. Alpha's losses continued to grow despite its efforts to keep up with competition.

In 1987 Beta decided to divest itself of Alpha. It eventually sold Alpha to one of its former competitors.

IDEALIZED DESIGNS

The portions of the two idealized designs presented here were selected for contrast, one prepared by a foreign company, the other American. The first is product oriented; the second focuses on the company itself.

Both were prepared by company personnel with outside assistance. Professor Wladimir Sachs of the University of Pennsylvania was the principal external consultant in both cases. The author was also involved, but to a lesser extent.

DESIGN 1

This design was prepared by a foreign company that develops resort areas in semitropical regions of its less-than-well-developed country. This portion of the design covers one of several regions in which it operates. The region involved contains three almost contiguous areas referred to here as *A, B,* and *C.* Changes have been made in the original to protect the identity of the company. It is referred to as "Gamma," its country as "Ituria," and the principal town in the region as "Aville."

Introduction

The general mission proposed for Gamma is:

Through land development and tourism to demonstrate the ability of the private sector of the Iturian economy to contribute significantly to national development while efficiently and effectively pursuing corporate objectives.

The specific mission proposed for Gamma in the coastal area is:

To create a wholesome, varied, pluralistic, multiclass recreational area incorporating tourist facilities and permanent residences, and to produce locally as much of the goods and services required by the area as possible, so as to improve the standard of living and quality of life of its inhabitants.

Both the general and specific missions guided the design that follows.

The Area as a Whole

1. The three subareas—*A, B,* and *C*—will cater to different life styles.

    1.1. *A* will cater primarily to the high-income segment of the recreational market.

    1.2. *B* will cater primarily to the upper-middle segment of the recreational market.

    1.3. *C* will cater primarily to the middle-income segment of the recreational market.

    (As people's incomes increase through their lifetimes, they will be encouraged to take advantage of the three areas in progression.)

2. The town of Aville will become a marketplace serving the entire area.

3. Gamma will create an Art Institute in the resort area.

    3.1. It will operate as a profit center.

    3.2. It will offer programs in the following fine arts, applied arts, performing arts, and crafts.

    3.2.1. *Fine Arts.* Drawing and painting, creative writing, art history, sculpture, film, and printmaking.

    3.2.2. *Applied Arts.* These will capitalize on the rich Iturian artistic capabilities in order to create a comparative advantage for Iturian products in foreign as well as domestic markets. They will include fashion design and photography, architecture and interior design (which could lead to a small R&D project on low-cost housing that is sorely needed in the area), photography, graphics, printing, advertising design, textile, arts, and industrial design.

(These could lead to such businesses as a greeting card company, business graphics and design, business printing, newspapers, publishing, etc. The students in applied arts will do practicums at the Applied Arts Center of the Industrial Management Institute [described in a portion of the design not included here] as well as in the appropriate centers in the Art Institute.)

3.2.3. *Performing Arts.* Dance (folk and modern), music, drama, and voice.

3.2.4. Glass, Jewelery, metalsmithing, woodworking, weaving, cooking, and ceramics.

3.3. The Art Institute will have a joint program with the Industrial Management Institute in Arts Management.

(Arts management is the complex process of creating art festivals, shows, contests, and coordinating artists in a profitable way. An art manager must have expertise in the world of business as well as the world of art. The program can use Gamma's resorts and activities as practicum sites where students can apply what they have learned by coordinating the arts for these areas.)

3.4. The Arts Management Program will be responsible for organizing and running art festivals and related events throughout Gamma's resort areas. These will include: (1) popular music, featuring internationally known singers and groups, (2) international "young talent" music contests and festivals, (3) jazz festivals, classical music festivals, and contests, attracting the best symphony and chamber orchestras in the world as well as virtuoso performers, (5) classical theater festivals, (7) international film festivals, (8) international painting, photography, sculpture, and cooking festivals and contests, (9) international fashion shows and contests, and (10) crafts contests and exhibitions.

3.5. The Institute will recruit famous artists and artisans for an "Artist in Residence" program.

3.5.1. Artists in residence will (1) help the Arts Management program organize festivals, shows, and other events, (2) offer "Minicourses" to guests in the resort area and regular courses to students in the Art Institute, and (3) help arrange for artists and artisans participating in special events to offer "minicourses."

3.6. The Art Institute will (1) market and promote the marketing of products generated by festivals, shows, and so on, and (2) create a fine arts museum to be located in the area (possibly in Aville).

3.7. Local residents will be encouraged to participate in events and activities organized by the Art Institute.

3.7.1. They will receive financial support for attending the Institute.

3.7.2. The Institute will offer courses and contests in local schools.

3.7.3. Gamma will create artistic job opportunities for local students.

3.8. Each summer the Art Institute will offer a program in aesthetics for managers. (This program can help increase managers' appreciation and use of the arts. they will be encouraged to bring their families along.)

4. Gamma will use communications and incentives to encourage identification with and repeated use of the three resort areas.

4.1. Gamma will form a club whose members will consist of anyone who has used resort areas *B* or *C*. Each will receive a reference number that will indicate the extent to which he or she has used these resorts. Discounts and site preferences based on this time will be offered to club members, except in area *A*.

4.2. Gamma will publish a newsletter that will be sent to everyone who has used the facilities.

4.2.1. It will contain news about developments and planning for the resort area, special events, and other club members. It will be prepared by the appropriate departments of the Art Institute.

4.2.2. Club members will receive the newsletter for a specified period of time after their last use of the facilities, or longer if they so request.

5. Gamma will develop a new feature in each of the three resort areas at least every two years. (This will keep the areas dynamic and continuously attractive.)

6. Gamma will determine which services, features, and events contribute positively to the vacation experience and which do not. It will do so by interviewing and sending questionnaires to to club members, current users, employees, and local residents.

6.1. Hosts, hostesses, and other staff personnel will conduct the interviews informally during the course of their activities. (They will be instructed on how to do so.)

6.2. Polls will be taken through the newsletter.

6.3. Resort staff will also be interviewed about possible improvements.

7. Gamma will arrange for cruise ships to stop in the area.

7.1. A plan will be developed to enable tourists from one ship to spend time in the area and leave on another ship. (This will expose potential clients to the resort complex. They will become club members and receive the newsletter.)

7.2. Gamma will organize an association of resort businesses along the coast and work through it to induce cruise ships to use these resorts. (This will increase the variety available to the ships and make their cruises more attractive.)

8. Gamma will develop group-travel discounts that will be offered in major markets. This will be facilitated by the development of Gamma travel agencies [described in another portion of the design not included here].

9. Gamma will build and operate a coliseum in the resort area with an initial capacity of 500 to 1000.

9.1. It will be used for special events and be available for local use (e.g., for graduation ceremonies).

9.2. In conjunction with athletic clubs and associations Gamma will organize athletic contests, games, meets, and so on.

10. Gamma will promote the use of its facilities by those staying in other resorts in the area by (1) operating a bus at least every half hour between its facilities and others in the area, and (2) providing sightseeing tours of its facilities and the region at least once per day.

Area C

(This area will cater primarily to the middle-income segment of the recreational market but will have some facilities for the upper and upper-middle segments as well.)

11. *C* will have a distinctive Iturian flavor. Its architecture will provide a showcase of native architectural styles and its staff will wear native costumes.

12. Gamma will direct the marketing of this area to a mixture of foreign and native vacationers.

13. *C*'s facilities will be operated bilingually.

14. There will be a variety of temporary and permanent housing in the area ranging from expensive to moderately priced. There will be (1) camping facilities with camping equipment for purchase or rental, (2) trailer facilities and trailer rentals, (3) simple native cottages, (4) moderately priced hotels, (5) an accredited international youth hostel, (6) moderate to expensive housing that will be used as second homes for vacationers, and first homes for *C* employees and local residents, and (7) houseboats for purchase or rental.

15. *C* will have a boat marina (possibly done in a fishing-village motif). (There is currently a shortage of such facilities on the coast of Ituria.)

   15.1. A unique feature of this marina will be a stage either built into the side of a hill that is visible from the marina, or on a barge in the marina. Performances will be arranged by the Art Institute.

   15.2. Boat races will be encouraged and developed. (This will be done with the association of resorts previously mentioned.)

   15.3. The marina will include boat repair and building facilities, a supply store, and a boat-fitting yard.

   15.4. A condominium complex will be located near the marina.

16. *C* will include a children's art camp that will provide opportunities for both creation and recreation.

   16.1. It will offer brief as well as extended camping experiences. (Parents who visit their children at the camp will be able to stay at any of the three resorts.) Day camping will be offered for children whose parents are staying at one of the resorts.

   16.2. The camp will operate bilingually and each child will be encouraged to use or learn a second language.

   16.3. The camp will offer instruction in all types of arts and crafts. (Students from the Art Institute will be employed to provide the instruction.)

   16.4. The camp will operate during the periods in which schools in the relevant markets are closed.

17. A large Iturian multipurpose entertainment center will be built near the beach and marina. It will be used as a showcase of arts and crafts and for the performing arts.

   17.1. The Center will be used for festivals and the sale of arts and crafts.

17.2. Local residents will be encouraged to use the facility for so-cial affairs and special events. (This will add local flavor and encourage interactions between vacationers and locals.)

17.3. The Center will be unique to *C* thus attracting guests from *A* and *B*, as well as from other resorts.

18. *C* will have an eighteen-hole golf course bordered by condomin-iums.

Area B

(This area will be aimed primarily at the upper-middle-income segment of resort clientele, but it will have some facilities for the middle and upper segments as well. Features in *B* can be transposed to other areas if necessary.)

19. *B* will have an international/continental flavor.

20. It will have a large entertainment complex with a wide variety of facilities.

20.1. A large disco-restaurant that will serve all the hotels and res-idential facilities in *B*.

20.2. An open-air covered bandstand on or near the beach.

20.3. A covered boardwalk cafe located near the bandstand.

20.4. A number of small restaurants featuring European foods. (These restaurants will be operated by the hotels in *B*. Each restaurant will feature the food of a different country.)

20.5. A large plaza leading into the complex in which people will be able to sit during the day and listen to licensed strolling musicians.

20.6. A movie theater complex with four to six screens. The Art Management Program will run international film festivals here.

21. An open-air Greek-style amphitheater for the performing arts will be built at the back of area *B*, using the foothills for seating. It will seat up to 5,000 people.

22. A restaurant boat will operate out of area *B* offering evening cruises with quiet dining and romantic dancing.

23. A sports complex will be built to serve area *B*. In addition to the usual courts and playing fields, it will have exercise rooms, saunas jacuzzis, pro shops, and a bar and restaurant.

24. The only other shops in *B* will be those selling sundries and arts and crafts from the Art Institute. (This is to encourage the guests to use the marketplace in Aville.)

25. Housing and hotel facilities will be available for nightly, weekly, or longer stays.

Area A

(*A* will remain much as it is now. It will continue to cater to people of high income and be secluded. There will be little movement of visitors in *B* and *C* to *A*, but guests in *A* will be encouraged to use facilities in *B* and *C*.)

The Surrounding Areas

28. Aville will be developed as a cluster of jewels whose center stone will be a native marketplace. This will done with the local residents and the Department of Regional Development.

    28.1. The marketplace will be developed to serve local residents as well as visitors. (It will encourage their interaction.) Prices will be normal for the area, thus a bargain for the visitors.

    28.2. The marketplace will feature outdoor cafes and local entertainment.

    28.3. Craftspeople and artists will live and work where the visitors can watch them at work, and shops around the open-air plaza will sell inexpensive souvenirs.

29. Inexpensive housing for employees of *B* and *A* and locals will be developed in the Aville area. (*C* employees will be housed in that area.)

30. The small villages around Aville will also be redeveloped, each with a different theme.

DESIGN 2

The idealized design from which the following two sections have been drawn relates to an American company of medium size, here referred to as "Eta," The company produces industrially consumed products in plants located in the United States and abroad.

The mission statement quoted in Chapter 5 was associated with this design.

The context of the two sections (II and IV) of the design reproduced here is best grasped from the table of contents of the source document:

I. Mission
II. The Business of Eta
   The Business Eta Would Be in
   Management of Eta's Portfolio
      Managing the Composition of the Portfolio
         Acquisitions and New Ventures
         Divestitures
         Portfolio Balance
      Activities in Support of Portfolio Management
   Management of New Ventures and Acquisitions
III. Organization and Management of Eta
   Ownership
   Organization
      Business Units
      Service Units
      Market Units
      Executive Office
   Management
      Management Information Systems
      Planning
         Planning Support Systems
      Control
IV. Acquisitions, Use, and Development of Resources
   Human Resources and Their Use
      All Personnel
      Nonmanagerial Personnel
   Raw Materials, Energy, Utilities, and Transportation
   Financial Resources
   Plants and Equipment
V. Society and Eta
   Evaluating Progress toward Fulfillment of the Mission

Participation of Societal Stakeholders
Eta's Image

THE BUSINESS OF ETA

1. Eta would be involved in two categories of business: *manufacturing* and *service*—selling services internally and externally (e.g., R&D).

   As seen later in this document, all of Eta's corporate service functions (e.g., MIS and personnel) would be managed as businesses. They would sell their services to users inside or outside Eta. Furthermore, users within Eta could choose between purchasing these services internally or externally.

Management of Eta's Portfolio

Managing the Composition of the Portfolio

As described in the section on organization [not included here], there would be a unit called Planning and Development (P&D) that would be entrusted with planning Eta's business portfolio. Its activities related to this function are described here.

2. P&D would prepare plans for new businesses, acquisitions, and divestitures, and submit these to relevant units and/or the Executive Office for consideration.
   2.1. Its target would be to double Eta's total revenue (in constant dollars) every ten years through development of new businesses and acquisitions. Its performance would be judged in terms of progress toward this objective.

3. Each year units would prepare separate profit and loss statements for each of their businesses.

   As described later, several businesses would be grouped into a unit that would be a profit center. These units would also have the freedom to organize each of their businesses as a profit center. Minimally, units would have to provide a means of calculating the profit and loss associated with each business (including service businesses).

4. Each year P&D would calculate an Eta-index for each of Eta's businesses. This index would be equal to the ratio of actual *earnings* of that business to the *earnings it would have had if it had not been part of Eta*. These calculations would be evaluated by an external consultant.

An Eta-index greater than 1 would signify that the business would suffer if it were separated from Eta. An index less than 1 would mean that the business would do better if it were separated from Eta.

Acquisitions and New Ventures

5. P&D would estimate the Eta-index, growth in sales, and profitability of each proposed acquisition and new venture. This would make it possible to place each of these in one of the eight categories shown in Figure A2.1.

> Figure A2.1 can be interpreted as follows. In general, when the Eta-index is less than 1, the business would not be a good candidate for Eta; indeed, it would do better outside Eta. Therefore, it would be unreasonable to allocate resources to it that could be used more profitably by businesses with indexes larger than 1.
>
> However, a *cow*—a business with high profitability but low growth in sales—could be of benefit to Eta as a source of cash for development even if it had an index of less than 1.
>
> A *star*—a business with high profitability and high growth—with an index less than 1 could have considerable value to Eta, but only if it were seen as a part of a diversification into a completely new area. Otherwise, it would not be acquired or developed so that it would not compete for cash with businesses that fit into Eta's development strategy.
>
> When the Eta-Index is greater than 1, the figure can be interpreted as follows. A *star*+ would be a very desirable business, growing both in profit and sales. A *cow*+ should be viewed as a source of cash to finance growth of *stars*. However, in the case of a *cow*-acquisition, one should ask whether the lack of growth has been due to external conditions (e.g., stable market and a very large share) or to the business's inability to obtain sales that are available. In the latter case a *cow*+ could be transformed into a *star*+. In general, a *dog*+ should not be acquired unless Eta has reasons for wanting to subsidize it (e.g., for prestige).
>
> A *nebula* should be viewed as potentially either a *star* or a *dog*. Plans should be developed for converting them into *stars*. This comment is summarized in Figure A2.2

5.1. P&D would employ the logic outlined above for proposing acquisitions and new ventures.

5.2. P&D would also prepare an assessment of the extent to which a new venture or acquisition would contribute to Eta's pursuit of each element of its mission.

For example, with respect to employees it would consider such things as the number of jobs created per dollar invested, the extent to which the jobs created would be satisfying, the opportunities for advancement they presented,

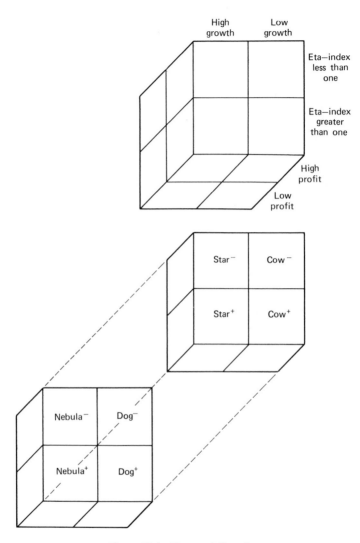

Figure A2.1 The portfolio cube.

and so on. Such an assessment would assure maintenance of a focus on organizational development, not just financial growth.

6. For every new venture or acquisition, once P&D had prepared its
recommendation, another group inside or outside the company
would be formed or selected to attack the recommendation.

Star$^-$ Do not acquire or develop unless it is a part of major diversification	Cow$^-$ Do not acquire or develop if another source of cash can be obtained
Star$^+$ Acquire/Develop	Cow$^+$ Acquire/Develop. Try to transform into a <u>star</u>$^+$

Nebula$^+$ Do not acquire or develop	Dog$^+$ Do not acquire or develop
Nebula$^-$ Acquire/Develop. Plan to transform into a <u>star</u>$^+$	Dog$^-$ Do not acquire/ develop (except for prestige, etc.)

Figure A2.2 Acquisition/development guidelines.

This means that a decision to launch or acquire, or not, would be made in the face of strong statements of the pros and cons. Such "dialectical confrontation" of opposing points of view would reduce both oversights and undersights.

Divestitures

7. P&D would annually classify each of the existing Eta businesses using the categories shown in Figure A2.1

In general, when the Eta-index is less than 1, the business should be a candidate for sale. It would do better if separated from Eta. Therefore, it should be possible to negotiate a good price for such a business. Its sale could provide resources for more profitable use in other businesses that have more synergy with Eta's current and future businesses (index greater than 1). Figure A2.3 interprets the relationship between the categories and divestiture.

7.1. P&D would propose to relevant units their divesting $dogs^+$, $dogs^-$, and $nebulae^-$. If a unit decided not to do so, it would have to present arguments to the Executive Office defending that decision.

7.2. P&D would also propose divesting $star^-$ businesses unless they were part of a diversification plan and the resources required for their growth were not taken from any $star^+$.

7.3. P&D would seek to develop or acquire $star^+$ or cow^+ businesses to replace cow^- businesses.

7.4. It would prepare plans for transforming cow^+ and $nebula^+$ businesses into $star^+$ businesses, and submit these to the Executive Office and relevant units.

    7.4.1. Efforts to convert a $nebula^+$ into a $star^+$ would have a specified cutoff after which, if the conversion had not taken place, efforts to divest would begin.

Portfolio Balance

8. Through acquisitions and development P&D would pursue a portfolio that would be balanced in the following ways: (a) the mix between *stars, cows,* and *nebulae* would satisfy Eta's profit and growth objectives; and (b) there would be enough *stars* and *nebulae* to absorb all the cash generated by Eta after meeting its dividend goals.

9. P&D would also employ other criteria that are conventionally used in portfolio management.

The system outlined above is intended to make sure that Eta would not spend resources on businesses or services that were not essential to its development strategy. The enforcement of portfolio-management principles would free all available cash for the pursuit of growth objectives.

Activities in Support of Portfolio Management

10. P&D would systematically search for promising technological opportunities by subscribing to existing relevant information services and by establishing contacts with relevant professionals and professional bodies.

11. P&D would formulate R&D projects aimed at development of products or processes on which new businesses might be built.

Star$^-$ Divest unless it is a part of a major diversification	Cow$^-$ Divest if it can be replaced as a major source of cash
Star$^+$ Keep	Cow$^+$ Keep and examine feasibility of converting it into a star$^+$

Nebula$^-$ Divest	Dog$^-$ Divest
Nebula$^+$ Plan transformation into a star$^+$	Dog$^+$ Divest (except for prestige, etc.)

Figure A2.3 Divestiture guidelines.

11.1. The Executive Office, P&D and other units could invest in such projects.

11.2. The cost of such projects could be recovered by selling their outputs or the rights to use them inside or outside Eta.

11.3. P&D could conduct market research in support of its business-development efforts.

11.4. P&D could completely or partially own small companies in relevant businesses. It could use such companies to gain understanding of the needs of Eta's customers and to develop and test products and processes.

Management of New Ventures and Acquisitions

As seen later, each unit would have a charter defining its product and market focuses.

12. Units would undertake ventures and acquisitions that would expand either their lines by adding products or services consistent with their charters, or their markets.

13. Other new ventures and acquisitions would be managed by a business unit called New Ventures.

   13.1. This unit would manage new ventures until they became profitable and could either be incorporated into other units or become units themselves.

   13.2. Newly acquired businesses (with the exception of those referred to in paragraph 14) would be managed by New Ventures until their Eta-index exceeded 1.

   13.3. New Ventures would operate on capital which it would replenish by selling developed businesses to either existing units or the executive office for establishment as new units.

14. An acquired business of the same size or larger than existing units would be set up as a separate unit.

   14.1. If, and as long as, its Eta-index were less than 1, such a new unit would be overseen by an integration board composed of a member of the executive office and heads of all business units and chaired by the head of New Ventures. The function of this Board would be to produce positive synergy.

ACQUISITIONS, USE, AND DEVELOPMENT OF RESOURCES

Human Resources and Their Use

All Personnel

39. Eta would be committed to providing continous employment to all those employees who performed satisfactorily and whose behavior at work or away from it was not detrimental to Eta's image.

40. Eta would be committed to providing opportunities for advancement to all qualified personnel.

41. All employees' performance would be evaluated anonymously once a year by their peers and immediate subordinates (if any). These evaluations would be submitted to immediate superiors, who would review employees' performances in private face-to-face meeting. Plans to repair any significant deficiencies would be prepared. The superiors would assist in implementing this plan. A complete record of each evaluation would be submitted to the personnel department.

42. Any employee who so desired could prepare a career development plan with guidance from a personnel officer. This could be reviewed annually and could be modified at any time. The personnel officer would assist in implementing this plan.

43. Eta would pay the full cost of any education or training an employee took on his or her own time and that was judged by a personnel officer to be relevant to Eta's present or future needs. Eta would pay half the cost of any education or training taken on an employee's own time that was not considered to be relevant to Eta.

44. Eta would provide internal educational and training programs or access to external programs that prevented obsolescence of its employees and promoted their work-related development.

45. Employees could receive leaves of absence to pursue further professional education, or even sabbaticals if the activities planned would clearly contribute to Eta's needs.

46. There would be a corporate ombudsman accessible in person or by phone to every employee. He would be responsible only to the president.

47. Eta would operate or help establish programs designed to deal with work- and nonwork-related personal problems of its employees and their families. These would include: (a) employee activity associations, such as music and sports clubs, supported by employee contributions but making free use of Eta's facilities or some administrative support; (b) employee/spouse training and development programs; (c) credit unions; (d) buying services; (e) an employee assistance program from which employees experiencing such problems as alcoholism or marital discord could receive assistance confidentially from an external counseling service—the cost to be covered largely by insurance; and (f) an out-placement program to assist departing employees in finding new jobs and ease their transition to them.

48. Eta would operate a "cafeteria-style" benefits system from which employees could assemble a package that best fits their individual needs.

49. Eta would maintain a pool of retired Eta personnel who could be employed on a part-time basis.

50. In addition to salary and benefits, all Eta employees would receive an annual bonus that was an increasing function of (a) their salary, (b) their individual performance, (c) their immediate unit's performance (if not an operating unit), (d) their operating unit's performance, and (e) the corporation's performance. This function would be so constructed that they would receive a bonus if their performance exceeded a specified target negotiated with superiors, no matter how the unit of which they were a part and the Corporation performed. On the other hand, if their performance were unsatisfactory they would receive no bonus, no matter how the unit or the Corporation performed.

The total compensation of an employee would depend on the performance of his or her unit and Eta as a whole. This would encourage constructive competitiveness between units and would simultaneously encourage the units to cooperate for the benefit of Eta as a whole.

Nonmanagerial Personnel

51. Nonmanagerial personnel would be members of work groups of no more than ten whenever possible.

52. Each work group would be given as much responsibility and autonomy as it could demonstrably handle.

53. Work groups could negotiate with each other for exchange of responsibilities and personnel.

54. Work groups would negotiate performance objectives and measures with their managers whose prime responsibility would be to encourage and facilitate their exceeding the negotiated objectives.

Raw Materials, Energy, Utilities, and Transportation

55. The Purchasing Unit would monitor the purchasing activities of other units.

55.1. It would identify areas in which there existed potential for reducing costs of materials, energy, and utilities, by combining unit purchases.

55.2. It would then propose to relevant units the creation and administration of a purchasing pool. The purchasing unit would produce earnings for itself through service fees charged for administering the purchasing pool.

55.3. Units could also contract with the purchasing unit for management of their individual purchasing activities.

56. The purchasing unit could own and operate a few small businesses whose products were used by Eta.

56.1. Through the operation of these businesses it would seek to understand their economics and thus determine a fair price to be paid to suppliers. It could use this understanding in negotiating purchase contracts and in guiding vertical integration of the Corporation.

57. The Executive Office would contract with Purchasing in conjunction with R&D for systematic studies of supply markets. Such studies would produce recommendations for areas in which sources ought to be diversified or substitute inputs sought. Costs and benefits of such actions would be computed. This information would serve as an input to the corporate planning process.

58. A similar system would be managed by the purchasing unit for the transportation needs of Eta.

Financial Resources

59. Acquisition of financial resources would be the responsibility of the board of directors and the executive office.

59.1. The board of directors would delineate the operational responsibilities of the executive office, specifying which financial decisions require its approval.

60. The executive office would contract with the finance and administration unit to manage designated corporate finances as well as assist other units in the financial aspects of their planning processes. Specifically, they would manage (a) credit lines, (b) major financing packages, (c) pension funds, (d) insurance, (e) taxation, (f) cash, (g) receivables, (h) securities investments, (i) foreign currency operations, (j) sales and purchase of stock, (k) sales of commercial paper, and (l) financial aspects of joint ventures.

61. Eta's total debt would be managed so as to maintain an AA credit rating.

62. In addition to retained earnings and borrowing, financing would be obtained by (a) sale of Eta stock to employees and their spouses and to financial institutions (as preferred stock), (b) divestitures, (c) sale of up to 99 percent of subsidiary stock to the investing public, and (d) joint ventures.

63. Finance and administration would change fees for services rendered. In addition, it would receive payment for short-term management of accounts payable.

Plants and Equipment

64. The facilities unit would lease plants and equipment or parts of them to other units. This would allow several units to operate out of the same facility.

65. Plants would be of modular design, capable of being expanded when needed.

   65.1. All modules used for the same purpose would have the same design. This would allow meaningful cost comparisons and sharing of experience among plants as well as provide for economies of scale in process engineering.

   65.2. Energy wasted in one part of a process would be captured and routed for use to other parts of that process that required it.

   65.3. Among Eta's plants there would be some that were mobile, mounted on barges and boats that could be transported anywhere in the world where there are navigable channels or rivers.

These plants would be useful for testing new markets or in areas of the world where Eta did not wish to risk nonremovable fixed assets.

66. Facilities would own a pilot plant and rent it for corporate and unit R&D activities.

67. Facilities would conduct process-engineering research aimed at improving plant quality and reducing costs and negative environmental impacts. It would recover its research costs through its charges for use of facilities.

As for everything else, units would be able to lease their production facilities outside Eta or even own them. The executive office would have to bear the cost of stopping them from doing so. Thus facilities would have an incentive to provide the best plants at the lowest possible price. Furthermore, they would have an incentive to find ways of reducing the risk of sinking assets into a fixed location because a business unit could pull out of any plant with appropriate notice. Facilities might find ways in which economical plants could be made completely mobile and/or usable for several purposes. This would clearly reduce Eta's vulnerability.

REFERENCES

1. Ackoff, Russell L., *Scientific Method: Optimizing Applied Research Decisions*, John Wiley & Sons, New York, 1962.

2. ———, *A Concept of Corporate Planning*, John Wiley & Sons, New York, 1970.

3. ———, *Redesigning the Future*, John Wiley & Sons, New York, 1974.

4. ———, *The Art of Problem Solving*, John Wiley & Sons, New York, 1978.

5. ———, "The Future of Operational Research Is Past," *Journal of the Operational Research Society*, **30** (1979), 93–104.

6. ———, T. A. Cowan, et al., *Designing a National Scientific and Technological Communication System*, University of Pennsylvania Press, Philadelphia, 1976.

7. ———, and F. E. Emery, *On Purposeful Systems*, Aldine-Atherton, Chicago, 1972.

8. ———, and J. R. Emshoff, "Advertising Research at Anheuser-Busch, Inc. (1963–1968)," *Sloan Management Review*, **16** (Winter 1975), 1–15.

9. ———, and M. W. Sasieni, *Fundamentals of Operations Research*, John Wiley & Sons, New York, 1968.

10. American Telephone and Telegraph Company, *1978 Annual Report*.

11. Argyris, Chris, and Donald A. Schön, *Theory in Practice: Increasing Professional Effectiveness*, Jossey-Bass, San Francisco, 1974.

12. ———, *Organizational Learning: A Theory of Action Perspective*, Addison-Wesley, Reading, Mass., 1978.

13. Balakrishnan, T. R., and G. D. Camp, *Family Planning and Old Age Security in India*, Indian Institute of Management, Calcutta, 1965.

14. Beer, Stafford, *Management Science*, Doubleday, Garden City, N. Y., 1968.

15. Bierce, Ambrose, *The Devil's Dictionary*, The World Publishing Co., Cleveland, 1911.

16. Bottiny, Walter, "Trends in Automobile Ownership and Indicators of Saturation," *Highway Research Record*, **106** (1966).

17. Bureau of Public Roads, *Highway Statistics, Summary to 1965*, Washington, D.C., 1967.

18. *Cars for Cities*, Report of the Steering Group and Working Group Appointed by the Ministry of Transport, Her Majesty's Stationery Office, London, 1967.

19. Churchman, C. W., R. L. Ackoff, and E. L. Arnoff, *Introduction to Operations Research,* John Wiley & Sons, New York, 1957.

20. Cohen, K. S., and Eric Rhenman, "The Role of Management Games in Education and Research," *Working Paper No. 22,* Graduate School of Industrial Administration, Carnegie Institute of Technology, Pittsburgh, September 1960.

21. Davis, Stanley, and Paul R. Lawrence, *Matrix,* Addison-Wesley, Reading, Mass. 1977.

22. Department of Housing and Urban Development, *Studies in New Systems of Evolutionary Urban Transportation,* Vol. II, Washington, D.C., 1968.

23. ———, Tomorrow's Transportation: *New Systems for the Urban Future,* Washington, D.C., 1968.

24. Dewey, John, *Logic: The Theory of Inquiry,* Henry Holt, New York, 1938.

25. Drucker, Peter F., *The Age of Discontinuity,* Harper & Row, New York, 1968.

26. Eden, C., "Operational Gaming in Action Research," *European Journal of Operational Research,* **3** (1979), 450–458.

27. Eldred, John C., "Labor Management Committee Improves the Quality of Working Life," *New Directions for Education and Work,* **3** (1978), 81–87.

28. Ellul, Jacques, *The Technological Society,* Vintage Books, New York, 1967.

29. Emery, F. E., *Futures We Are in,* Martinus Nijhoff, Leiden, 1977.

30. ———, and E. L. Trist, *Towards a Social Ecology,* Plenum Press, London, 1973.

31. Emery, M., *Searching,* Occasional Paper in Continuing Education No. 12, Australian National University, Centre for Continuing Education, Canberra, 1976.

32. Emshoff, J. R., and Ian I. Mitroff, "Improving the Effectiveness of Corporate Planning," *Business Horizons,* October 1978, pp. 49–60.

33. Frank, L. K., G. E. Hutchinson, W. K. Livingston, W. S. McCulloch, and N. Wiener, "Teleological Mechanisms," *Annals of the New York Academy of Sciences,* **50** (1948), Art. 4, 187–278.

34. Gall, John, *Systemantics,* Quadrangle/The New York Times Book Co., New York, 1975.

35. Glover, W. S., and R. L. Ackoff, "Five-Year Planning for an Integrated Operation," in *Proceedings of the Conference on Case Studies in Operations Research,* Case Institute of Technology, Cleveland, 1956, pp. 38–47.

36. Goggin, W. C., "How the Multidimensional Structure Works at Dow Corning," *Harvard Business Review,* January–February 1974, pp 54–65.

37. Gordon, W. J., *Synectics,* Harper, New York, 1961.

38. Guetzkow, Harold, "A Use of Simulation in the Study of Inter-Nation Relations," *Behavioral Science,* **4** (1959), 183–191.

39. Hirshman, A. O., and C. E. Lindblom, "Economic· Development, Research and Development, Polcy Making: Some Converging Views," in *Systems Thinking,* F. E. Emery, ed., Penguin Books, Harmondsworth, Middlesex, England, 1969, pp. 351–371.

40. Hoggatt, A. C., "An Experimental Business Game," *Behavioral Science,* **4** (1959), 192–203.

41. House, William C., ed., *Business Simulation for Decision Making,* Petrocelli, New York, 1977.

42. Howard, Nigel, *Paradoxes of Rationality: Theory of Metagames and Political Behavior,* MIT Press, Cambridge, 1971.

43. Hulme, Edward Maslin, *The Renaissance, the Protestant Revolution, and the Catholic Reformation in Continental Europe,* The Century Co., New York, 1920.

44. Jamestown Labor-Management Committee, "Improving the Quality of Work Life," in *Jobs through Economic Development,* U. S. Department of Commerce, Washington, D.C., January 1979.

45. Jennings, E. E., "The Worlds of the Executive," *TWA Ambassador,* **4** (1971), 28-30.

46. Kabayashi, S., *Creative Management,* American Management Association, New York, 1971.

47. Kuhn, Thomas S., *The Structure of Scientific Revolutions* (2nd ed.), The University of Chicago Press, Chicago, 1970.

48. Landsberg, Hans, L. Fleishman, and J. Fisher, *Resources in America's Future,* Johns Hopkins Press, Baltimore, 1963.

49. Lansing, J. B., and G. Hendricks, *Automobile Ownership and Residential Density,* Survey Research Center, University of Michigan, Ann Arbor, 1967.

50. Lyle C. Fitch and Associates, *Urban Transportation and Public Policy,* Chandler, San Francisco, 1964.

51. McClenehan, J. W., and H. J. Simkowitz, "The Effects of Short Cars on Flow and Speed in Downtown Traffic: A Simulation Model and Some Results," *Trasportation Science,* **3** (1969), 126-139.

52. Malcolm, D. G., "Bibliography on the Use of Simulation in Management Analysis," *Operations Research,* **8** (1960), 169-177.

53. Meadows, D. H., D. L. Meadows, J. Randers, and W. W. Behrens III, *The Limits to Growth,* Universe Books, New York, 1972.

54. Meier, Richard L., "Communication Overload: Proposals from the Study of a University Library," *Administrative Science Quarterly,* **7** (1963), 521-544.

55. Miller, G. A., "The Magical Number Seven, Plus or Minus Two: Some Limits on Our Capacity for Processing Information," *Psychological Review,* **63** (1956), 81-97.

56. *Minicar Transit System,* Final Report of Phase 1, Feasibility Study, prepared by the University of Pennsylvania for the U.S. Department of Transportation, 1968.

57. National Academy of Sciences, *U.S. Transportation Resources, Performance and Problems,* Proceedings of the Transportation Research Conference, Woods Hole, Mass., 1960.

58. Oren, T. I., "A Bibliography of Bibliographies on Modelling, Simulation and Gaming," *Simulation,* **23** (September 1974), 90-95.

59. Ortega y Gasset, José, *Mission of the University,* W. W. Norton, New York, 1966.

60. Osborn, A. F., *Applied Imagination,* Scribner's, New York, 1963.

61. Ozbekhan, Hasan, "The Future of Paris: A Systems Study in Strategic Urban Planning," *Philosophical Transactions of the Royal Society of London A,* **387** (1977), 523-544.

62. *Penn-Jersey Transportation Study,* Vol. 1: "The State of the Region," Philadelphia, 1964.

63. Prince, G. M., *The Practice of Creativity,* Harper, New York, 1970.

64. Rapoport, A., and A. M. Chammah, *Prisoner's Dilemma,* University of Michigan Press, Ann Arbor, 1965.

65. Richards, L., and R. Graham, "Identifying Problems through Gaming," *Interfaces,* **7** (1977), 76-79.

66. Rosenblueth, A., and N. Wiener, "Purposeful and Non-Purposeful Systems," *Philosophy of Science,* **17** (1950), 318-326.

67. Sagasti, Francisco, and R. L. Ackoff, "Possible and Likely Futures in Urban Transportation," *Socio-Economic Planning,* **5** (1971), 413-428.

68. Schön, Donald A., *Beyond the Stable State,* Random House, New York, 1971.

69. Shakeoff, Philip, *The New York Times,* December 22, 1973, p. 1.

70. Shim, J., "Management Game Simulations: Survey of New Directions," *University of Michigan Business Review,* **30** (May 1978), 26-29.

71. Shubik, Martin, "Bibliography on Simulation, Gaming, Artificial Intelligence and Allied Topics," *Journal of the American Statistical Association,* **55** (1960), 736-751.

72. Singer, E. A., Jr., *On the Contended Life,* Henry Holt, New York, 1923.

73. ———, *In Search of a Way of Life,* Columbia University Press, New York, 1948.

74. ———, *Experience and Reflection,* University of Pennsylvania Press, Philadelphia, 1959.

75. Smith, Hedrick, *The Russians,* Ballantine Books, New York, 1977.

76. Snow, C. P., *The Two Cultures: A Second Look,* Mentor Books, New York, 1964.

77. Sommerhoff, Gerd, *Analytical Biology,* Oxford University Press, London, 1950.

78. Thomas, C. J., "Military Gaming," in *Progress in Operations Research,* Vol. 1, R. L. Ackoff, ed., John Wiley & Sons, New York, 1961, pp. 421-463.

79. ———, and W. L. Deemer, Jr., "The Role of Operational Gaming in Operations Research," *Operations Research,* **5** (1957), 1-27.

80. Toffler, Alvin, *Future Shock,* Bantam Books, New York, 1971.

81. Vogel, E. H., Jr., "Creative Marketing and Management Science," *Management Decision,* Spring 1962, pp. 21-25.

82. Waid, C., D. F. Clark, and R. L. Ackoff, "Allocation of Sales Effort in the Lamp Division of the General Electric Company," *Operations Research,* **4** (1956), 629-647.

83. Wilbur Smith and Associates, *Transportation and Parking for Tomorrow's Cities,* New Haven, 1966.

84. Williams, T. A., "The Search Conference in Active Adaptive Planning," *The Journal of Applied Behavioral Science,* **15** (1979), 470-483.

85. ———, G. Calhoun, and R. L. Ackoff, "Stress, Alcoholism, and Personnality," *S³ Papers,* 79-10, Social Systems Sciences Unit, University of Pennsylvania, Philadelphia, 1979.

86. Young, J. P., "History and Bibliography of War Gaming," *Staff Paper ORO-SP-13,* Operations Research Office, Johns Hopkins University, Chevy Chase, Md., April 1957.

INDEX